VISUAL QUICKSTART GUIDE

Photoshop 4

FOR WINDOWS

Elaine Weinmann
Peter Lourekas

 **Peachpit Press**

Visual QuickStart Guide
Photoshop 4 for Windows
Elaine Weinmann and Peter Lourekas

Peachpit Press
2414 Sixth Street
Berkeley, CA 94710
510/548-4393
510/548-5991 (fax)

Find us on the World Wide Web at: http://www.peachpit.com
Peachpit Press is a division of Addison Wesley Longman

Colophon

This book was created with QuarkXPress 3.3 on a Macintosh Quadra 650 and Power Macintosh 8500. The fonts used were Sabon and Futura from Adobe Systems Inc. and Anna and Gillies Gothic from Image Club Graphics, Inc.

ISBN 0-201-68842-5
9 8 7 6 5 4 3

Printed and bound in the United States of America

In memory of Bert Weinmann
(1924-1996)
Loving, vivacious, and courageous spirit

Introduction

Photoshop 4.0 is not an earth-shaking upgrade, but, nevertheless, all the instructions needed revision and every dialog box and palette required reshooting for this edition (such is the life of computer book authors!). Also included in this new edition are scads of new keyboard shortcuts and a sprinkling of new features. Our favorite new feature is adjustment layers, which you can use to try out various color or tonal adjustments to underlying layers without having to make them permanent. We use adjustment layers so often, we honestly can't imagine Photoshop-ing without them.

And, to our great astonishment, we actually deleted or shortened some pages from the previous edition because many procedures have been streamlined and no longer require cumbersome work-arounds. When you create text in 4.0, for example, it automatically appears on its own layer—no more fiddling around with floating selections. It's as if the folks at Adobe spied on Photoshop power users and said, "Hmm, if we redesign this feature to work this way, people won't have to bother doing such-and-such, and they'll be much happier." Version 4.0 tries to do more with less. The streamlining process allowed us to sneak in oodles of new tips and suggestions, and new—and larger—illustrations (we couldn't resist). This book also includes a whole new and expanded color section, with imagery by real pros.

We've always encouraged our readers to be creative and to experiment with whatever application they're working in. We've resisted bogging down beginning Photoshoppers in the technical aspects of the program, especially since there are already so many humongous tomes in the marketplace that can be used as reference guides. These days, however, not only do you have to come up with a stunning visual concept and execute it with finesse—on a deadline—you must also navigate the image through other software applications and then shepherd it through the shark-infested waters of color separation, or get it onto the Web and make it look remotely like the dazzling image you started with (sound familiar?). So we've included more techy stuff in this edition, topics like getting Photoshop images onto the Web, and producing color separations. But this book is still light and thin enough to be called a Visual QuickStart Guide, stuff into a mini backpack, and leaf through without having to take your other hand off the mouse.

Whether you're a student learning Photoshop for the first time, or a seasoned freelance artist who uses our books as a "cheat sheet," you're certain to find something in this volume that will help you. Because what hasn't changed is our boil-it-down-to-the-essentials, haiku writing style and the fact that we think illustrations really do tell much of the story—certainly when it comes to computer graphics. In fact, this new and improved edition contains more than a thousand images! Dive in. ■

TABLE OF CONTENTS

Table of Contents

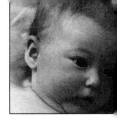

THE BASICS 1

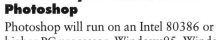

Hardware you'll need to run Photoshop

Photoshop will run on an Intel 80386 or higher PC processor; Windows95, Windows NT, or DOS 5.0 or later for Windows 3.1x; a hard drive with at least 20 megabytes of available space after loading Photoshop's 20 megabytes of data; and at least 16 megabytes of RAM (random access memory) allocated to the application. You'll also need a CD-ROM drive to install the software (though a floppy drive version can be ordered). Photoshop will run faster on a Pentium with 32 megabytes of RAM and a large hard drive with at least 50 megabytes of available space. For optimal speed, we recommend a 200 megahertz Intel processor, 32 megabytes or more of RAM, and a large, fast access hard drive (one to four gigabyte, 9-11 millisecond random seek time). For even better performance, add the new Intel MMX chipset. For those who need very fast processing, Photoshop 4.0 supports multi-processors on the Windows NT platform.

Photoshop requires a lot of RAM: about four times the size of the file! The number of layers, channels, and pixels in an image also impact on the amount of RAM required for processing and the amount of storage space an image occupies. To improve Photoshop's performance speed, try installing more RAM.

Color monitors display 8-bit, 16-bit, or 24-bit color, depending on the video card or Video RAM. With an 8-bit card, 256 colors are available for on-screen color mixing. With a 24-bit card, 16.7 million colors are available. A 24-bit card provides optimal display, because every color can be represented exactly. All Photoshop pictures are saved as 24-bit, regardless of the monitor's resolution.

LOUREKAS/WEINMANN

Hardware

File size units

Byte	=	8 bits of digital information *(approx. one black or white pixel, or one character)*
Kilobyte (KB)	=	1,024 bytes
Megabyte (MB)	=	1,024 kilobytes
Gigabyte (GB)	=	1,024 megabytes

You'll probably also need to purchase a removable storage device—such as an Iomega Zip or Jaz drive, an EZFlyer Syquest drive, or an optical drive—to back up files and to transport files to and from your print shop or other output service.

Memory allocation

To learn how much RAM you have available to allocate to Photoshop, launch Photoshop and any other applications that you want to run at the same time, click on the Start button in the Taskbar, choose Settings, then click on Control Panel. In the Control Panel window, double-click the System icon and click on the Performance tab to find the percentage of free system resources. The total amount of RAM is also indicated ■.

You should allocate as much RAM as possible to Photoshop. To do this, in Photoshop, choose File menu > Preferences, then click on Memory & Image Cache ■. The default percentage of RAM used by Photoshop is 75%. The Available RAM and Photoshop RAM are also indicated. To adjust the percentage of RAM to be used by Photoshop, click on the spinners or enter a percentage. Any changes you make will take effect when you re-launch Photoshop.

When Photoshop requires more RAM for processing than is assigned to it in the Memory & Image Cache dialog box, it uses available hard drive space that has been allocated as the scratch disk (see page 232), a technique known as using virtual memory. The amount of RAM assigned to Photoshop cannot be greater than the amount of available hard drive space, because Photoshop writes the entire contents of its RAM segment whenever it can. Processing is much faster in actual RAM than in virtual memory.

Purge

Use the Edit > **Purge** commands periodically to regain RAM used for the Clipboard or the Undo, Define Pattern, or Take Snapshot command. The Purge commands can't be undone.

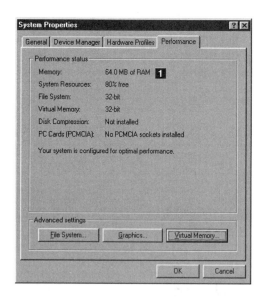

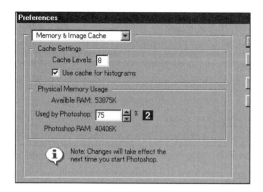

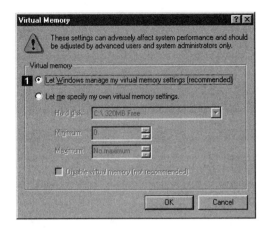

Virtual memory

In most cases, you should let Windows manage your virtual memory settings. If you decide, for some reason, that you want to specify your own virtual memory settings, you should not disable the virtual memory option in the Performance tab of the System Properies in the Control Panel. If you are using a PC with only 16MB of total RAM (which means you're really short on RAM), turn on the "Let Windows manage my virtual memory settings (recommended)" button **1**. Using virtual memory, Windows writes to its designated scratch disk drive when it runs out of RAM.

Accelerators

Application accelerators can speed up certain Photoshop functions, like RGB-to-CMYK conversions, Gaussian Blur filter, Sharpen filter, etc.). Third-party accelerators, in order to achieve Photoshop-like results when performing a filter function, use their own processes to alter pixels, not Photoshop's algorithms. If you opt to purchase a third-party product, choose one that bears the Adobe Charged logo. These accelerators will make some Photoshop functions run faster on older Pentium machines. The latest Intel MMX chipset is sufficiently powerful that the advantages of adding this type of accelerator are minimal.

With sufficient Video RAM installed on a graphics card (4 MB or more), a new Intel chipset will perform fast screen redraw. The faster the screen redraw, the faster you'll be able to work in Photoshop.

Scratch disk info

Choose **Scratch Sizes** (press the arrowhead at the bottom of an image window) to see how much RAM is currently used by all open Photoshop files (the left number) **2**, and how much RAM has been allocated to Photoshop (the right number) **3**. When the left number is greater than the right number, the scratch disk is being used. Choose **Efficiency** from the same drop-down menu to see what percentage of RAM is being used. A percentage below 100 also indicates the scratch disk is being used.

The Photoshop screen

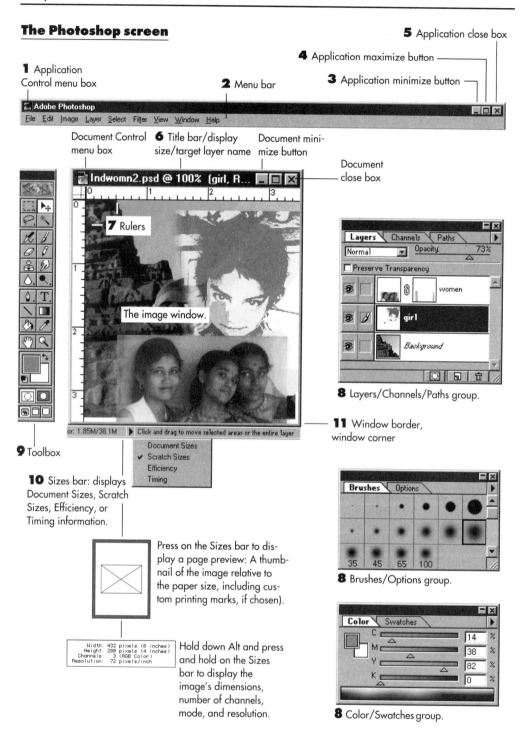

5 Application close box

4 Application maximize button

3 Application minimize button

1 Application Control menu box

2 Menu bar

Document Control menu box

6 Title bar/display size/target layer name

Document minimize button

Document close box

7 Rulers

The image window.

8 Layers/Channels/Paths group.

11 Window border, window corner

9 Toolbox

10 Sizes bar: displays Document Sizes, Scratch Sizes, Efficiency, or Timing information.

Press on the Sizes bar to display a page preview: A thumbnail of the image relative to the paper size, including custom printing marks, if chosen).

Width: 432 pixels (6 inches)
Height: 288 pixels (4 inches)
Channels: 3 (RGB Color)
Resolution: 72 pixels/inch

Hold down Alt and press and hold on the Sizes bar to display the image's dimensions, number of channels, mode, and resolution.

8 Brushes/Options group.

8 Color/Swatches group.

The Photoshop Screen

4

Key to the Photoshop screen

1 *Application (or Document) Control menu box*

The Application Control menu box commands are Restore, Move, Size, Minimize, Maximize, and Close. The Document Control menu box commands are Restore, Move, Size, Minimize, Maximize, Close, and Next.

2 *Menu bar*

Press any menu heading to access dialog boxes, submenus, and commands.

3 *Application (or Document) minimize button*

Click the Application Minimize button to shrink the document to an icon in the Taskbar. Click the icon on the Taskbar to restore the application window to its previous size.

Click the Document Minimize button to shrink the document to an icon at the bottom left corner of the application window. Click the icon to restore the document window to its previous size.

4 *Application (or Document) maximize/restore button*

Click the Application or Document Restore button to restore a window to its previous size. When a window is at the restored size, the Restore button turns into the Maximize button. Click the Maximize button to enlarge the window.

5 *Close box*

To close an image or a palette, click its close box.

6 *Title bar/display size/target layer name*

The image's title, color mode, and display size, and the name of the current target layer.

7 *Rulers*

Choose Show Rulers from the View menu to display rulers. The position of the cursor is indicated by a mark on each ruler. Choose ruler units in the Units & Rulers Preferences dialog box (see page 230).

8 *Palettes*

There are ten moveable palettes. Some palettes are grouped together: Layers/Channels/Paths, Brushes/Options, and Color/Swatches. Click a tab (palette name) to bring that palette to the front of its group. The other palettes are displayed individually.

9 *Toolbox*

Press Tab to hide the Toolbox and all open palettes. Press Tab again to display the Toolbox and all previously displayed palettes.

10 *Sizes bar*

When Document Sizes is chosen from the Sizes bar pop-up menu, the Sizes bar displays the file storage size when all layers are flattened and any alpha channels are removed (the first amount) and the file storage size when the layers are separate (the second amount).

When Scratch Sizes is chosen, the bar displays the amount of storage space Photoshop is using for all currently open pictures and the amount of RAM currently available to Photoshop. When the first amount is greater than the second amount, Photoshop is using virtual memory on the scratch disk.

When Efficiency is chosen, the bar indicates the percentage of RAM being used. A percentage below 100 indicates the scratch disk is being used.

11 *Window border, Window corner*

Press and drag a horizontal or vertical border or a corner to resize the window.

The Toolbox

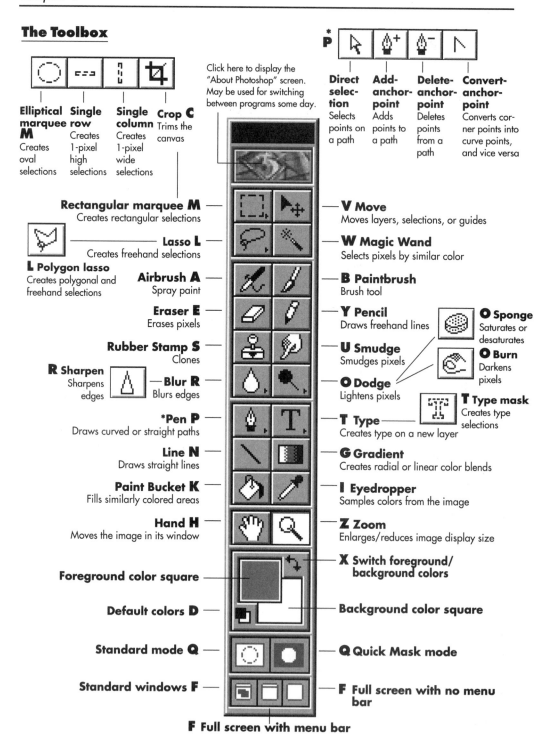

Elliptical marquee M
Creates oval selections

Single row
Creates 1-pixel high selections

Single column
Creates 1-pixel wide selections

Crop C
Trims the canvas

Click here to display the "About Photoshop" screen. May be used for switching between programs some day.

P

Direct selection
Selects points on a path

Add-anchor-point
Adds points to a path

Delete-anchor-point
Deletes points from a path

Convert-anchor-point
Converts corner points into curve points, and vice versa

Rectangular marquee M —
Creates rectangular selections

Lasso L —
Creates freehand selections

L Polygon lasso
Creates polygonal and freehand selections

Airbrush A —
Spray paint

Eraser E —
Erases pixels

Rubber Stamp S —
Clones

R Sharpen
Sharpens edges

Blur R —
Blurs edges

*Pen P —
Draws curved or straight paths

Line N —
Draws straight lines

Paint Bucket K —
Fills similarly colored areas

Hand H —
Moves the image in its window

— **V Move**
Moves layers, selections, or guides

— **W Magic Wand**
Selects pixels by similar color

— **B Paintbrush**
Brush tool

— **Y Pencil**
Draws freehand lines

— **U Smudge**
Smudges pixels

O Dodge
Lightens pixels

O Sponge
Saturates or desaturates

O Burn
Darkens pixels

T Type mask
Creates type selections

— **T Type**
Creates type on a new layer

— **G Gradient**
Creates radial or linear color blends

— **I Eyedropper**
Samples colors from the image

— **Z Zoom**
Enlarges/reduces image display size

Foreground color square —

Default colors D —

Standard mode Q —

Standard windows F —

— **X Switch foreground/background colors**

— **Background color square**

— **Q Quick Mask mode**

— **F Full screen with no menu bar**

F Full screen with menu bar

On-screen help

To learn a tool name or shortcut or a palette option in Photoshop 4.0 or later, simply rest the pointer—without clicking or pressing the mouse button—on the tool or palette icon you're interested in **1**. (Check the Show Tool Tips box in the File menu > Preferences > General dialog box to access this feature.)

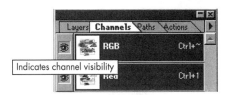

Context menus—try this!

To choose from an on screen context menu, right-click on a Layers, Channels, or Paths palette thumbnail or name or other area of a palette **3**. Or choose a tool, then right-click with the pointer over the image window to access options for that tool **4**.

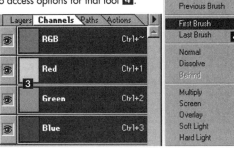

How to use the Toolbox

Press Tab to hide or show the Toolbox and all open palettes. Press Shift-Tab to hide/show all palettes except the Toolbox. Drag the top of the Toolbox to move it around.

To choose a tool whose icon is currently visible, click once on its icon. Press and drag to choose a hidden tool from a pull-out menu. Or choose tools using the shortcuts listed on the previous page. If you forget a tool's shortcut, just leave the cursor over the tool for a moment, and context sensitive help will remind you! **1** Keep pressing the same shortcut key to "cycle through" hidden, related tools, or Option-click the currently visible tool.

Choose attributes for a tool—like a blending mode or opacity percentage—from its Options palette **2**. If the Brushes palette is in front of the Options palette, double-click the tool to bring the Options palette to the front, or press Enter if the tool is already highlighted. You can also customize some tools using the Brushes, Swatches, and Color palettes. From the Brushes palette, you can choose a predefined brush tip or you can create your own brush tip. For example, you can make an Airbrush tool tip soft and transparent, or a Paintbrush stroke round and opaque.

To restore a tool's default settings, click the tool, then choose Reset Tool from the Options palette command menu. Choose Reset All Tools from the Options palette command menu to restore the default settings for all the tools.

To choose whether tool cursors look like their Toolbox icons or a crosshair, see page 228.

Mini-glossary

Target layer and layer transparency

The currently highlighted layer on the Layers palette, and the only layer that can be edited. An image can have just a Background (no layers) or it can be multi-layered. Layers can be restacked and moved, and are transparent where there are no pixels, so you can see through a whole stack of them. The advantage of working with multiple layers is that you can assign image components to separate layers and edit them individually without changing the other layers.

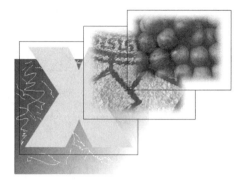

Layers are like clear acetate sheets: opaque where there is imagery and transparent where there is no imagery.

Adjustment layer

Unlike a standard layer, modifications made to an adjustment layer don't alter actual pixels until it is merged with the layers below it, so adjustment layers can be used for experimenting with color or tonal adjustments. Only layers below the adjustment layer are affected.

The Layers palette for a four-layer image. "water" is the target (currently active) layer.

Pixels (picture elements)

The dots used to display a bitmapped image on a rectangular grid on a computer screen.

Individual pixels are discernible in this image, which is shown at 500% view.

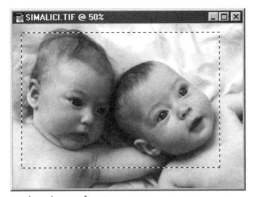

A selected area of an image.

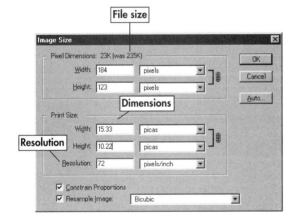

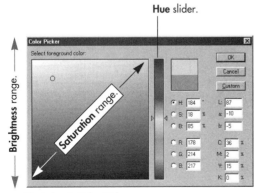

Photoshop's **Color Picker**.

Selection

An area of an image that is isolated so it can be modified while the rest of the image is protected. A moving marquee marks the boundary of a selection. If you move a non-floating selection, the cutout area that's left behind will be filled automatically with the current Background color if the selection is on the Background, or with transparency if the selection is on a layer.

Floating selection

A floating selection is created when a selection is Control-Alt-dragged or transformed, and, while it is still selected, it floats above and can be altered without affecting, the underlying pixels in the target layer. Once it is deselected (defloated), floating selection pixels are merged with the pixels in the layer directly below it.

Resolution

Image resolution is the number of pixels contained in an image, and is measured in pixels per inch. The monitor's resolution is also measured in pixels per inch. Output devices also have their own resolution, which is measured in dots per inch.

File size

The file size of an image, which is measured in bytes, kilobytes, megabytes, or gigabytes.

Dimensions

The width and height of an image.

Brightness

The lightness (luminance) of a color.

Hue

The wavelength of light that gives a color its name—such as red or blue—irrespective of its brightness and saturation.

Saturation

The purity of a color. The more gray a color contains, the lower is its saturation.

(See Appendix B: Glossary for more definitions.)

Mini-Glossary

The menus

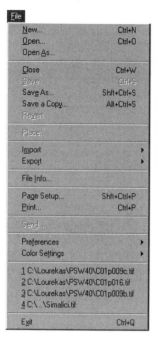

File menu

File menu commands are used to create, open, place, close, save, scan, import, export, or print an image, set preferences, and exit Photoshop.

Edit menu

Edit menu commands include Undo, which undoes the last modification made, the Clipboard commands Cut and Copy, and the Paste commands. The Fill, Stroke, and Define Pattern commands are also executed via the Edit menu. The Purge commands free up memory used by the Undo, Clipboard, Snapshot, or Pattern buffer.

Image menu

An image can be converted to any of eight black-and-white or color modes via the Mode submenu. The invaluable Adjust commands modify an image's color, saturation, brightness, or contrast. The Image Size command modifies an image's file size, dimensions, or resolution. The Canvas Size dialog box is used to add or subtract from an image's editable canvas area.

Layer menu

Layer menu commands add, duplicate, delete, modify, add masks to, group, transform, merge, and flatten layers. Many of these commands can also be accessed via the Layers palette command menu.

Select menu

The "All" Select menu command selects an entire layer. The None command deselects all selections. Other Select menu commands enlarge, contract, smooth, or feather selection edges, and save selections to and from channels. The Color Range command creates selections based on color.

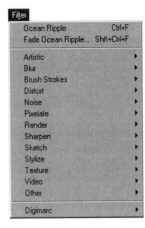

Filter menu

Filters, which perform a wide range of image editing functions, are organized in pop-up menu groups. The Fade command lessens the effect of the last applied filter or Adjust command. The Digimarc filter embeds a copyright watermark in an image.

View menu

View menu commands control new view creation, display sizes, and the display of rulers, guides, and grids. The Gamut Warning highlights colors that won't print on a four-color press. Choose CMYK Preview to see how your image looks in CMYK color without actually changing its mode.

Window menu

Window menu commands display or hide the palettes. Open images are also listed and can be activated via the Window menu.

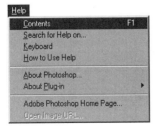

Help menu

Help menu commands provide access to on-screen support. Choose How to Use Help to learn about the Help commands. Plug-in information can also be accessed from this menu. If you are connected to the World Wide Web, you can access the Adobe Photoshop Home Page from this menu. If an image has a URL as part of its file information, you can click on Open Image URL to open the Web site from which the image was obtained.

The Menus

The palettes

How to use the palettes

There are ten moveable palettes that are used for image editing. To save screen space, some of the palettes are joined into groups: **Color/Swatches, Brushes/Options,** and **Layers/Channels/Paths.** The other palettes are **Navigator, Actions,** and **Info.**

You can **separate** a palette from its group by dragging its tab (palette name) **1–2.** You can **add** a palette to any group by dragging the tab over the group. When you release the mouse it will be the frontmost palette in the group. The Layers/Channels/ Paths group window can be widened, so if you want to gather more palettes together, use this one as your home base so the tabs (palette names) will be readable across the top.

To **open** a palette, choose Show [palette name] from the Window menu. The palette will appear in front in its group.

To **display** an open palette at the front of its group, click its tab (palette name).

Resize any palette other than Color, Options, or Info by dragging its size box (lower right corner).

Press Tab to hide or display all open palettes and the Toolbox. Press Shift-Tab to show/hide all open palettes except the Toolbox.

To shrink a palette, double-click its tab or click the palette zoom box (upper right corner, to the left of of the close button). If the palette is not at its default size, click the zoom box once to restore its default size, then click a second time to shrink the palette.

If the Save Palette Locations box is checked in the File menu > Preferences > General dialog box, palettes that are open when you exit Photoshop will appear in their same location when you re-launch Photoshop. To restore the palettes' default groupings when you launch Photoshop, click Reset Palette Locations to Default in the same dialog box.

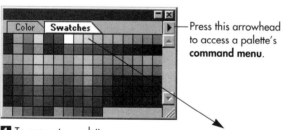

Press this arrowhead to access a palette's **command menu**.

1 To separate a palette from its group, drag the tab (palette name) away from the palette group.

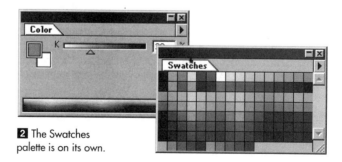

2 The Swatches palette is on its own.

You can resize a palette by clicking once on its Zoom box.

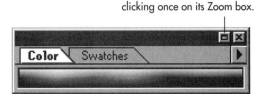

You can further shrink a palette by double-clicking its name or by Alt-clicking its Zoom box.

Color palette

The Color palette is used for mixing and choosing colors to apply with the painting, editing, and fill tools. Choose a color model for the palette from the palette command menu. Click the Foreground or Background color square to access the Color Picker, from which you can also choose a color. You can quick-select a color from the color bar on the bottom of the palette.

Foreground color square. The currently active square has a white border.

Background color square.

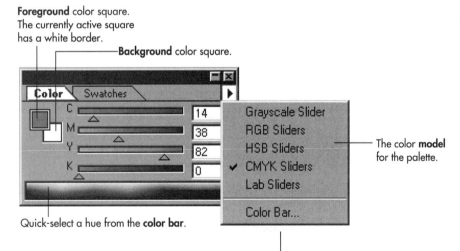

The color **model** for the palette.

Quick-select a hue from the **color bar**.

Choose Color Bar from the Color palette command menu or Control-click the color bar on the Color palette to open the Color Bar dialog box, then choose a **display style** for the color bar from the Style drop-down menu. Or Shift-click the color bar to cycle through the Styles.

Color Palette

Swatches palette

The Swatches palette is used for selecting already mixed colors to be applied with the painting, editing, and fill tools. Individual swatches can be added to and deleted from the palette. Custom swatch palettes can also be loaded, appended, and saved using Swatches palette commands.

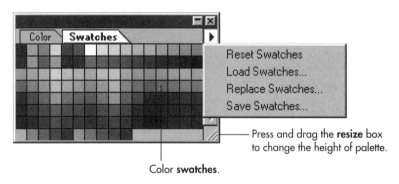

Press and drag the **resize** box to change the height of palette.

Color **swatches**.

Channels palette

The Channels palette is used to display one or more of the channels that make up an image and any specially created alpha channels, which are used for saving selections. The Channels palette can also be used to display layer masks.

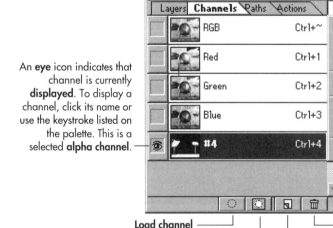

An **eye** icon indicates that channel is currently **displayed**. To display a channel, click its name or use the keystroke listed on the palette. This is a selected **alpha channel**.

Load channel as selection

Save selection as channel

Create new channel

Delete current channel

Brushes palette

The Brushes palette is used for defining a tool's tip size, edge, and angle. You can choose from preset brushes or you can create your own brushes. You can also load, append, and save brushes using the Brushes palette command menu.

Hard-edged tips in this row.

Soft-edged tips in these rows.

Large brush tips. The number is the tip diameter in pixels.

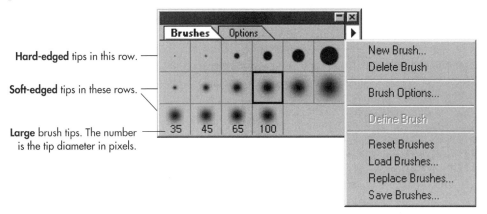

Options palette

The Options palette is used to define attributes for a tool, such as its Opacity, Fade distance, or mode. Options are set for each tool individually. You can reset the currently selected tool or all tools using Options palette commands. If the Brushes palette is in front of the Options palette, click the Options tab, or double-click a tool to bring the Options palette to the front, or press Enter if the tool is already highlighted.

The **Pressure** or **Opacity** slider.

The **mode** drop-down menu.

The Options palette when the Paintbrush tool is selected.

Layers palette

Normally, when you create a new image, it will have an opaque Background. Using the Layers palette, you can add, delete, hide/show, duplicate, and rearrange layers on top of the Background. Each layer can be assigned its own mode and opacity and can be edited separately without changing the other layers. You can also attach a mask to a layer. (To specify that the bottommost tier of a new image be a layer with transparency instead of an opaque Background, click Content: Transparent in the New dialog box.)

If you're using Photoshop 4 or later, you can also create **adjustment layers**, which are temporary layers that are used for trying out various color or tonal adjustments using the Adjust commands. An adjustment layer's effects do not become permanent until it's merged with the layer below it.

Only the currently highlighted layer, called the **target layer**, can be edited. Click on a layer name on the Layers palette to highlight it. The name of the target layer will be listed on the image window title bar.

Layers take up storage space, so when you're done with your multi-layer image, you can merge or flatten the layers into one.

Layer icon. **Layer mask** icon. **Opacity** slider.

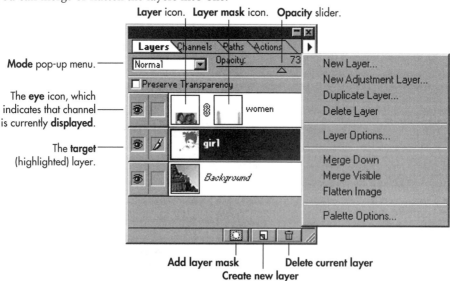

Mode pop-up menu.

The **eye** icon, which indicates that channel is currently **displayed**.

The **target** (highlighted) layer.

Add layer mask

Create new layer

Delete current layer

Paths palette

Paths are composed of curved and straight line segments connected by anchor points. A path can be drawn directly with the Pen tool or a selection can be converted into a path. The Pen tool and its relatives, the Add-anchor-point tool, Delete-anchor-point tool, and Convert-anchor-point-tool, can be used to reshape a path. Paths are saved and accessed via the Paths palette.

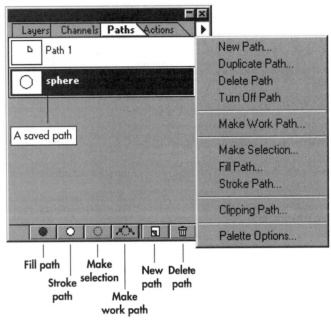

Fill path
Stroke path
Make selection
Make work path
New path
Delete path

Navigator palette

The Navigator palette is used for moving an image in its window, and for changing an image's display size.

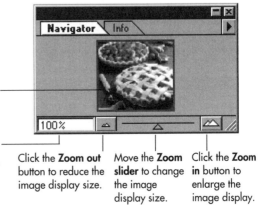

Drag in the preview box to **move** the image in the image window. Control-drag in the preview box to marquee the area you want to magnify.

Enter the desired **zoom percentage** (or ratio, like 1:1 or 4:1), then press **Enter**. To zoom to the percentage and keep the field highlighted, press Shift-Enter.

Click the **Zoom out** button to reduce the image display size.

Move the **Zoom slider** to change the image display size.

Click the **Zoom in** button to enlarge the image display.

Info palette

The Info palette displays a breakdown of the color of the pixel currently under the pointer. The Info palette also shows the *x/y* position of the pointer on the image. If a color adjustment dialog box is open, the palette will also display before and after color readouts. Other information, such as the distance between points when a selection is moved or a line is drawn, the dimensions of a crop marquee, or the angle of a selection as it's rotated, may display on the palette, depending on which tool is being used.

An exclamation point indicates the color currently under the pointer is **out of gamut** (isn't printable on a four-color press).

RGB and **CMYK readouts** for the pixel currently under the pointer.

Choose a **color model, Total Ink,** or **Opacity** for the readout by pressing this arrowhead.

Press on this arrowhead to choose a different **unit of measure** for the palette.

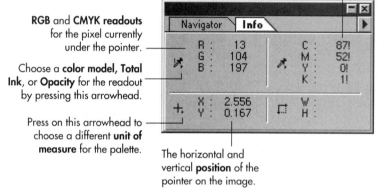

The horizontal and vertical **position** of the pointer on the image.

Actions palette

Alas, the Commands palette is no longer. You can use the Actions palette, however, to create and access command shortcuts. The Actions palette's main purpose is to automate image processing by recording a series of commands and then replaying those commands on one image or on a batch of images.

Turn an action command on or off

A recorded command

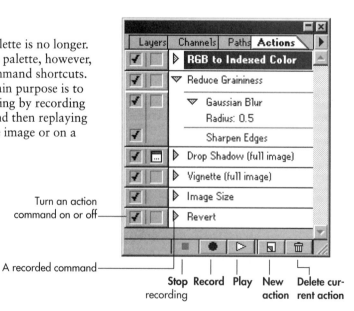

Stop recording   Record   Play   New action   Delete current action

Info Palette; Actions Palette

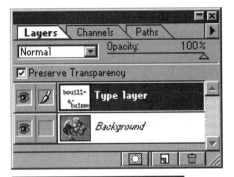

Build your image using layers

You can work on one layer at a time without affecting the non-target layers, and discard any layers you don't need. Merge two or more layers together periodically as you work, though, to conserve memory for large images. And using a **layer mask**, you can temporarily hide pixels on an individual layer so you can experiment with different compositions. When you're finished using a layer mask, you can discard the effects or permanently apply them to the layer.

To speed up screen redraw

Choose small **thumbnails** or no palette thumbnails for Layers, Channels, and Paths. Choose Palette Options from the palette command menu, then click Thumbnails: None or the smallest thumbnail option.

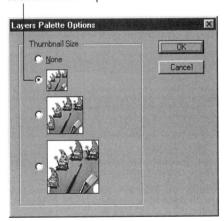

Production techniques

■ To undo the last modification, choose the Edit menu > **Undo** (Control-Z) (some commands can't be undone).

■ To restore the last saved version of an image, choose File menu > **Revert**, then click Revert.

■ Restore part of the last saved version of an image by dragging across it using the **Rubber Stamp** tool with its **From Saved** option, or using the **Eraser** tool with its **Erase to Saved** option, or by applying the **Fill** command with its **Saved** option to a selected area.

■ Save flattened versions of an image as you work on it using the **Save a Copy** command. When you're satisfied with one of the versions, discard the copies.

■ Use **adjustment layers** to try out tonal and color adjustments, and then merge the adjustment layer downward to apply the effect or discard the adjustment layer. Use the Layers palette Opacity slider to lessen the effect of an adjustment layer. Create a clipping group with the layer directly below the adjustment layer to limit the adjustment effect to that layer.

■ Use the Filter > **Fade** command (Control-Shift-F) to lessen a filter effect or Adjust command without having to undo and redo, and also choose a mode or opacity for the filter or color adjustment while you're at it.

■ **Interrupt screen redraw** after executing a command or applying a filter by choosing a different tool or command. (To cancel a command while a progress bar is displayed, press Esc.)

■ Choose the lowest possible **resolution** and **dimensions** for your image, factoring in your output requirements. You can create a practice image at a low resolution, saving the commands you use in an **action**, and then replay the action on a higher resolution version.

- Make sure your **hardware** requirements are sufficient for your production needs (see pages 1–3).

- Display your image in **two windows** simultaneously, one in a larger display size than the other, so you don't have to change displays sizes constantly.

- Save a complicated selection to a special grayscale channel called an **alpha channel,** which can be loaded and reused on any image whenever you like. Or create a **path,** which occupies significantly less storage space than an alpha channel, and can be converted into a selection.

- Since CMYK Color files process more slowly than RGB Colors files, use the **CMYK Preview** command to preview your image as CMYK Color mode, and convert to the real CMYK Color mode when the image is completed.

- Memorize as many **keyboard shortcuts** as you can. Start by learning the shortcuts for choosing tools (see page 6) or the shortcut for accessing a particular tool while another tool is chosen. Use on-screen tool tips to refresh your memory (rest your pointer on the icon of the tool you're interested in), or refer to Appendix B. Shortcuts are included in many instructions in this book. Use the **Actions** palette to organize and quickly execute frequently used commands.

- If color accuracy isn't critical, you can speed up screen redraw by choosing 256 color/**8-bit display** for your monitor.

- Use **Quick Mask** mode to turn a selection into a mask, which will cover the protected areas of the image with transparent color and leave the unprotected area as a cutout, and then modify mask contours using painting tools. Turn off Quick Mask mode to convert the cutout area back into a selection.

Production Techniques

Open and edit part of an image to speed up processing

Using **Quick Edit**, you can open and edit part of an image in the uncompressed TIFF, Scitex CT, or Photoshop 2.0 file format. Choose File menu > Import > Quick Edit, highlight the image you want to open, click Open, marquee the area of the image you want to work on, then click OK. Other techniques you can use to zero in on an area of an image: click Grid in the Quick Edit dialog box, then click on a tile ■, or press F to choose the first tile, or press N to cycle through the tiles. Click a plus or minus button to change the number of tiles. When you're ready to save the edited portion back to its original file, choose File menu > Export > Quick Edit Save. But be careful: changes will save instantly, and without a save dialog box.

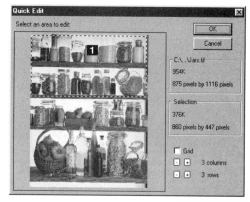

Context menus save time

To choose from an on screen context menu, right-click on a Layers, Channels, or Paths palette thumbnail or name or other area of a palette. Or, choose a tool, then right-click the pointer over the image window to access options for that tool ■.

MINI COLOR PRIMER 2

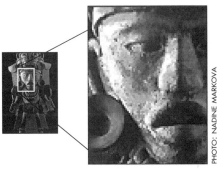

PHOTO: NADINE MARKOVA

1 Close-up of an image, showing individual pixels.

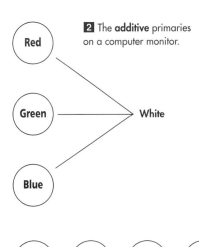

2 The **additive** primaries on a computer monitor.

Red

Green → White

Blue

Cyan Magenta Yellow Black

3 The **subtractive** primaries—printing inks.

THE **FOLLOWING** is a brief explanation of color basics: color models, image modes, and blending modes.

Pixels

The screen image in Photoshop is a bitmap, which is a geometric arrangement (mapping) of a layer of dots of different shades or colors on a rectangular grid. Each dot, called a pixel, represents a color or shade. By magnifying an area of an image, you can edit pixels individually **1**. Every Photoshop image is a bitmap, whether it originates from a scan, from another application, or entirely within the application using painting and editing tools. (Don't confuse Bitmap image mode with the term "bitmapped.") Bitmap programs are ideal for producing painterly, photographic, or photorealistic images that contain gradations of color.

If you drag with a painting tool across an area of a layer, pixels below the pointer are recolored. Once modified, the pixels' original attributes can be restored only by choosing Undo or Revert or by using the Rubber Stamp tool with its From Saved option.

RGB vs. CMYK color

Red, green, and blue (RGB) light are used to display a color image on a monitor. When these additive primaries in their purest form are combined, they produce white light **2**.

The three subtractive primary inks used in four-color process printing are cyan (C), magenta (M), and yellow (Y) **3**. When combined, they produce a dark, muddy color. To produce a rich black, printers usually mix black (K) ink with small quantities of cyan, magenta, and/or yellow ink.

The display of color on a computer monitor is highly variable and subject to the variables of ambient lighting, monitor temperature, and room color. All monitors display color using the RGB model, and simulate the display of CMYK colors. Many colors seen in nature cannot be printed, some colors that can be displayed on screen cannot be printed, and some printable colors can't be displayed on screen. You don't need to worry about RGB-to-CMYK conversion if you're doing multimedia work or are going to output your file to a film recorder.

An exclamation point will appear on the Color palette if you choose a non-printable (out of gamut) color **1**. An exclamation point will also display on the Info palette if the color currently under the pointer is out of gamut **2**. Using Photoshop's Gamut Warning command, you can display non-printable colors in your image in gray, and then, using the Sponge tool, you can desaturate them to bring them into gamut.

You can use the grayscale, RGB (red-green-blue), HSB (hue-saturation-brightness), CMYK (cyan-magenta-yellow-black), or Lab (lightness-a axis-b axis) color model when you choose colors in Photoshop via the Color Picker or Color palette.

Channels

Every Photoshop image is a composite of one or more semi-transparent, colored-light overlays called channels. For example, an image in RGB Color mode is composed of red, green, and blue channels. To illustrate, open a color image, choose Show Channels from the Window menu, then click Red, Green, or Blue on the Channels palette to display only that channel. Click RGB (Control-~) to restore the full channel display. (For this exercise, choose File menu > Preferences > Display & Cursors, then check the Color Channels in Color box.)

Web graphics

If you're creating an image for a Web site, use the RGB color model. Bear in mind that RGB colors—or colors from any other color model, for that matter—may not match the color palette of your Web browser (see pages 271–272). For the best results, load in the Web palette color table from the Indexed Color mode onto the Swatches palette.

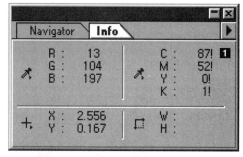

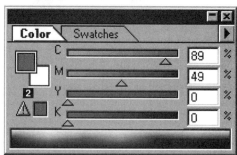

Default number of channels for each image mode

One	Three	Four
Bitmap	RGB	CMYK
Grayscale	Lab	
Duotone		
Indexed Color		

Only currently highlighted channels can be edited.

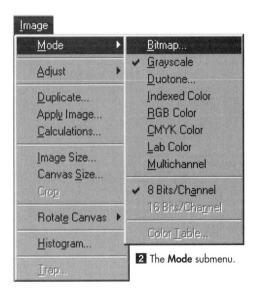

1 An Alpha channel

2 The **Mode** submenu.

Color adjustments can be made to an individual channel, but normally modifications are made and displayed in the multichannel, composite image (the topmost channel name on the Channels palette), and affect all of an image's channels at once. Special grayscale channels that are used for saving selections as masks, called alpha channels, can be added to an image **1**.

The more channels an image contains, the larger its file storage size. The storage size of an image in RGB Color mode, which is composed of three channels (Red, Green, and Blue), will be three times larger than the same image in Grayscale mode, which is composed of one channel. The same image in CMYK Color mode will be composed of four channels (Cyan, Magenta, Yellow, and Black), and will be even larger.

Image modes

An image can be converted to, displayed in, and edited in eight image modes: Bitmap, Grayscale, Duotone, Indexed Color, RGB Color, CMYK Color, Lab Color, and Multichannel. Simply choose the mode you want from the Image menu > Mode submenu **2**. To access a mode that is unavailable (whose name is dimmed), you must first convert your image to a different mode. For example, to convert an image to Indexed Color mode, it must be in RGB Color or Grayscale mode.

Some mode conversions cause noticeable color shifts; others cause subtle color shifts. Very dramatic changes may occur if an image is converted from RGB Color mode to CMYK Color mode, because printable colors are substituted for rich, glowing RGB colors. Color accuracy may diminish if an image is converted back and forth between RGB and CMYK Color mode too many times.

Medium to low-end scanners usually produce RGB scans. If you're creating an image that's going to be printed, for faster editing and to access all the filters, edit it in RGB

Image Modes

Color mode and convert it to CMYK Color mode when you're ready to imageset it. You can use the CMYK Preview command (Control-Y) to preview an image in CMYK Color mode without actually changing its mode. You can CMYK preview your image in one window and open a second window to display the same image without the CMYK preview. Also bear in mind that some conversions cause layers to be flattened, such as a conversion from Indexed Color mode to Multichannel or Bitmap mode. For other conversions, you'll have the option to click Don't Flatten if you want to preserve layers.

High-end scanners usually produce CMYK scans, and these images should be kept in CMYK Color mode to preserve their color data. If you find working on such large files is cumbersome, you can work out your image-editing scheme on a low resolution version of an image, save the commands using the Actions palette, and then apply the action to the high resolution, CMYK version. You will still, however, have to perform selection, painting, and editing tool operations manually.

Some output devices require that an image be saved in a particular image mode. Commands and tool options in Photoshop also vary depending on the currently selected image mode.

These are the image modes, in brief:

In **Bitmap** mode , pixels are 100% black or 100% white only, and layers, filters, and Adjust commands are unavailable, except the Invert command. An image must be in Grayscale mode before it can be converted to Bitmap mode.

In **Grayscale** mode , pixels are black, white, or up to 255 shades of gray. If an image is converted from a color mode to Grayscale mode and then saved, its luminosity (light and dark) values remain intact, but its color information is deleted and cannot be restored.

1 Bitmap mode, Method: Diffusion Dither.

2 Grayscale mode

The **Channels** palette for an image in various modes:

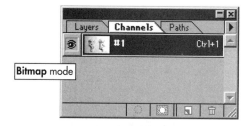

Bitmap mode

Grayscale mode

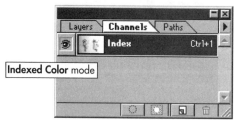

Indexed Color mode

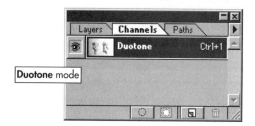

Duotone mode

Image Modes

The **Channels** palette for an image in various modes:

RGB Color mode

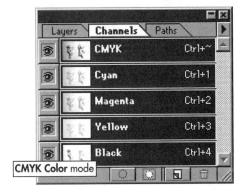

CMYK Color mode

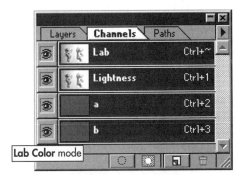

Lab Color mode

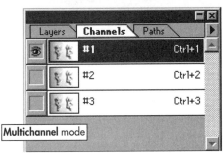

Multichannel mode

An image in **Indexed Color** mode has one channel and a color table containing a maximum of 256 colors or shades. To display a Photoshop image on a Web page or in certain painting or animation programs, it is sometimes better to first convert it to Indexed Color mode. You can also convert an image to Indexed Color mode to create arty color effects.

RGB Color is the most versatile mode because it is the only mode in which all Photoshop's tool options and filters are accessible. Some video and multimedia applications can import an RGB Photoshop image, and the GIF89a Export command, which is one of the best options for Web graphics, is available only for an RGB image.

Photoshop is one of few Macintosh programs in which images can be displayed and edited in **CMYK Color** mode. You can convert an image to CMYK Color mode when you're ready to output it on a color printer or color separate it (unless the output device is a PostScript Level 2 printer, in which case you'd choose Lab Color mode).

Lab Color is a three-channel mode that was developed for the purpose of achieving consistency among various devices, such as printers and monitors. The channels represent lightness, the colors green-to-red, and the colors blue-to-yellow. Photo CD images can be converted to Lab Color mode or RGB Color mode in Photoshop. Save an image in Lab Color mode to print it on a PostScript Level 2 printer or to export it to another operating system.

A **Duotone** is a printing method in which two or more plates are used to add richness and tonal depth to a grayscale image.

A **Multichannel** image is composed of multiple, 256-level grayscale channels. This mode is used for certain grayscale printing situations. You could use multichannel mode to assemble individual channels from several images before converting the new image to a color mode.

Image Modes

The blending modes

You can select from 16 blending modes from the Options palette, the Layers palette, the Fill, Stroke, or Fade dialog box, or the Fill Path dialog box. The mode you choose for a tool or a layer affects how that tool or layer modifies underlying pixels, which in the following text is called the base color. "Blend layer" refers to the layer for which a layer mode is chosen.

NOTE: If the Preserve Transparency box is checked on the Layers palette for the target layer, only non-transparent areas can be recolored or otherwise edited.

Opacities add up

When you choose a mode and an opacity for a tool, be sure to factor in the mode and opacity of the target layer you're working on. If you choose 60% opacity for the Paintbrush tool on a layer that has a 50% opacity, for example, your resulting brush stroke will have a 30% opacity.

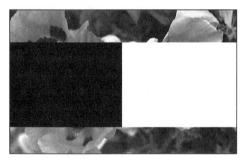

NORMAL
All base colors are modified.

DISSOLVE
Creates a chalky, dry brush texture with the paint or blend layer color. The higher the pressure or opacity, the more solid the stroke or color area.

BEHIND
(Paint color only) Only transparent areas are modified, not existing base color pixels. The effect is like painting on the reverse side of clear acetate. Good for creating shadows.

CLEAR
(Paint color only) Makes the base color transparent where strokes are applied. Only available for a multi-layer image when using the Line or Paint Bucket tool, the Fill command, or the Stroke command. Cannot be used on the Background.

MULTIPLY
A dark paint or blend layer color removes the lighter parts of the base color to produce a darker base color. A light paint or blend layer color darkens the base color less. Good for creating semi-transparent shadow effects.

Blending Modes

SCREEN

A light paint or blend layer color removes the darker parts of the base color to produce a lighter, bleached base color. A dark paint or blend layer lightens the base color less.

OVERLAY

Multiplies (darkens) dark areas and screens (lightens) light areas of base color. Preserves luminosity (light and dark) values. Black and white are not changed, so detail is maintained.

SOFT LIGHT

Lightens the base color if the paint or blend layer color is light. Darkens the base color if the paint or blend layer color is dark. Preserves luminosity values in the base color. Creates a subtle, soft lighting effect.

HARD LIGHT

Screens (lightens) the base color if the paint or blend layer color is light. Multiplies (darkens) the base color if the paint or blend layer color is dark. Greater contrast is created in the base color and layer color. Good for painting glowing highlights and creating composite effects.

COLOR DODGE

Lightens the base color where the paint or blend layer color is light. A dark paint or blend layer color tints the base color slightly.

COLOR BURN

A dark paint or blend layer color darkens the base color. A light paint or blend layer color tints the base color slightly.

Blending Modes

DARKEN

Base colors lighter than the paint or blend layer color are modified; base colors darker than the paint or blend layer color are not. Use with a paint color that is darker than the base colors you want to modify.

LIGHTEN

Base colors darker than the paint or blend layer color are modified; base colors lighter than the paint or blend layer color are not. Use with a paint color that is lighter than the base colors you want to modify.

DIFFERENCE

Creates a color negative effect on the base color. When the paint or blend layer color is light, the negative (or invert) effect is more pronounced. Produces noticeable color shifts.

EXCLUSION

Grays out the base color where the paint or blend layer color is dark. Inverts the base color where the paint or blend layer color is light.

HUE

The paint or blend layer color hue is applied. Saturation and luminosity values are not modified in the base color.

SATURATION

The paint or blend layer color's saturation is applied. Hue and luminosity values are not modified in the base color.

COLOR

The paint or blend layer color's saturation and hue are applied. The base color's light and dark (luminosity) values aren't changed, so detail is maintained.

LUMINOSITY

The base color's luminosity values are replaced by tone (luminosity) values from the paint or blend layer color. Hue and saturation are not affected in the base color.

STARTUP 3

N THIS CHAPTER you will learn how to get started in Photoshop: launch the application, scan an image, create a new image, open an existing image, and place an Illustrator image into Photoshop. You'll also learn how to change an image's dimensions, resolution, or file storage size; apply the Unsharp Mask filter to resharpen after resampling; enlarge an image's canvas size; crop, flip, rotate, save, copy, and close an image; and exit the application.

To launch Photoshop:

In Windows 95, click the Start button on the Taskbar **1**, choose Progams, choose Adobe, then click Adobe Photoshop 4.0. If you don't have a shortcut icon for Photoshop on your desktop, open the Photoshop folder, then drag the Photoshop application icon to the desktop.

or

Open the Adobe Photoshop folder in My Computer, then double-click the Photoshop application icon **2**.

or

Double-click a Photoshop file icon **3**.

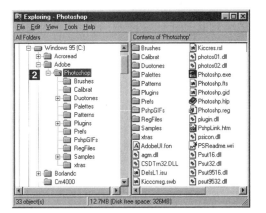

Where images come from

An image can be created, opened, edited, and saved in 18 different file formats in Photoshop 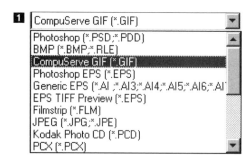. Of these, you may use only a few, such as TIFF, PICT, EPS, and the native Photoshop file format. Because Photoshop accepts so many formats, images can be gathered from a wide variety of sources, such as scans, drawing applications, PhotoCDs, still image and video captures, and other operating systems—and they can be output from Photoshop on many types of printers. And, of course, images can also be created entirely within the application.

Scanning

Using a scanning device and scanning software, a slide, flat artwork, or a photograph can be translated into numbers (digitized) so it can be read, displayed, edited, and printed by a computer. You can scan directly into Photoshop or you can use other scanning software and save the scan in a file format that Photoshop opens.

To produce a high-quality scan, start with as high quality an original as possible. Some scanners will compress an image's dynamic range and increase its contrast, so use a photograph with good tonal balance, and, if you're doing your own scanning, set the scanning parameters carefully, weighing such factors as your final output device and storage capacity.

The quality of a scan will partially depend on the type of scanner you use. If your print shop is going to use the original photograph for printing and the scan will only be used to indicate the image's position or you're going to dramatically transform the image in Photoshop, you can use an inexpensive flat-bed scanner, which will produce an RGB scan. If color accuracy and crisp details are critical, scan a transparency on a slide scanner. An image that is going to be printed electronically should be scanned by a service bureau on a high-resolution CCD scanner, such as a Scitex Smart-Scanner,

Scanning

or on a drum scanner. High end scanners usually produce CMYK scans. Unfortunately, high-resolution scans also usually have very large file sizes.

Scanning software basics

Scanning software usually offers most of the following options, although terms may vary. The quality and file storage size of a scan are partially defined by the mode, resolution, and scale you specify, and whether you crop the image.

Preview: Place the art in the scanner, then click Preview or PreScan.

Scan mode: Select Black-and-White Drawing (no grays), Grayscale, or Color (choose millions of colors, if available). An image scanned in Color will be approximately three times larger in file size than the same image scanned in Grayscale.

Resolution: Scan resolution is measured in pixels per inch (ppi). The higher the resolution, the finer the detail in the image, but the larger its file size. Choose the minimum resolution necessary to obtain the best possible printout from your final output device. Don't choose a higher resolution than required, because the image will be larger in storage size than necessary, it will take longer to render on screen, display on the Web, or print, and there will be no improvement in output quality. On the other hand, too low a resolution will cause a printed image to look coarse and jagged, and its details will be lost.

Before selecting a resolution for print output, determine the resolution of the printer or imagesetter and the halftone screen frequency your print shop plans to use. (The scan resolution is different from the resolution of the output device.)

As a general rule, for a grayscale image, you should choose a resolution that is one-and-a-half times the halftone screen frequency (lines per inch) of your final output device, twice the halftone screen frequency

72 ppi

150 ppi

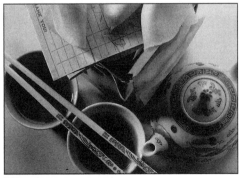

300 ppi

Scanning

for a color image. Use a high scanning resolution (600 ppi or higher) for line art. For example, if your print shop intends to use a 133-line screen frequency for black-and-white printing, you should use 200 ppi as your scan resolution. Ask your prepress shop if they're using an imagesetter that doesn't use the halftoning technology, in which case you should ask them to recommend an appropriate scan resolution. To calculate the appropriate file size for a scan, see the instructions on page 34.

Cropping: If you plan to use only part of an image, reposition the handles of the box in the preview area to reduce the scan area. Cropping can significantly reduce the storage size of a scan.

Scale: To enlarge an image's dimensions, choose a scale percentage above 100%. Enlarging an image or increasing its resolution in Photoshop or any other software program may cause it to blur, because the program uses mathematical "guesswork" (interpolation) to fill in additional information. An image's original information is recorded only at the time of scanning.

Scan: Click Scan and choose a location in which to save the file.

NOTES: To scan into Photoshop, the scanner's plug-in module or Twain module must be in the Import folder inside the Photoshop Plugins folder. The first time you choose a scanning module from the File > Import submenu, choose select Twain_32 Source and choose a Twain device (the scanner), then choose Twain_32 Source. Thereafter, to access the scanning software, just choose Twain_32 Source. (See the Photoshop documentation for information about scanning modules.)

If your scanner doesn't have a Photoshop compatible scanner driver, scan your image outside Photoshop, save it as a TIFF, then open it in Photoshop as you would any other image.

To calculate the proper resolution for a scan, follow the instructions on the next page.

To scan into Photoshop:

1. Choose a scanning module or choose File menu > Import > Twain_32 Source.

2. Following the guidelines outlined on the previous two pages, choose a Mode or Type **1**.
and
Choose a Resolution or Path.

3. *Optional:* Choose a different Scale percentage.

4. *Optional:* Crop the image preview.

5. Click Scan or Final. The scanned image will appear in a new, untitled window.

6. Save the image (see pages 49–51). If the image requires color correction, see pages 248–261.

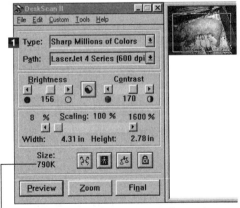

Note how the **file size** changes as you change the mode, resolution, and scale settings.

The resolution of a Photoshop image, like any bitmapped image, is independent of the monitor's resolution, so it can be customized for a particular output device, with or without modifying its file storage size. An image whose resolution is greater than the monitor's resolution (96 ppi for a typical PC monitor) will appear larger than its print size when it's displayed in Photoshop at 100% view. It's always best, though, to scan your image at the final size and resolution that are required for your final output device.

To calculate the proper resolution for a scan or for an existing image:

1. Create a new RGB document and choose 96 ppi, and enter your final width and height dimensions, if you know what they are.

2. Choose Image menu > Image Size.

3. Click the Auto button on the right side of the dialog box.

4. Enter the screen resolution of your final output device (i.e., the lines per inch (lpi) setting that your print shop will use) **1**.

5. Click Draft (1x screen frequency), Good (1½ x screen frequency), or Best (2 x screen frequency).

6. Click OK.

7. Jot down the Print Size: Resolution value, which is the proper value to enter when you scan your image.
   NOTE: If you're going to scale the final image up or down in Photoshop, you should multiply the resolution by the scale factor to calculate the proper resolution for the scan. You don't need to multiply the resolution if you scale the original image when you scan it.

8. Click OK or press Return.

Is the Web the final destination for your image?

Create the appropriate image size by settting the resolution to 96 ppi in the Image Size dialog box and entering the pixel dimensionss (height and width) for the maximum desired view size of the image. For an online image, determine the most common monitor size and pixel dimensions your viewers will use. Images are usually formatted for a 13-inch monitor—640 by 480 pixels. The total number of pixels in the image determines the file size.

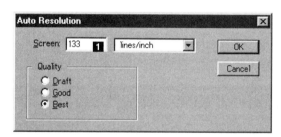

To calculate scanning parameters based on the required file size

Some scanners require that you enter the final file storage size in order to produce the necessary number of pixels for the image. To determine the final file size, choose File menu > New, enter the final width and height, choose RGB Color mode, then click Cancel. Now, keep increasing the resolution until the Image Size figure at the top of the dialog box reaches the size recommended by your print shop or service bureau, and enter that Image Size figure when you scan the image. You can readjust the width and height of the scanned image later in Photoshop, if necessary.

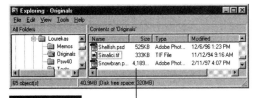

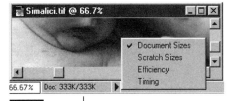

Storage size

If you're courious to know the actual **storage size** of an image, use Windows Explorer to open the folder that contains the file you are interested in, and look in the Size Column. Or, for an even more accurate figure, right-click the file icon and click on Properties.

RAM

To see how much **RAM** an image requires, choose Document Sizes from the bottom of the image window. The figure on the left is the RAM required for the flattened image with no extra channels; the figure on the right is the RAM size for the image with layers and extra channels, if any.

File storage sizes of scanned images

Size (In inches)	PPI (Resolution)	Black/White 1-Bit	Grayscale 8-Bit	CMYK Color 24-Bit
2 x 3	150	17 K	132 K	528 K
	300	67 K	528 K	2.06 MB
4 x 5	150	56 K	440 K	1.72 MB
	300	221 K	1.72 MB	6.87 MB
8 x 10	150	220 K	1.72 MB	6.87 MB
	300	879 K	6.87 MB	27.50 MB

Potential gray levels at various output resolutions and screen frequencies

	Output Resolution (DPI)	Screen Frequency (LPI)				
		60	85	100	133	150
Laser printers	300	26	13			
	600	101	51	37	21	
Image-setters	1270	256*	224	162	92	72
	2540		256*	256*	256*	256*

Note: Ask your print shop what screen frequency (lpi) you will need to specify when image-setting your file. Also ask your prepress shop what resolution (dpi) to use for imagesetting. Some imagesetters can achieve resolutions above 2540 dpi.

*At the present time, PostScript Level 1 and Level 2 printers produce a maximum of 256 gray levels.

File Storage Sizes, Potential Gray Levels

To create a new image:

1. Choose File menu > New (Control-N) .

2. Enter a name in the Name field **2**.

3. Choose a unit of measure from the drop-down menus next to the Width and Height fields.

4. Enter Width and Height values.

5. Enter the Resolution required for your final output device—whether it's an imagesetter or the Web (resolution issues are discussed on page 34).

6. Choose an image mode from the Mode drop-down menu. You can convert the image to a different mode later (see "Image modes" on pages 23–25).

7. Click Contents: White, Background Color, or Transparent for the Background. To choose a Background color, see pages 112–114. If you choose the Transparent option, you can only save the image in the Photoshop file format, because the background will actually be a layer. Photoshop's layer transparency cannot be read by any other software. (More about layers and transparency in Chapters 7 and 12).

8. Click OK or press Enter. An image window will appear **3**.

TIP If you want the New dialog box settings to match those of another open document, with the New dialog box open, choose the name of the image that has the desired dimensions from the Window menu.

TIP If there is an image on the Clipboard, the New dialog box will automatically display its dimensions. To prevent those dimensions from displaying, hold down Alt when you choose File menu > New.

1 Choose **New** from the File menu.

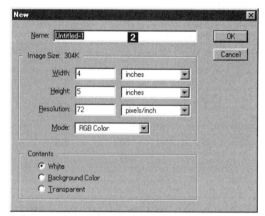

In the New dialog box, enter a **Name** and enter numbers in the **Width, Height,** and **Resolution** fields. Also choose an **image Mode** and click a **Contents** type for the **Background**.

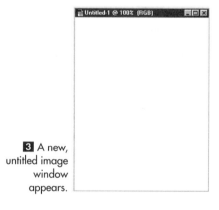

3 A new, untitled image window appears.

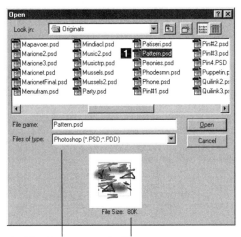

The file's **format**.   The file's **size**.

Double-click a file name in the Open dialog box. If the name of the file you want to open doesn't appear on the scroll list, click the drop-down button in the Files of type box, then choose a format.

Thumbnails

To create image icons for **Windows Explorer** when the View menu is set to Large Icon, click the Save Thumbnail checkbox for individual files as you save them. Thumbnail icons appear only if the file extension is PSD.

To create a thumbnail of any subsequently saved image for display in the Open dialog box, choose File menu > Preferences > Saving Files, then choose Image Previews: Always Save **2**. A thumbnail icon will only appear for an image that has a PSD, JPG, or TIF file extension.

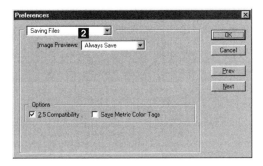

NOTE: To open an Adobe Illustrator file, follow the instructions on page 40 or 41.

To open an image within Photoshop:

1. Choose File menu > Open (Control-O).

2. Locate the file you want to open **1**.

> **NOTE:** If the name of the file you want to open doesn't appear on the scroll list, it means the plug-in module for its file format isn't installed in your system, so you'll have to convert the file to a format that Photoshop supports. To do this, choose the All file format from the Files of type drop-down menu. Once opened, an image can be saved in any format that Photoshop supports. Don't leave the format as Raw.

4. Highlight the file name, then click Open.

or

Double-click the file name.

For some file formats, a further dialog box will open. For example, if you open a file saved in the EPS or Adobe Illustrator format that hasn't yet been rasterized (converted from object-oriented to bitmap), the Rasterize Generic EPS Format dialog box will open. Follow steps 4–9 on page 40.

TIP To open a QuarkXPress page in Photoshop, save it in QuarkXPress using the Save Page as EPS command, then follow the steps on page 40.

TIP To open images in some file formats, like Scitex CT, you must use a special plug-in module, which will be accessed via the File menu > Import submenu.

Open an Image within Photoshop

To open a Photoshop image from Windows Explorer:

Double-click a Photoshop image file icon in Windows Explorer 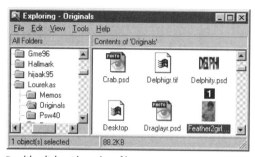. Photoshop will launch if it hasn't already been launched.

Double-click a Photoshop file icon.

To open Kodak Photo CD images, Photoshop uses the Kodak CMS Photo CD plug-in, which is accessed from the File menu. Kodak's Color Management System is used to enhance the accuracy of image translation from the Kodak file format into Photoshop's RGB Color or Lab Color mode.

To open a Kodak Photo CD file:

1. Choose File menu > Open (Control-O).

2. Locate and double-click the Photo CD file name 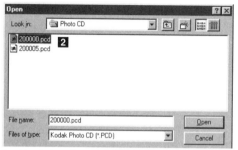.
   or
   Highlight the Photo CD file name and click Open.

3. Choose a Resolution 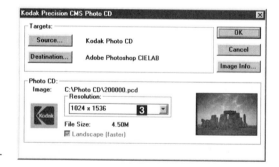. The base resolution is 512 by 768 pixels, which will produce an image about 7 by 10.5 inches at 72 pixels/inch. A higher resolution will produce a larger image at 72 pixels/inch.

   Leave the Landscape box checked to open the image quickly. (Use one of Photoshop's Rotate commands if you need to change the orientation of the image after opening it.)

4. Click Image Info to read about the original film medium. Make a note of the Medium of Original and Product Type of Original info (the type of film used to create the image) . Color Reversal is the term for a color slide; 52/xx is Ektachrome slide; and 116/xx is Kodachrome slide. Click OK.

5. Click Source.

Double-click a Photo CD file name in the Open dialog box. The Format will be listed as Kodak CMS Photo CD.

Open an Image; Open Kodak Photo CD

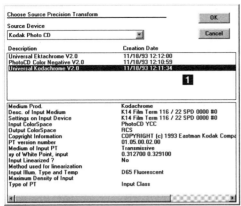

Click on the **Description** that most closely matches the film medium of the original photo that was listed in the Image Info dialog box. The image info dialog box for this image listed Color Reversal as the Medium of Original and the Product Type as 116/-XX, so we chose Universal Kodachrome V2.0 as the profile. Kodak recommends choosing Universal Ektachrome when the Medium of Original is Color Reversal and the Product Type of Original is unknown.

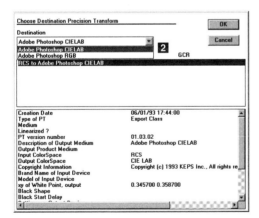

6. Click on the closest available match to the Image Info description **1**, then click OK.

7. Click Destination.

8. From the Device drop-down menu, choose Adobe Photoshop RGB or Adobe Photoshop CIELAB (Lab) as the color mode for the image in Photoshop **2**, then click OK.

9. Click OK in the Photo CD Plug in dialog box. The image will open in Photoshop.

Stop press!

Kodak has upgraded its film scanners to the 4045 and 4050 models and has also upgraded its PhotoCD transform descriptions (version 3.x instead of version 2.x). The product types and film choice for the new upgrades are as follows:

052/72   4050E6
116/72   4050K14
052/xx   Universal Ektachrome
116/xx   Universal Kodachrome

Open Kodak Photo CD File

When an EPS or Adobe Illustrator file is opened or placed in Photoshop, it is rasterized, which means it's converted from its native object-oriented format into Photoshop's pixel-based format. Follow these instructions to open an EPS file, such as an Adobe Illustrator graphic, as a new document. Follow the instructions on the next page to place an EPS file into an existing Photoshop file.

To open an EPS or Illustrator file as a new image:

1. Choose File menu > Open (Control-O).

2. If the file name isn't listed, click on All Formats in the Files of type box.

3. Locate and highlight an EPS image to be opened, then click Open.
   or
   Double-click a file name.

4. *Optional:* In the Rasterize Generic EPS Format dialog box, check the Constrain Proportions box to preserve the file's height and width ratio **1**.

5. *Optional:* Choose a unit of measure from the drop-down menus next to the Height and Width fields, and enter new dimensions.

6. Enter the final resolution required for your image in the Resolution field. Entering the correct final resolution before rasterizing produces the best rendering of the image.

7. Choose an image mode from the Mode drop-down menu. (See "Image modes," beginning on page 23.)

8. Check the Anti-aliased box for optimal rendering of the image, and soft edge transitions.

9. Click OK or press Enter.

Drag-and-drop from Illustrator 7

You can drag-and-drop an object from an Illustrator 7 image window into a Photoshop 4 image window. The object will automatically become bitmapped in Photoshop, and it will appear on its own layer. If you want to import an Illustrator shape as a path in Photoshop, hold down Control as you drag-and-drop.

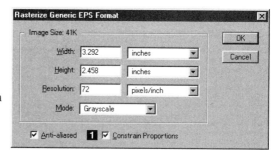

PHOTO: E. WEINMANN

1 The word "Delphi" was created in Adobe Illustrator, and then placed in a Photoshop file.

When you place an object-oriented (vector) image into a Photoshop image, it becomes bitmapped and is rendered in the resolution of the Photoshop image. The higher the resolution of the Photoshop image, the better the rendering (200 ppi minimum).

NOTE: You can also drag a path from an Illustrator 7 image window into a Photoshop image window, where it will appear on a new layer.

To place an Adobe Illustrator image into an existing Photoshop image:

1. Open a Photoshop image.

2. Choose File menu > Place.

3. Locate and highlight the Illustrator file you want to open.

4. Click Place. A box will appear on top of the image. Pause to allow the image to draw inside it **1**.

5. *Perform any of these optional steps (use the Undo command to undo any of them):*

To resize the placed image, drag a handle of the bounding border. Hold down Shift while dragging to preserve the proportions of the placed image.

To move the placed image, drag inside the bounding border.

To rotate the placed image, position the pointer outside the bounding border, then drag.

6. To accept the placed image, press Enter or double-click inside the bounding border. The placed image will appear on a new layer.

TIP By default, the Anti-alias PostScript box is checked in the File menu > Preferences > General dialog box, and this setting produces the most optimal, but slowest, rendering of placed images.

TIP To remove the placed image, press Esc before or while it's rendering. If the image is already rendered, highlight its layer name on the Layers palette, then click the trash icon.

To produce this image, artist Wendy Grossman created the musical notes and other shapes in Illustrator and then imported them into Photoshop.

Place an Adobe Illustrator Image

NOTE: Changing an image's dimensions in Photoshop while preserving its current resolution (leaving the Resample Image box checked) will cause resampling, which degrades image quality. That's why it's always best to scan or create an image at the desired size. If resample you must, apply the Unsharp Mask filter afterward to resharpen (see pages 44–45).

To change an image's dimensions for print output:

1. Choose Image menu > Image Size.

2. To preserve the image's width-to-height ratio, check the Constrain Proportions box **1**. To modify the image's width independently of its height, uncheck the Constrain Proportions box.

3. *Optional:* To preserve the image's resolution, check the Resample Image box **2** and choose Nearest Neighbor, Bilinear, or Bicubic as the interpolation method. Bicubic causes the least degradation in image quality.

4. Choose a unit of measure from the drop-down menu next to the Print Size: Width and Height fields.

5. Enter new numbers in the Width and/or Height fields. The Resolution will change if the Resample Image box is unchecked.

6. Click OK or press Enter.

TIP To restore the original Image Size dialog box settings, hold down Alt and click Reset.

TIP If you modify an image's dimensions and/or resolution with the Resample Image box checked, you will not be able to use the Rubber Stamp tool with its From Saved option to restore a portion of it. Save an image immediately after modifying its dimensions and/or resolution to establish a new From Saved reference.

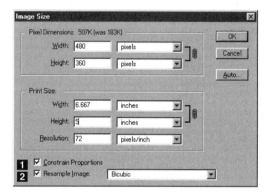

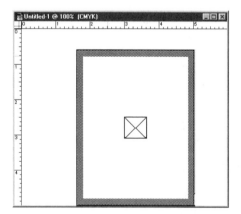

Print preview

To see the image size relative to the paper size, press and hold on the sizes bar at the bottom of the image window. To display the image on screen at the size it will print, choose View menu > Print Size. (By the way, at 100% view, the on-screen display size will match the print size only if the image resolution is the same as the monitor's resolution, which is usually 72 ppi.)

Change Dimensions for Print

To change an image's pixel dimensions for on-screen output:

1. Choose Image menu > Image Size.

2. Make sure the Resample Image box is checked.

3. To preserve the image's width-to-height ratio, leave the Constrain Proportions box checked.

4. Set the Resolution to 96 ppi, the resolution commonly used for PC on-screen display.

5. Enter new values in the Pixel Dimensions: Width and/or Height fields.

6. Click OK or press Enter.

Cashing in on too high a resolution

An image contains a given number of pixels after scanning, and its print dimensions and its resolution are interdependent. If an image's resolution or dimensions are changed with the Resample Image box unchecked (Image Size dialog box), the file's total pixel count is preserved. Increasing an image's pixels per inch resolution will shrink its print dimensions; lowering an image's pixels per inch resolution amount will enlarge its print dimensions.

If your file has a higher resolution than needed (more than twice the screen frequency), you can allocate the extra resolution to the print size dimensions by unchecking the Resample Image box (the width, height, and resolution are now interdependent), and then lowering the resolution to twice the screen frequency. The width and height values will automatically increase, and the file size will remain constant—no pixels will be added or deleted from the image.

If you must further enlarge the image's dimensions, click in the Width field, check the Resample Image box, and enter a new Width value. The Height will change proportionately, and the file size will increase, but you'll be resampling, so after clicking OK, apply the Unsharp Mask filter to resharpen (see pages 44–45).

NOTE: If you increase an image's resolution (resample up) with the Resample Image box checked, pixels will be added and the image's file storage size will increase, but its sharpness will diminish. If you decrease an image's resolution (downsample), information is deleted from the file and it can't be retrieved once the image is saved. Blurriness caused by resampling may only be evident when the image is printed; it may not be discernible on screen. It's best to scan or create an image at the proper resolution. Follow the instructions on the next page to resharpen a resampled image. (And see "Resolution" on page 34.)

To change an image's resolution:

1. Choose Image menu > Image Size.

2. *Optional:* To preserve the image's dimensions (Width and Height), check the Resample Image box **1**. To preserve the total pixel count in the image, uncheck Resample Image. The Width and Height dimensions must change to preserve the current pixel count.

3. Enter a number in the Resolution field.

4. Click OK or press Enter.

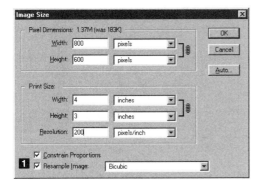

On-Screen Dimensions; Change Resolution

If you change an image's dimensions or resolution with the Resample Image box checked, convert it to CMYK Color mode, or transform it, blurring may occur due to the resampling process. Despite its name, the Unsharp Mask filter has a focusing effect. It increases contrast between adjacent pixels that already have some contrast. You can specify the amount of contrast to be created (Amount), the number of surrounding pixels that will be modified around each pixel that requires more contrast (Radius), and determine which pixels the filter effects or ignores by specifying the minimum degree of existing contrast (Threshold).

NOTE: The Unsharp Mask effect is more discernible on screen than on high-resolution print output.

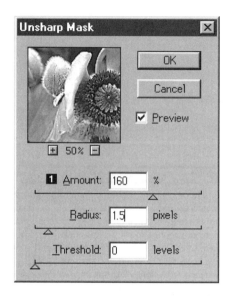

To apply the Unsharp Mask filter:

1. Choose Filter menu > Sharpen > Unsharp Mask.

2. Enter a number in the Amount field (the percentage increase in contrast between pixels) or move the Amount slider **1**. Use a low setting (below 45) for figures or natural objects and a higher setting if the image contains sharp-edged objects. Too high a setting will produce obvious halos around high contrast areas. The larger the image, the less sharpening may be required.

3. To choose an appropriate Radius value, which is a little trickier, you need to consider the final size, the resolution, and the subject matter of the image. Enter a number between 0.1 and 100 in the Radius field or move the Radius slider to specify the number of pixels surrounding high contrast edges that will be modified. Try between 1 and 2. Higher values will produce too much contrast in areas that already have high contrast.

The higher the resolution of the image, the more pixels there are on the border

The original image, a bit blurry.

After Unsharp Masking with a high Amount (160%). Radius 1.5, Threshold 0. Notice the halos around the edges and the centers of the flowers.

After Unsharp Masking with a high Radius (6.0). Amount of 130, Threshold of 0. The soft gradations have become choppy and the image has an unnatural contrast and sharpness.

After Unsharp Masking with a high Threshold (15). Amount of 160, Radius of 1.5. Even with the same Amount setting as in the top image, the soft gradations in the petals and the background are preserved.

between high contrast areas, so the higher the Radius setting is required. Try a high Radius setting for a low contrast image, and a lower Radius setting for an intricate, high contrast image.

NOTE: The higher the Radius setting, the lower the Amount setting can be, and vice versa.

4. Enter a number between 0 and 255 in the Threshold field or move the Threshold slider. The Threshold is the minimum amount of contrast an area must have before it will be modified. At a Threshold of 0, the filter will be applied to the entire image. A Threshold value above 0 will cause sharpening along already high contrast edges, less so in low contrast areas. If you increase the Threshold value, you can then increase the Amount and Radius values without adding sharpening noise to areas that require less sharpening. To prevent noise from distorting skin tones, specify a Threshold between 10 and 20.

5. Click OK or press Enter.

TIP To soften a grainy scan, apply the Gaussian Blur filter (Blur submenu) at a low setting (below 1) and then apply the Sharpen Edges filter (Sharpen submenu) once or twice afterward to resharpen.

TIP If you're Unsharp Masking a large image, uncheck the Preview box to avoid waiting for full screen previews. First, get close to the right settings using just the preview window, then check the Preview box to preview the results on the full screen, and finally, readjust the settings, if needed.

TIP Try applying the Unsharp Mask filter to one or two individual color channels (the Red or Green channel, for example, in an RGB image). If you sharpen two separate channels, use the same Radius value in both.

Unsharp Mask

The Canvas Size command changes the live, editable image area.

NOTE: If you want to crop right on the image, use the Crop tool or the Crop command.

To change the canvas size:

1. If the image has a Background, choose a Background color (see pages 112–114).

2. Choose Image menu > Canvas Size.

3. *Optional:* Choose a different unit of measure from the drop-down menus.

4. Enter new numbers in the Width and/or Height fields **1**. Changing the Width won't change the Height, and vice versa.

5. *Optional:* To reposition the image in its new canvas size, click on a gray Anchor square. The white square represents the existing image relative to the new canvas area.

6. Click OK or press Enter. Any added areas will automatically fill with the current Background color (unless the background is a layer with transparency, in which case added canvas areas will also be transparent) **2**–**3**.

Note the new and current file sizes as you change the canvas size.

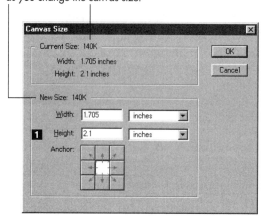

2 The original image.

PHOTO: E. WEINMANN

3 The same image with added canvas pixels.

To specify dimensions and resolution as you crop

Double-click the Crop tool, check the Fixed Target Size box on the Cropping Tool Options palette, enter values in the Width, Height, and Resolution fields, then follow steps 2–4 at right. Click Front Image to insert the current image's Width, Height, and Resolution values into the fields.

Having clicked Front Image, the crop marquee will match the current width-to-height ratio. The cropped image's resolution will increase or decrease to fit the width and height values you enter. If you increase only the resolution, the print size won't change, but the image's pixel count will increase. Entering a higher resolution value will cause pixel resampling, and will probably add distortion to the image.

To crop one image to fit exactly inside another image

Open both images, activate the destination image, choose the Crop tool, check the Fixed Target Size box and click Front Image on the Cropping Tool Options palette, activate the image you want to crop, then draw a marquee. After cropping, drag-and-drop the layer or copy and paste the layer onto the destination image.

To crop an image:

1. Choose the Crop tool (C) ⊐, from the Marquee tool pop-out menu.

2. Drag a marquee over the portion of the image you want to keep **1**.

3. *Do any of these optional steps:*

   To resize the marquee, drag any handle (double-arrow pointer) **2**. Hold down Shift while dragging to preserve the marquee's proportions.

   To reposition the marquee, drag from inside it.

   To rotate the marquee, position the cursor outside the bounding box, then drag in a circular direction.

4. Press Enter **2**.
   or
   Double-click inside the marquee. If you rotated the marquee, the rotated image will be squared off in the image window.

TIP To stop the cropping process before accepting it, press Esc.

TIP To resharpen an image after cropping, apply the Unsharp Mask filter (see pages 44–45).

1 Drag a marquee over the portion of the image you want to keep.

PHOTO: PAUL PETROFF

2 The cropped image.

NOTE: The Rotate Canvas command flips all the layers in an image. To flip one layer at a time, use the Layer menu > Transform > Flip Horizontal or Flip Vertical command.

To flip an image:

To flip the image left to right, choose Image menu > Rotate Canvas > Flip Horizontal **1**–**2**.

or

To flip the image upside-down to produce a mirror image, choose Image menu > Rotate Canvas > Vertical **3**.

1 The original image.

2 The image flipped horizontally.

3 The image flipped vertically.

NOTE: The Rotate Canvas commands rotate all the layers in an image. To rotate one layer at a time, use a Layer menu > Transform submenu rotate command.

To rotate an image a preset amount:

Choose Image Menu > Rotate Canvas > Rotate 180°, 90° CW (clockwise), or 90° CCW (counterclockwise).

To rotate an image by specifying a number:

1. Choose Image Menu > Rotate Canvas > Arbitrary.

2. Enter a number between -359.9° and 359.9° in the Angle field **4**.

3. Click °CW (clockwise) or °CCW (counterclockwise)

4. Click OK or press Enter **5**.

5 After rotating an image 180°. Compare with the flipped images, above.

What the Photoshop format does and doesn't do

Photoshop is the only format in which multiple layers are available. You'll also need to use the Photoshop format if you want to work with adjustment layers, grids, guides, or the KP Color Management profiles. Few other applications can read an image in the Photoshop file format, though, so you should keep a copy of your layered RBG image if you think there's any chance you'll want to rework it, and flatten the copy or the second version (see pages 51 and 98). Painter versions 4 and later will import a layered Photoshop image with its layers intact; they'll appear as floaters.

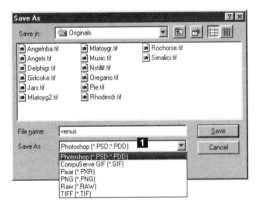

Special instructions for saving in the EPS, PICT, and TIFF file formats are on pages 244–245. Other file formats are covered in the Photoshop User Guide.

To save a new image:

1. Choose File menu > Save (Control-S).
or
If the image contains multiple layers, follow the Save a Copy instructions on page 51.

2. Type a name in the "File name" field **1**.

3. Choose a location in which to save the file. If you need to locate a drive, choose My Computer from the Save in drop-down list. Double-click a folder in which to save the file or create a new folder by clicking the Create New folder icon.

4. Choose a file format from the Save As drop-down list. If the document contains more than one layer, only the native Photoshop format will be available.

5. Click Save.

The prior version of a file is overwritten when the Save command is chosen.

To save an existing image:

Choose File menu > Save (Command-S).

To revert to the last saved version:

1. Choose File menu > Revert.

2. Click Revert when the prompt appears **2**.

TIP To revert only a portion of an image, use the Rubber stamp tool with its From Saved option.

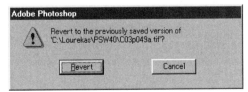

2 Click **Revert** when this warning prompt appears.

Using the Save As command, you can save a copy of an image in a different image mode or use the copy to do a design variation. For example, you can save a version of an image in CMYK Color mode and keep the original version in RGB Color mode.

NOTE: Use the Save a Copy command to copy a file and continue working on the original (instructions on the next page).

To save a new version of an image:

1. Open a file. If the image contains layers and you want to save it in a format other than Photoshop's native file format, flatten the image now.

2. Choose File menu > Save As (Control-Shift-S).

3. Enter a new name or modify the existing name in the File name field **1**.

4. Choose a location in which to save the new version.

5. Choose a different file Format (available for a single-layer document only). Hold down Alt while choosing a format to append the format's three-character extension to the file name.

6. Click Save. For an EPS file, follow the instructions on page 244. For a TIFF or PICT file, follow instructions on page 245. Consult the Photoshop manual for other formats. The new version will remain open; the original file will close automatically.

TIP If you don't change the name of the file and you click Save, a warning prompt will appear. Click Yes to save over the original file or click No to return to the Save As dialog box.

TIP Your image may need to be in a particular mode for some formats to be available.

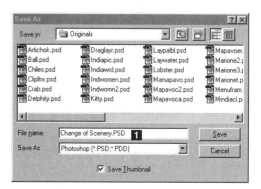

What does the Duplicate command do?

The Image menu > Duplicate command copies an image and all its layers, layer masks, and channels into currently available memory. A permanent copy of the file is not saved to disk unless you then choose File > Save. An advantage of the Duplicate command is that you can use the duplicate to try out variations quickly without altering the original file. HOWEVER, Duplicate should be used with caution, because if an application freeze or a system crash occurs, you'll lose whatever's currently in memory, including your duplicate image. (The original image probably occupied a considerable amount of memory and the duplicate occupied even more memory. If you're curious, both sizes are reflected in the Scratch Sizes on the Info bar.)

The Save a Copy command creates and saves a flattened version of a multi-layer image in any file format you choose. The multi-layer version of the image will stay open so you can continue to work on it. The flattened version of an image will be smaller in file size than its multi-layer counterpart.

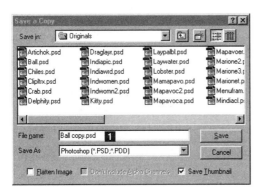

To copy a file and continue to work on the original:

1. With the file open, choose File menu > Save a Copy (Control-Alt-S).

2. *Optional:* Type a new name or change the name in the File name field **1**. The word "copy" will automatically append to the file name.

3. Choose a location in which to save the copy.

4. *Optional:* For an image in the Photoshop file format, check the Flatten Image box to flatten all layers.

5. *Optional:* Choose a different file Format. If you choose any format other than Photoshop, the Flatten Image box will be checked automatically and layers will be flattened.

6. *Optional:* You can delete alpha channels from a Photoshop, PDF, Pixar, PNG, Targa, or TIFF file by checking the Don't Include Alpha Channels box.

7. Click Save. For an EPS file, follow the instructions on page 244. The original file will remain open.

Copy a File, Keep Working on Original

To close an image:

Click the close box in the upper right corner of the document window **1**.

or

Choose File menu > Close (Control-W).

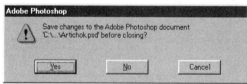

If you attempt to close an image and it was modified since it was last saved, a warning prompt will appear. Click **No** to close the file without saving, click **Yes** to save the file before closing, or click Cancel to cancel the Close operation.

To exit Photoshop:

Choose File menu > Exit (Control-Q).

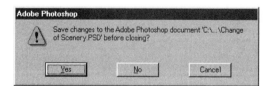

If you exit Photoshop, all open Photoshop files will close. If changes were made to an open file since it was saved, a prompt will appear. Click **No** to close the file without saving, click **Yes** to save the file before exiting, or click Cancel to cancel the Exit operation.

Close an Image; Exit Photoshop

NAVIGATE 4

THIS **CHAPTER** covers how to change the display size of an image, how to move an image in its window, how to display an image in two windows simultaneously, and how to switch screen display modes. The new Navigator palette can be used to move an image in its window or to change the view percentage.

You can display an entire image within its window, or magnify part of an image to work on a small detail. The display size is indicated as a percentage on the image window title bar, in the lower left corner of the image window, and in the lower left corner of the Navigator palette. The display size of an image neither reflects nor affects its printout size.

To change the display size using the Navigator palette:

Drag in preview box to **move** the image in the image window. Control-drag in the preview box to marquee the area you want to **magnify**.

Enter the desired **zoom percentage** (or ratio, like 1:1 or 4:1), then press **Enter**. To zoom to the percentage and keep the field highlighted, press Shift-Enter. (You can also change the display size by typing the desired zoom percentage, and then presssing Enter.)

Click the **Zoom out** button to reduce the image display size.

Move the **Zoom slider** to change the image display size.

Click the **Zoom in** button to enlarge the image display.

To change the display size using the Zoom tool:

1. Choose the Zoom tool (Z). 🔍

2. To **magnify** the image, click in the image window **1**. Or, drag a marquee across an area to magnify that area.
or
To **reduce** the display size, Alt-click on the image **2**.
or
To display the entire image in the largest possible size that will fit on your screen, click Fit on Screen on the Zoom Tool Options palette **3**.

TIP Uncheck the Resize Windows To Fit box on the Zoom Tool Options palette if you want to prevent the image window from resizing when you change the image's display size.

TIP To display the image at actual pixel size, click Actual Pixels on the Zoom Tool Options palette or double-click the Zoom tool. An image's display size equals its actual size only when the display ratio is 100% (1:1) and the image resolution and monitor resolution are the same.

TIP Control-Space bar-click to magnify the display size when another tool is selected or a dialog box with a Preview option is open. Control-Alt-Space bar-click to reduce the display size.

TIP You can also change the display size by choosing Zoom In or Zoom Out from the View menu.

1 Click on the image with the Zoom tool to enlarge the display size. Note the plus sign in the magnifying glass pointer.

2 Alt-click on the image with the Zoom tool to reduce the display size. Note the minus sign in the magnifying glass pointer.

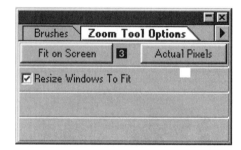

Shortcuts for changing the display size

Magnify	Control +
Zoom Out	Control –
Zoom in (window doesn't resize)	Control Alt +
Zoom out (window doesn't resize)	Control Alt –
Actual pixels/100% view	Control Alt 0
Fit on screen	Control 0

Zoom in or Out

1 Click on or drag the preview box on the Navigator palette to move an image in its window.

NOTE: If the scroll bars aren't active, the entire image is displayed, and there is no need to move it.

To move a magnified image in its window:

Click or drag the preview box (image thumbnail) on the Navigator palette **1**.
or
Click the up or down scroll arrow. Drag a scroll box to move the image more quickly.
or
Choose the Hand tool (H) ✋, then drag the image.

TIP To fit the entire image in the largest document window your monitor accommodates, double-click the Hand tool or click Fit on Screen on the Zoom Tool Options palette or choose View menu > Fit on Screen.

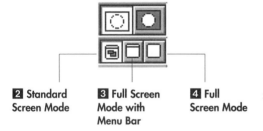

2 Standard Screen Mode   **3** Full Screen Mode with Menu Bar   **4** Full Screen Mode

To change the screen display mode:

Click the Standard Screen Mode button on the bottom of the Toolbox (F) **2** to display the image, menu bar, scroll bars on the document window. This is the Standard mode.
or
Click the Full Screen Mode with Menu Bar button (F) **3**–**4** to display the image and menu bar, but no scroll bars. The area around the image will be gray.
or
Click the Full Screen Mode button (F) **5** to display the image, but no menu bar or scroll bars. The area around the image will be black.

TIP Press Tab to show/hide the Toolbox and any open palettes; press Shift-Tab to show/ hide the palettes, but not the Toolbox.

TIP Use the Hand tool (H) to move the image in its window when the scroll bars are hidden and the image is magnified, or use the Navigator palette. Hold down Space bar to use the Hand tool while another tool is selected.

5 Full Screen Mode with Menu Bar

Move Image in its Window; Screen Modes

The number of images that can be open at a time depends on available RAM and scratch disk space. You can open the same image in two windows simultaneously: one in a large display size, such as 400%, to edit a detail and the other in a smaller display size, such as 100%, to view the whole image. Or, leave the image in RGB Color mode in one image window and choose View menu > CMYK Preview for the same image in a second window.

To display an image in two windows:

1. Open an image.

2. Choose View menu > New View. The same image will appear in a second window **1**.

3. *Optional:* Move either window by dragging its title bar, and/or resize either window by dragging its resize box.

To recolor the work canvas
Choose a Foreground color (see pages 111–115), choose the Paint Bucket tool, ✋ then Shift-click on the work canvas **2**. You can't undo this. To restore the default gray, choose 50% gray for the Foreground color, then Shift-click the work canvas again.

Work canvas

1 An image displayed in two windows simultaneously: one in a large display size for editing, the other in a smaller display size for previewing.

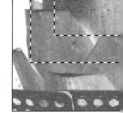

SELECT 5

YOU CAN USE any Photoshop selection tool—Marquee, Lasso, or Magic Wand—to isolate an area of an image. If a command, such as a filter, is applied to a selection, only the selection is affected—the rest of the image is protected. A selection is defined by a moving marquee.

The creation of selections is covered in this chapter, including using the Marquee tool to create rectangular or elliptical selections, the Lasso tool to create irregular or polygonal selections, and the Magic Wand tool and Color Range command to select areas by color or shade. In this chapter you will also learn how to create a frame selection, how to deselect a selection, how to move or hide a selection marquee, how to flip, rotate, resize, add to, subtract from, feather, defringe, and smooth a selection, and how to create a vignette. You can convert a selection into a path for precise reshaping, and then convert it back into a selection (see pages 166 and 172).

The selections covered in this chapter are non-floating—they contain a layer's underlying pixels. If a non-floating selection is moved on the Background **1**, the exposed area is covered with the current Background color. If a non-floating selection is moved on a layer, the exposed area will be transparent.

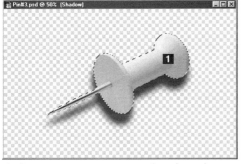

Pixels—not transparent areas—selected on a layer.

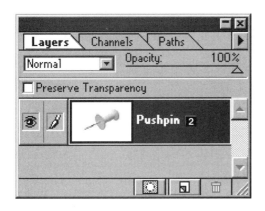

To select an entire layer:

Choose Select menu > All (Control-A). A marquee will surround the entire layer **1**.

To select only pixels—not the transparent areas—on a layer, Control-click the layer name on the Layers palette **2**.

To create a rectangular or elliptical selection:

1. Choose a target layer.

2. Choose the Rectangular Marquee or Elliptical Marquee tool 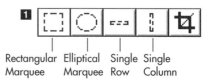. To toggle between those two tools, press M.

Rectangular Elliptical Single Single
Marquee Marquee Row Column

3. *Optional:* To specify the exact dimensions of the selection, with the Rectangular or Elliptical Marquee tool highlighted, press Enter to open the Marquee Options palette (or double-click the tool), choose Fixed Size from the Style drop-down menu 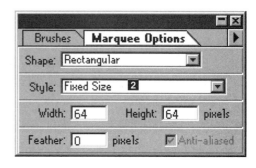, then enter Width and Height values. Remember, though, you're counting pixels based on the file's resolution, not the monitor's resolution, so the same Fixed Size marquee will appear larger in a low resolution file than in a high resolution file.

To specify the width-to-height ratio of the selection (3-to-1, for example), choose Constrained Aspect Ratio from the Style drop-down menu, then enter Width and Height values. Enter the same number in both fields to create a circle or a square.

4. *Optional:* To soften the edges of the selection before it's created, enter a Feather amount on the Options palette. Enter 0 to produce no feathering.

5. If you specified Fixed Size values, click on the image. For any other Style, drag diagonally . A marquee will appear. Hold down Space bar to move the marquee while drawing it. To move the marquee after releasing the mouse, follow the instructions on page 65.

3 Drag diagonally to create a rectangular selection...

TIP As you drag the mouse, the dimensions of the selection will be indicated in the W and H fields on the Info palette.

TIP To drag from the center of a selection, hold down Alt and drag. Release the mouse, then release Alt.

TIP Hold down Shift while dragging to create a square or a circular selection.

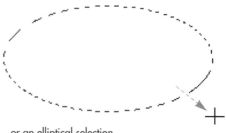

...or an elliptical selection.

Anti-aliasing

Check the **Anti-aliased** box on the Options palette to create a selection with a softened edge that steps to transparency. Uncheck Anti-aliased to create a crisp, hard-edged selection.

 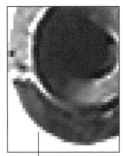

Aliased   Anti-aliased

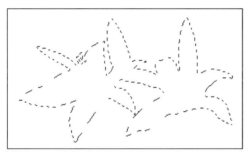

1 A **Lasso** tool selection.

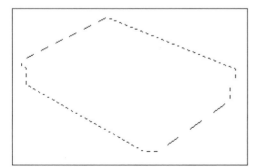

2 A **Polygon Lasso** tool selection.

NOTE: It's a good idea to make all your modifications to a selection before deselecting it, because it is very difficult to precisely reselect an area, unless you save it as a mask in an alpha channel. If the shape you want to select isn't too complex, use the Pen tool to select it instead of the Lasso— you'll get a smoother selection. You can also convert a selection into a path for precise reshaping.

To create a freeform selection:

1. Choose a target layer.
2. Choose the Lasso tool.
3. *Optional:* Enter a value in the Feather field to soften the edges of the selection. This amount will remain in effect until it's changed or the tool is reset.
4. Drag around an area of the layer **1**. When you release the mouse, the open ends of the selection will automatically join.

TIP To feather a selection after it's created, use the Select menu > Feather command (Control-Shift-D).

TIP To create a straight side as you're using the Lasso tool, with the mouse button still down, press Alt, and click to create corners. Release Alt to resume drawing a freehand selection.

To create a polygonal selection:

1. Choose a target layer.
2. Choose the Polygon Lasso tool from the Lasso tool pop-out menu.
3. To create straight sides, click to create points **2**. To join the open ends of the selection, click on the starting point (a small circle will appear next to the pointer). Or Control-click or double-click to close the selection automatically.

   Alt-drag to create a curved segment as you draw a polygonal selection. Release Alt to resume drawing straight sides.

Freeform or Polygonal Selection

If you click on a layer pixel with the Magic Wand tool, a selection will be created that includes adjacent pixels of a similar shade or color. You can then add similarly colored, non-adjacent pixels to the selection using the Similar command, or non-similar colors by Shift-clicking.

To select by color (Magic Wand):

1. Choose a target layer.

2. Choose the Magic Wand tool (W). ✎

3. Check the Sample Merged box on the Magic Wand Options palette to sample from colors in all the currently displayed layers to create the selection. Only pixels on the current target layer can be edited, but you can apply changes within the same selection marquee through successive target layers.
or
Uncheck the Sample Merged box to sample from colors on the target layer only.

4. Click on a shade or color on the target layer.

5. *Optional:* To enlarge the selection based on the current Tolerance setting on the Magic Wand Options palette, choose Select menu > Grow one or more times.

6. *Optional:* To select other, non-contiguous areas of similar color or shade on the layer, choose Select menu > Similar.

7. *Optional:* To specify a different Tolerance range, enter a number between 0 and 255 in the Tolerance field on the Magic Wand Options palette **1**, then click on the image again (see "Tolerance," at right).

TIP Choose Edit > Undo to undo the last created selection.

TIP To quickly select all the pixels on a target layer (not the Background), Control-click the layer name.

TIP If you have created a floating selection by moving a selection using the Move tool, you can Alt-drag with

To silhouette an object on a flat-color background

Select the background of the image using the Magic Wand tool, choose Select menu > Inverse (Control-Shift-I), choose Edit menu > Copy, then Edit menu > Paste. The object will paste onto its own layer. You can then fill the layer the object originally came from with a flat color.

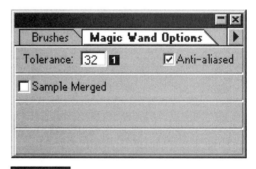

Tolerance

To expand or narrow the range of shades or colors the Magic Wand tool selects, enter a number between 0 and 255 in the **Tolerance** field on the Magic Wand Options palette. With a Tolerance of 32, the Magic Wand will select within a range of 16 shades below and 16 shades above the shade on which it is clicked. Enter 1 to select only one color or shade. To gradually narrow the range of shades or colors the Magic Wand tool selects, modify the Tolerance value between clicks.

another selection tool to remove pixel areas from the selection, if necessary.

TIP To add to a selection with the Magic Wand tool, Shift-click outside the selection. To subtract from a selection, Alt-click inside the selection. You can also use another selection tool, such as the Lasso, to add to or subtract from a selection (see page 67).

TIP To Expand or Contract the selection by a specified number of pixels, choose either command from the Select menu > Modify submenu.

A Magic Wand selection using a Tolerance of 10.

A Magic Wand selection using a Tolerance of 40.

PHOTO: PAUL PETROFF

Select by Color (Magic Wand)

Using the Color Range command, you can select areas based on existing colors in the image or based on a particular luminosity or hue range.

To select by color (Color Range):

1. Choose a target layer. The Color Range command samples colors from all the currently visible layers, but, of course, only the target layer will be available for editing. You can limit the selection range by first creating a selection.

2. Choose Select menu > Color Range.

3. Choose from the Select drop-down menu. You can limit the selection to a color range (Reds, Yellows, etc.), to a luminosity range (Highlights, Midtones, or Shadows), or to Sampled Colors (shades or colors you'll click on with the Color Range eyedropper).

4. Choose a Selection Preview option for the image window.

5. To preview the selection, click the Selection button; to redisplay the whole image, click the Image button. Or, hold down Control with either option selected to toggle between the two. If the image extends beyond the edges of your monitor, use the Image option—

the entire image will be displayed in the preview box to facilitate sampling.

6. If you chose Sampled Colors in step 3, click in the preview box or in the image window with the eyedropper cursor to sample colors in the image.

7. *Optional:* Move the Fuzziness slider to the right to expand the range of colors or shades selected, or move it to the left to narrow the range.

8. *Optional:* If you chose Sampled Colors in step 3, Shift-click with the eyedropper cursor in the image window or in the preview box to add more colors or shades to the selection. Alt-click to remove colors or shades from the selection. Or, click the "+" or "-" eyedropper icon button in the Color Range dialog box, then click on the image or in the preview box without holding down Shift or Alt.

9. Click OK or press Enter.

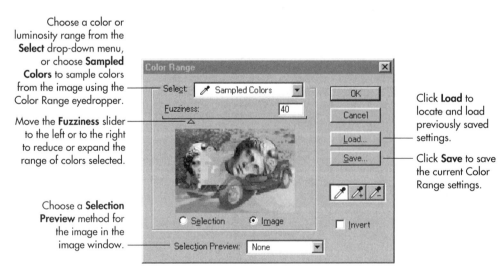

Choose a color or luminosity range from the **Select** drop-down menu, or choose **Sampled Colors** to sample colors from the image using the Color Range eyedropper.

Move the **Fuzziness** slider to the left or to the right to reduce or expand the range of colors selected.

Choose a **Selection Preview** method for the image in the image window.

Click **Load** to locate and load previously saved settings.

Click **Save** to save the current Color Range settings.

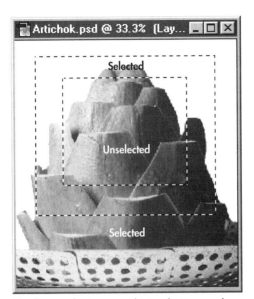

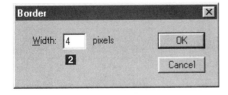

1 A **frame** selection created using the Rectangular Marquee tool.

To create a frame selection:

1. Choose a target layer.

2. Choose the Rectangular or Elliptical Marquee tool (M), then press and drag to create a selection, or choose Select menu > Select All (Control-A).

3. Alt-drag a smaller selection inside the first selection **1**.

PHOTO: PAUL PETROFF

To produce this image, a frame selection was created a different way: First the Marquee tool was used to select the center area, then the Inverse command was used to reverse the selected and non-selected areas so the outer area became the selection. The Levels command was used to screen back the selected area.

To select a narrow border around a selection:

1. Create a selection.

2. Choose Select menu > Modify > Border.

3. Enter the desired Width of the border in pixels **2**. The allowable range is 1 to 64.

4. Click OK or press Enter. The new selection will evenly straddle the edge of the original selection **3**.

Frame Selection; Border Selection

To deselect a selection:

With any tool selected, choose Select menu > None (Control-D).

or

Click anywhere on the layer using a Marquee tool or the Lasso tool , but not the Polygon Lasso tool.

or

Click **inside** the selection with the Magic Wand tool. (If you click outside the selection with the Magic Wand, you will create a new selection.)

TIP It's difficult to reselect the same area twice, so deselect a selection only when you're sure you've finished using it. If you unintentionally deselect, choose Edit menu > Undo immediately. If you think you might want to reuse a selection, save it as a path or in an alpha channel.

1 Click **outside** a selection to deselect it with a Marquee or Lasso tool. Click **inside** a selection to deselect it with the Magic Wand tool.

PHOTO: NADINE MARKOVA

If you delete a non-floating selection from a layer, the original selection area will become transparent. If you delete a non-floating selection from the Background, the selection area will fill with the current Background color.

A selection deleted from a **layer**.

To delete a selection:

Press Delete.

or

Choose Edit menu > Clear.

or

Choose Edit menu > Cut (Control-X) if you want to place the selection on the Clipboard.

A selection deleted from the **Background**.

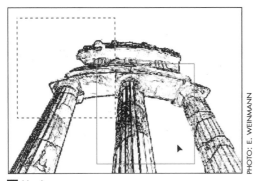

1 **Moving** a marquee.

PHOTO: E. WEINMANN

To move a selection marquee:

1. *Optional:* To aid in positioning the marquee, choose View menu > Show Grid or drag a guide or guides from the horizontal or vertical ruler, and also turn on Snap to Guides (View menu > Snap to Guides, or Control-Shift-;).

2. Choose any selection tool.

3. Drag inside the selection **1**. Hold down Shift after you start dragging to constrain the movement to 45° increments.
or
Press any arrow key to move the marquee one pixel at a time.

TIP If you drag a selection on a layer using the Move tool, the selection will be cut from its layer and the empty space will be replaced by layer transparency. If a selection is moved from the Background, the empty space will be filled with the current Background color. In either case, the selection will become a floating selection.

2 The original selection—the **angels** are selected.

To switch the selected and unselected areas:

Choose Select menu > Inverse (Control-Shift-I) **2**–**3**.

TIP Choose Inverse again to switch back.

TIP It's easy to select a shape on a flat color background: Choose the Magic Wand tool, enter 5 in the Tolerance field on the Magic Wand Options palette, click on the flat color background to select it entirely, then choose Select menu > Inverse.

3 The selection **inverted**—the **background** is selected.

Move Selection Marquee; Inverse Selection

To hide a selection marquee:

Choose View menu > Hide Edges
(Control-H). The selection will remain
active.

TIP To redisplay the selection marquee,
choose View menu > Show Edges.

TIP To verify that a selection is still active,
press on the Select menu. Most com-
mands will be available if a selection is
active.

TIP You can choose the Hide Edges command while some Image menu and
Filter menu dialog boxes are open.

To transform a selection:

To apply the transform commands (flip,
rotate, or scale) **1**–**2**, follow the instructions for transforming a layer on pages
89–91.

If you transform a selection on a layer, any
remaining empty space will be replaced by
layer transparency. If the selection was on
the Background, the empty space will be
filled with the current Background color. In
either case, if you transform a selection—
unlike if you transform a layer—the selection will automatically turn into a floating
selection.

To resize a selection marquee using a
command, choose Select menu > Modify >
Expand or Contract, enter a number of
pixels in the Expand By or Contract By
field, then click OK.

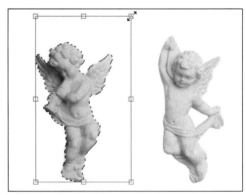

1 Scaling a selection.

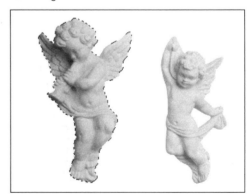

2 The selection enlarged.

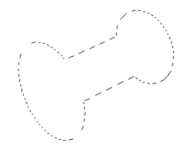

1 The original selection.

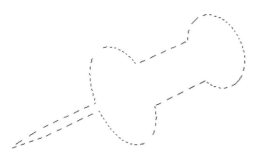

2 The selection enlarged.

To add to a selection:

Choose any selection tool other than the Magic Wand, position the cursor over the selection, then Shift-drag to define an additional selection area **1**–**2**.
or
Click the Magic Wand tool, then Shift-click on any unselected area.

TIP If the additional selection overlaps the original selection, it will become part of the new, larger selection. If the addition does not overlap the original selection, a second, separate selection will be created.

To subtract from a selection:

Choose any selection tool other than the Magic Wand, then Alt-drag around the area to be subtracted.
or
Choose the Magic Wand tool, then Alt-click on the area of shade or color in the selection to be subtracted.

TIP Alt-Shift-drag to select the intersection of an existing selection and the new selection.

To vignette an image:

1. For a multi-layer image, choose a target layer, and uncheck the Preserve Transparency box. The vignette you create is going to appear to fade into the layer or layers below it.

For an image with a Background only, choose a Background color (see pages 111–115) for the area around the vignette.

2. Choose the Rectangular Marquee ⬚, Elliptical Marquee ○, or Lasso tool ♪.

3. On the Options palette, enter 15 or 20 in the Feather field. Or to feather the selection after it's created instead, choose Select menu > Feather after step 4.

4. Create a selection **1**.

5. Choose Select menu > Inverse (Control-Shift-I).

6. Press Delete **2**.

7. Deselect (Control-D).

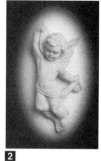

1 **2**

The original image.

The vignette.

Vignette an Image

COMPOSITING 6

THIS **CHAPTER** covers methods for rearranging image elements using the Move tool and using the Clipboard commands: Cut, Copy, Paste, and Paste Into. Compositing is accomplished using layers. In order to place imagery on its own layer, you'll need to learn how to select pixels in a one-layer document so you can move them from one layer to another or copy them between images. (Instructions for moving a selected area of a layer or a whole layer to another document are on pages 94–96.)

pages 94–96.)

1 Moving a selection on a **layer**...

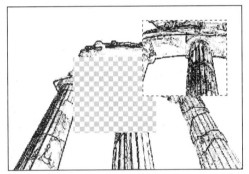

2 ...a **transparent** hole is left behind.

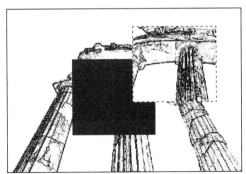

3 Moving a selection on the **Background**: the exposed area fills with the current **Background color**.

To move a selection:

1. *Optional:* To help you position the selection, choose View menu > Show Grid (Control-") or drag a guide or guides from the horizontal or vertical ruler, and also turn on Snap to Guides (View menu > Snap to Guides, or Control-Shift-;).

2. If the selection is on the Background, choose a Background color. The area the moved selection exposes will fill with this color automatically. If the selection is on a layer, the exposed area will fill with transparency.

3. Choose the Move tool (V). ▶⊕ Or hold down Control to access the Move tool while any tool other than the Pen or Hand tool is chosen.

4. Position the cursor over the selection, then drag. The selection marquee and its contents will move together **1**–**3**. A floating selection layer will be created. Read about floating selections on the next page.

TIP Press any arrow key to move a selection in 1-pixel increments.

If you follow the instructions on the previous page to move a selection or the instructions below to drag-copy a selection, a new, temporary Floating Selection layer will be created automatically ■. You can modify floating selection pixels without changing pixels in the layer below it.

What to do with a floating selection:

To merge a floating selection into the layer below it, click on any other layer. Any areas that extend beyond the selection will be preserved and can be dragged into view using the Move tool. The selection marquee will remain active, though now it will surround pixels on the new target layer. Deselect the marquee if you're done with it.

or

To turn the floating selection into its own layer and leave pixels on the underlying layer unchanged, double-click the Floating Selection layer name, enter a name, then click OK.

or

To remove the floating selection altogether, with the "Floating Selection" name active, click the Layers palette Trash icon, or press Delete, or choose Edit menu > Cut or Edit menu > Clear, or choose Delete Selection from the Layers palette command menu.

To drag-copy a selection:

1. Choose the Move tool. (Use the Control key to access the Move tool while another tool is selected.)

2. Hold down Alt before and as you drag the selection you want to copy. Release the mouse before you release Alt. The copied selection will appear on the Layers palette as a floating selection ■–■.

What's the difference between a floating and a non-floating selection?

A **non-floating selection** is created when any selection tool or the Color Range command is used. If you Delete or Cut selected non-floating pixels from the Background, the area left behind will automatically fill with the current Background color. If you remove pixels from a layer, the area left behind will be transparent.

A **floating selection** layer is created automatically if a selection is dragged or Alt-dragged with the Move tool. Pixels in a floating selection are temporarily suspended above the former target layer.

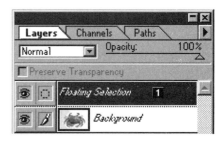

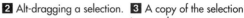

PHOTO: E. WEINMANN

■ Alt-dragging a selection. ■ A copy of the selection is moved.

An object in motion

Hold down **Alt** and press an **arrow** key a bunch of times to generate multiple copies of a selection, one pixel apart: Each time you create a new copy, the prior floating selection layer copy will merge into the underlying layer. Hold down **Alt** and **Shift** and press an **arrow** key to offset each new copy by ten pixels.

Know your image dimensions and resolution before copying between images

■ Before using the Clipboard commands, compare the **dimensions** of the image to be Cut or Copied with the dimensions of the layer onto which it will be pasted (the "destination layer"). If the image on the Clipboard is larger than the destination layer, the Clipboard image will extend beyond the image window. You can use the Move tool to reposition the extended areas after pasting.

■ The size of a selection may change when pasted, because it is rendered in the **resolution** of the destination layer. If the resolution of the destination layer is higher than that of the imagery you are pasting, the Clipboard image will become smaller when pasted. Conversely, if the resolution of the destination layer is lower than the resolution of the Clipboard imagery, the Clipboard image will be enlarged when pasted. You can use the Image Size dialog box to choose the same resolution (and dimensions, if desired) for both images. Follow the instructions on page 74 to paste into a smaller image.

Clipboard facts

You can use the Cut or Copy command to save a selection to a temporary storage area called the Clipboard, and then use the Paste or Paste Into command to paste the Clipboard imagery onto another layer in the same image or in another image. The Cut, Copy, and Paste Into commands are available only when an area of a layer is selected.

If you create a selection and choose the Cut command, the selection will be placed on the Clipboard. (The Clear command doesn't use the Clipboard.) If you Cut or Clear a non-floating selection from the Background, the exposed area will be filled with the current Background color. If you remove pixels from a layer, the area left behind will be transparent. For the most seamless transition, check the Anti-aliased box on the Options palette for your selection tool before creating your selection.

The Paste command pastes the Clipboard contents into a new layer and preserves any areas that extend beyond the selection. You can move the entire layer to reveal the extended areas. If you then save your document, the extended areas will save with it. If you crop the layer, however, the extended areas will be discarded.

The Clipboard can contain only one selection at a time, and it is replaced each time Cut or Copy is chosen. The same Clipboard contents can be pasted an unlimited number of times, and will be retained if you exit Photoshop. They will also be retained if you switch to another application if the Export Clipboard box is checked in the General Preferences dialog box.

One more info bite: The dimensions in the New dialog box automatically match the dimensions of imagery on the Clipboard.

TIP If the Clipboard imagery is large, the remaining available memory for processing is reduced. To reclaim memory, empty the Clipboard by choosing Edit > Purge > Clipboard.

To copy and paste a selection in the same image:

1. Select an area on a layer or the Background. To feather the selection, choose Select menu > Feather, and enter a value.

2. Choose Edit menu > Copy 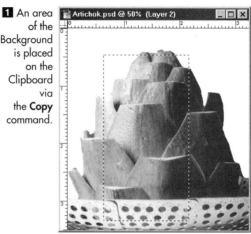 (Control-C) (or choose Edit menu > Cut to cut the selection).

3. Choose a target layer.

4. Choose Edit menu > Paste (Control-V) **2**.

5. *Optional:* Restack, move, or defringe the new layer.

If you drag selected pixels from one image to another, presto, those selected pixels will be copied onto a new layer in the destination image. This drag-and-drop method bypasses the Clipboard, so it both saves memory and preserves the Clipboard contents. If your monitor it too small to display two image windows simultaneously, use the copy-and-paste method instead.

To drag-and-drop a selection between images:

1. Open the source and destination images, and make sure the two image windows don't completely overlap.

2. Select an area of a layer.

3. Choose the Move tool.
   or
   Hold down Control.

4. Drag the selection into the destination image window, and release the mouse where you want the pixels to be dropped. You can always move the new layer around later using the Move tool.

TIP Hold down Shift before and as you drag to automatically drop the selection in the exact center of the destination image. You can release the mouse when the pointer is anywhere inside the destination image window.

TIP To drag-and-drop a whole layer to another image, see pages 95–96.

1 An area of the Background is placed on the Clipboard via the **Copy** command.

2 The pasted imagery appears on the target layer.

Copy/Paste Selection; Drag-Drop Selection

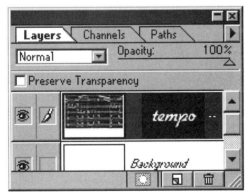

1 The music layer was selected in another image, then pasted into a Type Mask tool selection.

2 The layer contents can be repositioned within the layer mask, since the two aren't linked together. For this image, the music layer icon was activated, and then the layer contents were moved upward using the Move tool.

3 The pasted image appeared on a new layer and the layer mask was created automatically when the Paste Into command was chosen. The pasted image (the music) is only visible within the white areas in the layer mask, in this case, the letter shapes.

If you use the Paste Into command to paste the Clipboard contents into the boundary of a selection, a new layer is created automatically and the active marquee becomes a layer mask. The pasted image can be repositioned within the boundary of the visible part of the layer mask, and the mask itself can also be edited.

To paste into a selection:

1. Select an area of a layer. If you want to feather the selection, choose Select menu > Feather and enter a value.

2. Choose Edit menu > Copy to copy pixels only from the target layer, or choose Edit menu > Copy Merged (Control-Shift-C) to copy pixels within the selection area from all the currently visible layers.

3. Leave the same layer active, or activate a different layer, or activate a layer in another image.

4. Select an area (or areas) into which the Clipboard image will be pasted.

5. Choose Edit menu > Paste Into (Control-Shift-V). A new layer and layer mask will be created **1**–**3**.

6. *Optional:* The entire Clipboard contents were pasted onto the layer, but the layer mask may be hiding some of them. Use the Move tool to reposition the imagery within the area the layer mask reveals.

To select the layer mask, click on the layer mask thumbnail. Drag the layer mask to reposition the area the layer mask reveals. Paint on the layer mask with white to reveal parts of the image, or with black to hide parts of the image.

To move the layer and layer mask in unison, first, on the Layers palette, click in the space between the layer and layer mask thumbnails to link the two layer components together. (Click the link icon to unlink the layer and layer mask.)

Normally, in Photoshop 4.0 or later, if you move a large selection or layer or paste into another image, all the pixels on a layer are preserved, even those that may extend beyond the visible edge of the layer (Adobe calls this "Big Data"), regardless of the dimensions of the image into which the layer is moved. If you want to trim the pasted imagery as it's pasted, follow the instructions below, but please read the sidebar on page 71 before proceeding.

To paste into a smaller image:

1. Click on the destination image, then hold down Alt and press and hold on the Sizes bar in the lower left corner of the image window. Jot down the image's dimensions.

2. Create a selection on another (larger) image.

3. Choose Edit menu > Copy.

4. Choose File menu > New.

5. Type a name in the Name field, then click OK. The Width, Height, Resolution, and Mode will automatically conform to that of the Clipboard imagery.

6. Choose Edit menu > Paste.

7. Choose Image menu > Image Size.

8. Check the Resample Image box to make the resolution the same as that of the destination image **1**. Enter smaller numbers than the dimensions of the destination image (step 1, above) in the Width and Height fields **2**, then click OK or press Return.

9. Choose Select menu > All to reselect the pasted layer.

10. Choose Edit menu > Copy, click in the destination image, then choose Edit menu > Paste.
    or
    Shift-drag the layer name into the destination image window.

Trim or include Big Data

■ To **remove** pixels that extend beyond the edge of a layer, make sure the layer is active, choose Edit menu > Select All, then choose Image menu > Crop. Trimming off Big Data will reduce a file's storage size.

■ If you apply an image editing command, like a filter, to a whole layer, any big data that is part of the layer will also be modified. To **include** Big Data by making it visible in the image window, use the Canvas Size command.

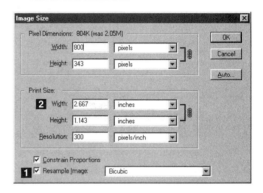

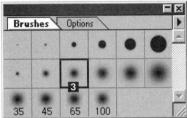

4 The original image.

5 After using the **Sharpen** tool on the strawberry in the center, and the **Blur** tool on the rest of the image.

The Blur tool decreases contrast between pixels. Use it to soften edges between shapes. The Sharpen tool increases contrast between pixels. Use it to delineate edges between shapes. Neither tool can be used on a image in Bitmap or Indexed Color mode.

To sharpen or blur edges:

1. Choose the Blur tool ○ or the Sharpen tool △ (R to toggle between the two). Each tool has its own Options palette settings.

2. On the Focus Tools Options palette, choose a Pressure percentage **1**. Try a setting of around 30% first.
and
Choose a mode **2**. Choose Normal to sharpen or blur pixels of any shade or color. Choose Darken to sharpen or blur only pixels darker than the Foreground color. Choose Lighten to sharpen or blur only pixels lighter than the Foreground color. (The blending modes are described on pages 26–28.)

3. *Optional:* Click the Sample Merged box on the Options palette to pick up pixels from other visible layers under the pointer to place on the target layer.

4. Click the Brushes tab on the palette, then click a hard-edged or soft-edged tip **3**.

5. Drag across the area of the image that you want to sharpen or blur **4**–**5**. Stroke again if you want to intensify the effect.

TIP To avoid creating an overly grainy texture, use the Sharpen tool with a medium Pressure setting and stroke only once on an area.

Sharpen or Blur

Grids, rulers, and guides can help you position objects precisely.

To hide or show rulers:

Choose View menu > Show Rulers (Control-R). Rulers will appear on the top and left sides of the image window, and the current position of the pointer is indicated by a dotted marker on each ruler 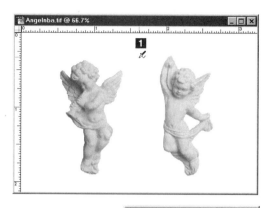. To hide the rulers, choose View menu > Hide Rulers.

TIP To quickly access the Units & Rulers Preferences dialog box to change the ruler units, double-click inside the either ruler.

To change the rulers' zero origin:

1. To make the new ruler origin snap to gridlines, choose View menu > Snap to Grid (Control-Shift-"). To make the ruler origin snap to guidelines, choose View menu > Snap to Guides (Control-Shift-;).

2. Drag from the intersection of the rulers in the upper left corner of the image window diagonally into the image –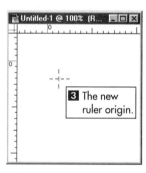.

TIP To reset the ruler origin, double-click where the rulers intersect in the upper left corner of the image window.

The grid is a non-printing framework that can be used to align image elements. Guides are individual guidelines that you drag into the image window yourself. With View > Snap To Guides turned on, selections and tool pointers will snap to a guide if it's moved near (with 8 screen pixels of) a guide. Ditto for View > Snap to Grid.

To hide or show the grid:

Choose View > Show Grid (Control-") 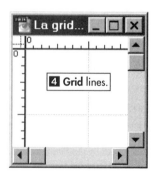. To hide the grid, choose View > Hide Grid.

2 Dragging the **ruler origin**.

3 The new ruler origin.

4 Grid lines.

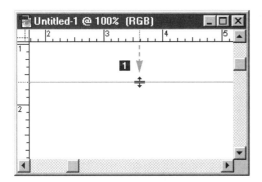

To create a guide:

Make sure the rulers are displayed, then drag from the horizontal or vertical ruler into the image window **1**. Hold down Shift as you drag to snap the guide to ruler increments as you drag. If the grid is displayed and View > Snap to Grid is turned on, the guide can be snapped to a grid line.

TIP To lock all ruler guides, choose View menu > Lock Guides (Control-Alt-;).

TIP To switch a guide from vertical to horizontal, or vice versa, hold down Alt as you drag.

TIP To move an existing guide, drag it using the Move tool.

TIP File menu > Preferences > Guides & Grid to choose a new guide color or style.

To remove guides:

To remove one guide, drag it out of the image window using the Move tool.
or
To remove all guides, choose View menu > Clear Guides.

Take Snapshot copies the contents of the target layer into the snapshot buffer. The buffer contents can be recouped manually by dragging the Rubber Stamp tool (From Snapshot option) or into a selection using the Fill command (Use: Snapshot option).

To use the Take Snapshot option:

1. Edit or apply a filter to a target layer.

2. Choose Edit menu > Take Snapshot. Choose Take Merged Snapshot to copy the contents from all visible layers.

3. Choose Edit menu > Undo.

4. Use the Rubber Stamp tool, Option: From Snapshot, to restore parts of the prior effect manually.
or
Select part of a layer and use the Edit menu > Fill (Use: Snapshot) command **2**–**3**. Choose Edit menu > Purge > Snapshot when you're finished.

2 The original image.

3 We applied the Glass filter to a layer, chose Undo, selected the area around the tree, and then filled the selection (Use: Snapshot). Try doing the same thing using the Distort > Wave or Ripple filter or an Artistic or Sketch filter.

Create, Remove Guides; Take Snapshot

Cloning

The Rubber Stamp tool can be used to clone and rearrange imagery from one layer to another within an image or to clone imagery from one image to another. The same tool can be used with its From Saved option to restore part of the last saved version of an image.

The other Rubber Stamp options

No source point is needed for these steps.

- ■ To Rubber Stamp a **pattern**, before step 1, at left, select a rectangular area to become the pattern tile, choose Edit menu > Define Pattern, choose Pattern (aligned) or Pattern (non-aligned) from the Rubber Stamp Options palette drop-down menu, then drag on the layer to stamp the pattern. Choose Pattern (aligned) to stamp pattern tiles in a perfect grid, regardless of how many separate strokes you use. If you don't want the tiles from each stroke to align, choose Pattern (non-aligned).

- ■ To clone areas from the last saved version of the image, choose **From Saved**.

- ■ To create Impressionistic strokes, choose **Impressionist**, and use short strokes as you clone.

To clone areas within an image:

1. Choose the Rubber Stamp tool (S). ♨

2. On the Rubber Stamp Options palette, choose a mode.
and
Choose an Opacity percentage.
and
Choose "Clone (aligned)" from the Option drop-down menu **1**. The other options are explained at right.

3. Check the Sample Merged box on the Options palette to have the Rubber Stamp tool sample pixels from all currently visible layers that you Alt-click over. Uncheck Sample Merged to sample pixels from only the current target layer.

4. Click the Brushes tab, then click a small brush tip to clone a small detail or a medium- to large-size tip to duplicate larger areas.

5. Activate the layer you want to clone from.

6. In the image window, Alt-click on the area of the layer you want to clone from to establish a source point. Don't click on a transparent part of a layer— nothing will be cloned.

1 Drag the mouse where you want the clone to appear. To produce this illustration, **Clone (aligned)** was chosen for the Rubber Stamp tool.

2 Choose **Clone (non-aligned)** for the Rubber Stamp tool to create multiple clones from the same source point.

3 An opacity of 45% was chosen for the Rubber Stamp tool to create this double exposure effect.

7. On the same layer, drag the mouse back and forth where you want the clone to appear **1**.

or

For the most flexibility in editing the image layer, choose another target layer, then drag the mouse.

NOTE: If the Preserve Transparency box is checked on the Layers palette, cloning will only appear where existing pixels are on that layer.

Two cursors will appear on the screen: a crosshair cursor over the source point and a Rubber Stamp cursor where you drag the mouse. Imagery from the source point will appear where the mouse is dragged, and it will replace the underlying pixels.

TIP Using the Rubber Stamp tool with the Clone (aligned) option, you can clone the entire layer, as long as you don't change the source point. The distance between the source point cursor and the Rubber Stamp cursor will remain constant, so you can release the mouse and drag in another area. To establish a new source point to clone from, Alt-click on a different area of the source image.

TIP Choose Clone (non-aligned) for the Rubber Stamp tool to create multiple clones from the same source point. The crosshair cursor will return to the same source point each time you release the mouse. You can create a pattern with Clone (non-aligned) chosen by cloning an image element over and over **2**.

TIP You can change the Options palette settings for the Rubber Stamp tool between strokes. To create a "double exposure" on one layer, choose a low Opacity percentage so the underlying pixels will partially show through the cloned pixels **3**.

To clone from image to image:

1. Open two images, and position the two windows side by side.

2. If both images are color, choose the same image mode for both. You can also clone between a color image and a Grayscale image. **NOTE:** Choose the Don't Flatten option to preserve layers.

3. Choose the Rubber Stamp tool. 🖐

4. From the Rubber Stamp Options palette, choose Option: Clone (aligned) to reproduce a continuous area from the source point **1**.
   or
   Choose Clone (Non-aligned) to produce multiple clones from the source point.
   and
   Choose an Opacity and a mode.

5. Click the Brushes tab, then click a brush tip.

6. Click on the image where the clone is to appear, and choose a target layer for the clone.

7. Alt-click on the area of the source (non-active) image that you want to clone from **2**.

8. Drag back and forth on the destination (active) image to make the clone appear.

TIP To create a brush stroke version of an image, clone to a new document with a white or solid-colored background **3**.

TIP To test a mode for the Rubber Stamp tool, create a new document with a white background, make part of the background black, choose Clone (non-aligned) and choose a mode from the Rubber Stamp Options palette, then clone to the new document. Choose Darken mode to clone onto a light background, Lighten mode to clone onto a dark background, Luminosity mode to produce a grayscale clone from a color image, or Dissolve mode with an opacity below 100% to produce a grainy, chalky clone.

Destination image. Source image.

PHOTO: PAUL PETROFF

2 **Alt-click** on the non-active image to establish a source point, then drag back and forth in short strokes on the active (destination) image to make the clone appear.

3 To create this effect, an image was cloned to a new document with a white background.

Physique Medley, David Humphrey. To produce this image, Humphrey composited scanned embroidery and his own charcoal drawings and photographs, among other things. He adjusted luminosity levels of the various components on individual layers using blending modes (Darken, Multiply) and the Eraser and Burn tools.

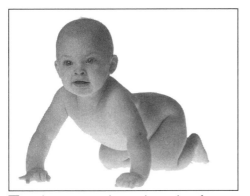

1 A selection copy with a Feather Radius of 0.

2 A selection copy with a Feather Radius of 30 pixels.

Apply the Feather command to fade the edge of a selection a specified number of pixels inward and outward from the marquee. A feather radius of 5, for example, would create a feather area 10 pixels wide.

NOTE: The feather won't appear until the selection is modified with a painting tool, copied, pasted, moved, or filled, or a filter or an Image menu command is applied to it.

To feather a selection:

1. Choose Select menu > Feather (Control-Shift-D).

2. Enter a number up to 250 in the Feather Radius field. The actual width of the feather is affected by the image resolution. A high resolution image will require a wider feather radius to produce the same degree of feathering than a low resolution image will require.

3. Click OK or press Enter **1**–**2**.

TIP To specify a feather radius for a selection before it's created, choose a Marquee or Lasso tool and enter a number in the Feather field on the Options palette.

If you save an image and then modify one of its layers, you can restore portions of the saved version to contrast with the modifications using the Rubber Stamp tool with its From Saved option. Save your image at the stage at which you would like it restored.

NOTE: The From Saved option cannot be used if you added or deleted a layer or a layer mask from the image, cropped the image, or changed its mode, dimensions, or resolution since it was last saved.

To restore part of the last saved version of an image:

1. Save the image.

2. Modify a layer.

3. Choose the Rubber Stamp tool. 🖐

4. Choose From Saved from the Options drop-down menu on the Rubber Stamp Options palette.
and
Choose an opacity. Choose a low opacity to restore a faint impression of the saved image.
and
Choose a mode.

5. Click the Brushes tab, then click a brush tip.

6. Drag across any area of the layer **1**–**2**. Each subsequent stroke over the same area will restore it more. To undo the last stroke, choose Edit menu > Undo (Control-Z) immediately.

1 The original image, to which we applied the Graphic Pen filter.

2 The Rubber Stamp tool was used with 95% opacity to restore part of the image.

Erase to saved

You can also use the Eraser tool (E) 🧽 with its Erase to Saved option **3** to restore pixels from the last saved version of an image. An advantage of using the Eraser is that in addition to choosing an opacity and mode for the tool, you can also choose a tool type (Paintbrush, Airbrush, Pencil, or Block) and other options from its Options palette.

Restore Part of the Last Saved Version

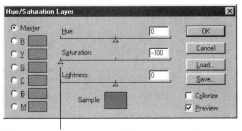

1 In the Hue/Saturation dialog box, move the Saturation slider all the way to the left to remove the color from the layer.

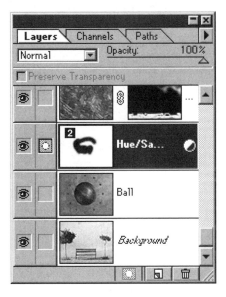

Another nifty technique

Duplicate a color layer, use the Hue/Saturation command to make the layer grayscale, choose Image menu > Add Layer Mask > Hide All to create a layer mask for that layer, and then paint with white to reveal parts of the grayscale layer above the color layer. You can gradually reshape the mask this way, alternately painting with black to add to the mask or white to remove the mask.

To convert a color layer to grayscale and selectively restore its color:

1. Choose a target layer in a color image. Layers below this layer will be affected by the adjustment layer you're about to create.

2. Control-click the Create New Layer button on the Layers palette to create an adjustment layer, choose Type: Hue/Saturation, then click OK.

3. Move the Saturation slider all the way to the left (to -100) **1**.

4. Click OK or press Enter.

5. Set the Foreground color to black.

6. On the adjustment layer, paint across the image where you want to restore the original colors from the underlying layers **2**. (Paint with white to reset areas to grayscale.)

7. *Optional:* You can also move a layer above the adjustment layer to fully restore that layer's color.

TIP Choose any of the following mode and opacity combinations for the adjustment layer:

Dissolve with a 40%–50% Opacity to restore color with a chalky texture.

Multiply with a 100% Opacity to restore subtle color in the darker areas of the image layers.

Color Burn to darken and intensify color in the image layers.

TIP To limit the adjustment layer effect to just the layer directly below it, Alt-click the line between them on the Layers palette to create a clipping group.

Convert to Grayscale, then Restore Color

To eliminate a noticeable "seam" after pasting or moving layer pixels, use the Defringe command. It recolors pixels from the edge of the selection with pixel colors from just inside the edge within a specified radius. (If the edges of the selection or pasted imagery were originally anti-aliased and were originally on a black or white background, use the Select menu > Matting > Remove Black Matte or Remove White Matte command, respectively, to remove unwanted remnants from the original background.)

To defringe a layer:

1. With the target layer or floating selection layer chosen, choose Layer menu > Matting > Defringe.

2. Enter a Width for the Defringe area . Try a low number first (1, 2 or 3) so your edges don't lose definition. Some non-edge areas may also be affected.

3. Click OK or press Enter.

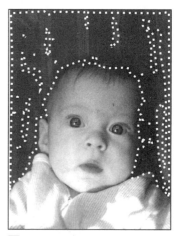

3 The original Magic Wand tool selection.

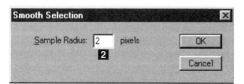

The Smooth command adds unselected pixels to a selection from within a specified radius.

To smooth a selection or a layer:

1. Choose Select menu > Modify > Smooth.

2. Enter a Sample Radius value between 1 and 16 **2**. The larger the Sample Radius, the more unselected pixels will be added to the selection.

3. Click OK or press Enter **3**–**4**.

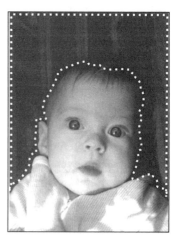

4 After applying the Smooth command, Sample Radius of 3.

LAYERS 7

Topics that are covered in this chapter

Topics that are covered in Chapter 12, More Layers

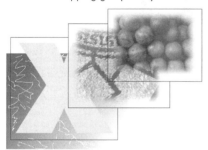

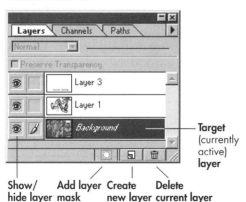

Show/ hide layer

Add layer mask

Create new layer

Delete current layer

Target (currently active) layer

LAYERS ARE LIKE clear acetate sheets: opaque where there is imagery and transparent where there is no imagery. You can assign to each layer a different opacity and choose a mode to control how each layer blends with the layers below it. You can change the stacking order of layers, and you can also assign a layer mask to any layer.

If you choose Contents: White or Background Color for a new image, the bottommost area of the image will be the Background, which is not a layer. If you choose Contents: Transparent, the bottommost component of the image will be a layer. Other layers can be added to an image at any time using the Layers palette or the Layer menu. Only one layer can be edited at a time, so you can easily modify one part of an image without disturbing the other layers.

Layers are listed on the Layers palette from topmost to bottommost, with the Background, of course, at the bottom of the list. The target layer, which is the layer currently highlighted on the palette, is the only layer that can be edited. Click on a layer name to make it the target layer. The target layer name is listed on the image window title bar.

If you're using Photoshop version 4.0 or later, you can create an adjustment layer to see how various color adjustments affect the layers below it, and then you can make the effect permanent or discard the adjustment layer altogether if you want to leave the underlying layers unchanged.

Layers

VERY IMPORTANT NOTES: Only the Photoshop file format supports multiple layers and the option to create a transparent bottommost layer. If you save your image in any other file format via the Save a Copy command, all the layers will be flattened, and any transparency in the bottommost layer will become opaque white. If you change image modes (i.e. from RGB to CMYK), click Don't Flatten to preserve layers.

An image can contain as many layers as available memory and storage allow, but since the pixel (non-transparent) areas on each layer occupy storage space, when your image is finished, you can merge two or more layers together or flatten all the layers into one to reduce the file's storage size.

To create a new layer:

1. To create a layer with 100% opacity and Normal mode, simply click the Create New Layer button at the bottom of the Layers palette **1**.

To choose options for the new layer when it's created, choose New Layer from the Layers palette command menu or Alt-click the Create New Layer button at the bottom of the palette, and then follow the remaining steps.

2. *Optional:* Enter a new name for the layer in the Name field **2**.

3. *Optional:* Choose a different opacity or mode (they can be changed later).

4. *Optional:* Click the Group With Previous Layer box to make the new layer a part of a clipping group (see pages 154–155).

5. Click OK or press Enter. The new layer will appear directly above the previously active layer.

TIP To change the size of the Layers palette thumbnails or turn off thumbnail display altogether, choose Palette Options from the Layers palette command menu, then click a different Thumbnail Size **3**. Choose None or the smallest size thumbnail to improve Photoshop's performance speed.

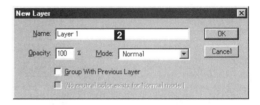

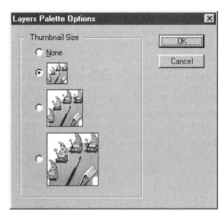

3 You can click a different **Thumbnail Size** or turn off thumbnail display altogether (None) via the Layers Palette Options dialog box.

Before adding a new layer to your image, choose **Document Sizes** from the Sizes bar pop-up menu and note the current **image size**.

The second figure is the amount of **RAM** the layered, unflattened file is using. Note how much the file's storage size increases when you add a new layer. The image in this illustration contains three layers.

(sidebar, left margin) Create a New Layer

If you create a floating selection by dragging or Alt-dragging a selection with the Move tool, the selection will automatically be placed on a new, temporary layer above the target layer (the layer currently highlighted on the Layers palette), and will bear the name "Floating Selection." You can edit a floating selection, but it's better to convert it into a layer right away, because simply clicking on another layer name will cause a floating selection to merge with the layer directly below it.

To turn a floating selection into a layer:

1. With the "Floating Selection" name highlighted, Alt-click the Create New Layer button on the Layers palette **1**.
or
Double-click the "Floating Selection" layer name on the Layers palette.

2. *Optional:* Rename the layer, choose a different opacity or mode for it, or check the Group With Previous Layer box to make the new layer part of a clipping group (see page 155).

3. Click OK or press Enter.

TIP To delete a floating selection, with the "Floating Selection" name active, click the Layers palette Trash icon, or choose Delete Selection from the Layers palette command menu, or press Delete.

2 An area of the Background is selected.

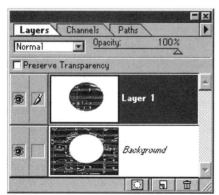

3 After choosing the **Layer Via Cut**, the selection is cut from the Background and placed on **its own layer**.

To turn a selection into a layer:

1. Create a selection.

2. To place a copy of the selected pixels on a new layer and leave the original layer untouched, choose Layer menu > New > Layer Via Copy (Control-J).
or
To place the selected pixels on a new layer and remove them from the original layer, choose Layer menu > New > Layer Via Cut (Control-Shift-J) **2**–**3**.

Turn a Selection into a Layer

You can hide layers you're not currently working on if you find them distracting. Remember, as you're working, that only currently visible layers can be merged (or printed). And when layers are flattened, hidden layers are discarded.

To hide or show layers:

Click the eye icon on the Layers palette for any individual layer you want to show or hide **1**–**3**. Click again where the eye icon was to redisplay the layer.

or

Drag in the eye column to hide or show multiple layers.

or

Alt-click an eye icon to hide all other layers except the one you click on. Alt-click again to redisplay all the other layers.

To duplicate a layer in the same image:

To create a new layer without naming it, drag the name of the layer you want to duplicate over the Create New Layer button at the bottom of the Layers palette. The duplicate layer will appear above the original target layer, and it will be the active layer.

or

To name the duplicate as you create it, on the Layers palette, activate the Layer you want to duplicate, choose Duplicate Layer from the Layers palette command menu or choose Layer menu > Duplicate Layer, type a name for the duplicate layer, then click OK or press Enter.

To flip a layer:

1. On the Layers palette, activate the layer you want to flip. Any layers that are linked to the active layer will also flip.

2. Choose Layer menu > Transform > Flip Horizontal **4** or Flip Vertical.

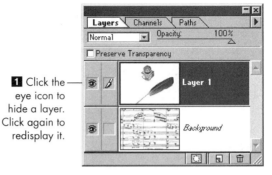

1 Click the eye icon to hide a layer. Click again to redisplay it.

2 Layer 1 hidden.

3 Layer 1 redisplayed.

4 Layer 1 flipped horizontally.

Hide/Show, Duplicate, Flip Layer

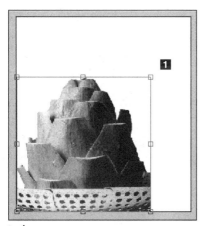

Scale

Rotate

Distort

To transform (scale, rotate, skew, distort, or apply perspective to) a layer by dragging:

1. On the Layers palette, activate the layer you want to transform. Any layers that are linked to the active layer will also transform. **NOTE:** You can also transform a selection on a layer; it will turn into a floating selection layer automatically.

2. Choose Layer menu > Transform > Scale, Rotate, Skew, Distort, or Perspective. A bounding border box will appear.

NOTE: If you want to perform multiple transformations, to save time and preserve image quality, after performing step 3 for the first command you choose, you can choose and then perform additional transform commands, and then accept them all at once (step 4).

3. To **scale** the layer horizontally and vertically, drag a corner handle **1**. To scale only the horizontal or vertical dimension, drag a side handle. Hold down Shift while dragging to scale proportionately. Hold down Alt to scale from the center of the layer.

To **rotate** the layer, position the cursor outside the bounding border (the cursor will become a curved arrow pointer), then drag in a circular direction **2**. Hold down Shift while dragging to constrain the rotation to 15-degree increments.

To **skew** the layer, drag a corner handle to reposition just that handle **3**, or drag a side handle to skew along the current horizontal or vertical axis. Hold down Alt while dragging to skew symmetrically from the center of the layer.

To **distort** the layer, drag a corner handle to freely reposition just that handle. Drag a side handle to distort the side of the bounding border along the horizontal and/or vertical axis. Hold down Alt while dragging to distort symmetrically

(Continued on the following page)

Transform a Layer

from the center of the layer. The distort transformation relies less on the horizontal/vertical axes than skew does, so it can produce a greater degree of transformation.

To apply **perspective** to the layer, drag a corner handle along the horizontal or vertical axis to create one-point perspective along that axis –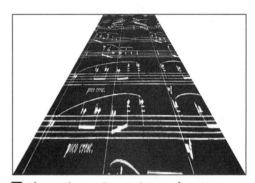. The adjacent corner will move in unison. Or drag a side handle to skew along the current horizontal or vertical axis.

4. To accept the transformation(s), double-click inside the bounding border.
or
Press Enter.

TIP Press Esc to cancel the entire transformation.

TIP Use Edit menu > Undo to undo the last handle modification.

TIP Position the cursor inside the bounding border to move the layer image.

1 The original image.

2 After applying a **Perspective** transformation.

Once you become acquainted with the individual Transform commands, you'll probably want to start using the Free Transform command when you want to perform a series of transform commands. With Free Transform, the various commands are accessed using keyboard shortcuts—you don't have to choose each command from the Layer menu. The image data will be resampled only once—when you accept the changes.

To free transform:

Follow the instructions starting on the previous page, but for step 2, choose Layer menu > Transform > Free Transform (Control-T), and for step 3, the instructions are the same, with these exceptions:

To **Skew**, hold down Control and Shift as you drag.

To **Distort**, hold down Control as you drag.

To apply **Perspective**, hold down Control, Alt, and Shift as you drag.

Also hold down Alt to scale, skew, or distort symmetrically from the center of the layer image.

Use the Numeric command if you'd rather transform a layer by entering exact numeric values than by dragging the mouse.

To transform a layer using numeric values:

1. On the Layers palette, activate the layer you want to transform. Any layers that are linked to the active layer will also transform.

   NOTE: You can also transform a selection on a layer; it will turn into a floating selection layer automatically.

2. Choose Layer menu > Transform > Numeric (Control-Shift-T).

3. For any of the following transformations that you don't want to perform, just uncheck that transformation's check box.

   To **move** the layer, enter *x* and *y* Position values **1**. Choose units for those values from the drop-down menu. Leave the Relative box checked to move the layer relative to its current position. Uncheck the Relative box to position the layer relative to the upper-left corner of the image.

   To **scale** the layer, enter Width and/or Height values **2**. Choose units for those values from the drop-down menu. Check the Constrain Proportions box to scale proportionately.

   To **skew** the layer, enter degree values (for the amount of slant) in the Horizontal and/or Vertical Skew fields **3**.

   To **rotate** the layer, enter a Rotate Angle or move the dial in the circle **4**.

4. Click OK or press Enter.

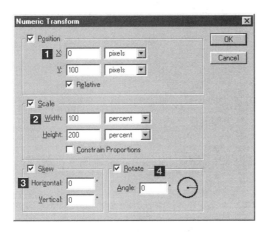

The standard things that you can do to a layer—move it upward or downward in the layer stack, choose a mode or opacity for it, or create a layer mask for it—can't be done to the Background—unless you first convert it into a layer.

To convert the Background into a layer:

1. Double-click Background on the Layers palette **1**.

2. Type a new name **2**, and choose a mode and opacity for the layer.

3. Click OK or press Enter **3**.

TIP If you move the Background using the Move tool, it will turn into a layer.

Let's say you've converted the Background into a layer so you could move it upward in the layer stack or for some other purpose, but now you want a flat, white Background. In other words, your image doesn't have a Background and you'd like to create one.

To create a Background for an image:

1. Choose New Layer from the Layers palette command menu.
or
Alt-click the Create New Layer button at the bottom of the Layers palette **4**.

2. Choose Background from the bottom of the Mode drop-down menu. You can't rename the Background or change its opacity or mode.

3. Click OK or press Enter. The Background will, of course, appear at the bottom of the layer stack.

TIP If you turned the Background into a layer and now you want to turn it back into the Background, do steps immediately above, make sure the former Background is above the new bottommost layer, then choose Merge Down from the Layers palette command menu. It will merge with the new Background.

1 Double-click the Background.

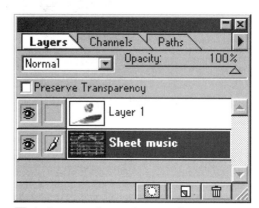
3 The former **Background** is now a **layer**.

Background into Layer; Create Background

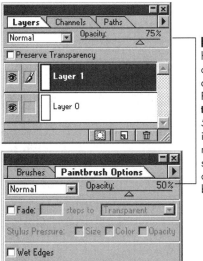

1 Layer 1 has a 75% opacity and the Paintbrush **tool** has a 50% opacity: The resulting stroke opacity will be 37%.

A few more things to know about layers

Tools and the layers

You can use any painting or editing tool to edit pixels on the target layer, but keep in mind that in addition to the Options palette mode and opacity settings for each tool, a tool's effect will also be controlled by the current target layer's opacity and mode **1**. For example, if a layer has a 60% opacity, a painting or editing tool with an opacity of 100% will work at a maximum opacity of 60% on that layer, and less if the tool's opacity is below 100%.

Preserve Transparency

With the Preserve Transparency box on the Layers palette checked, only areas of a layer that contain pixels can be edited **2**; blank areas will remain transparent. You can turn this option on or off for individual layers.

TIP Press / to toggle Preserve Transparency on or off.

If you want to change the size or color of the checkerboard pattern that is used to indicate transparent areas on a layer or turn off the checkerboard pattern altogether, use the File > Preferences > Transparency & Gamut dialog box.

Sample Merged

With the Sample Merged box checked on its Options palette, the Rubber Stamp, Paint Bucket, Blur, Sharpen, Smudge, and Magic Wand sample pixels from all the currently visible layers, though pixels will only be altered on the currently active layer.

Changing image modes

Click Don't Flatten to preserve layers in a multi-layered image if you change its color mode.

To easily try out different fill colors

2 With **Preserve Transparency** turned on for a type layer, the Fill command recolors only the type shapes, not transparent areas.

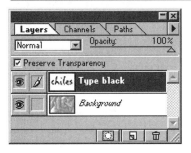

More About Layers

To restack a layer:

1. Click on a layer name on the Layers palette.

2. Drag the layer name up or down on the palette, and release the mouse when a dark horizontal line appears where you want the layer to be **1**–**2**.

TIP You can also restack a target layer by choosing Bring to Front, Bring Forward, Send Backward, or Send to Back from the Arrange submenu under the Layer menu.

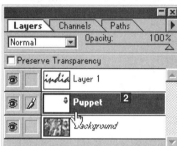

Dragging the "Puppet" layer downward.

The "Puppet" layer is in a new position in the stack.

To move multiple layers at one time, see page 154.

To move the contents of a layer:

1. On the Layers palette, click the name of the layer that you want to move.

2. Choose the Move tool (V) ⊹ or hold down Control.

3. Drag in the image window to move the contents of the target layer. The entire layer will move **3**–**4**.
NOTE: If you move the Background, it will become Layer 0, and the exposed area will become transparent.

TIP Press an arrow key to move a target layer one pixel at a time. Press Shift-arrow to move a layer in 10 screen-pixel increments.

TIP Any part of a layer that is moved beyond the edge of the image will be saved with your image.

TIP With the Move tool selected, Control-Alt-right-click on an object in the image window to quickly activate that object's layer.

3 The original image.

PHOTO: E. WEINMANN

4 After moving the "cow toy" layer with the **Move** tool.

Restack a Layer; Move Layer Contents

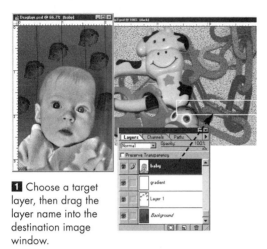

1 Choose a target layer, then drag the layer name into the destination image window.

2 The destination image after dragging the "baby" layer name onto the image.

PHOTOS: E. WEINMANN

3 The new layer name appears on the Layers palette, and is the topmost layer in the destination image.

The method you use to copy a layer (or linked layers) to another image depends on what part of the layer(s) you want to copy. The quickest way to copy a layer to another image is by dragging its name from the Layers palette to the destination image window. With this method, any areas that extend beyond the edge of the image boundary (called the "Big Data") will also move. Use the method on the next page if you want to trim the layer as you copy it. Also, you can't copy linked layers using this method. To copy linked layers, use the method described on page 96.

To drag-and-drop a layer to another image (Layers palette method):

1. Open the image containing the layer you want to move and the image the layer is to be placed into (the "destination image"), and make sure the two windows don't completely overlap.

2. Click in the source image window.

3. Click on the name of the layer you want to move on the Layers palette **1**. Any tool can be selected.

4. Drag the layer name from the Layers palette into the destination image window. Release the mouse when the darkened border is where you want the layer to appear. It will be stacked above the previously active layer in the destination image **2**–**3**.

TIP If the dimensions of the layer being moved are larger than those of the destination image, the moved layer will extend beyond the edges of the destination image window. Use the Move tool to move the layer in the image window. The "hidden" parts will save with the image.

Drag-and-drop a Layer to Another Image

Use this method to copy a single layer or linked layers to another image. In order to drag-copy linked layers, you must use the Move tool and you must drag the source layer from the source image window—not the Layers palette.

To drag-and-drop a layer to another image (Move tool):

1. Open the image containing the layer you want to move (the "source image") and the image to which the layer is to be moved (the "destination image").

2. On the Layers palette, click the name of the layer that you want to copy. (To move multiple layers, link them first. See page 154.)

3. *Optional:* Click in the destination image window, then click on the name of the layer on the Layers palette that you want the added layer to appear on top of.

4. Choose the Move tool (V). ▶⊹

5. Click in the source image window. Drag the target layer from the current image window to the destination image window **1**. The new layer will be positioned where you release the mouse, on top of the target layer in the destination image **2**.

6. *Optional:* Use the Move tool ▶⊹ to move the layer in the destination image window.

7. *Optional:* Restack the new layer or layers (drag them upward or downward).

TIP To copy a layer into the center of another image, start dragging the layer, hold down Shift, then continue to drag. If the two images have the same pixel count, the moved layer will be positioned in the exact *x/y* location as in the source image.

A nifty way to zero in on the layer you want to copy

Position the Move tool over a layer in the image window, right-press to view a menu of layers that are directly below the cursor, then choose a layer from the menu. With any other tool selected, Control-right-press.

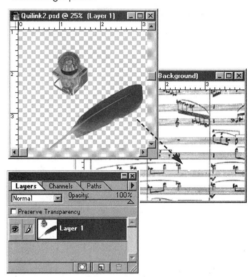

1 Drag the target layer from the **source image window** into the **destination image window**.

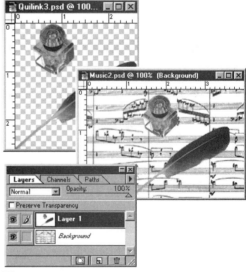

2 The new layer appears in the destination image.

Not quite as simple as it seems

Bear in mind when you copy and paste that the size of the layer imagery may change when pasted, because it is rendered in the **resolution** of the destination image. If the resolution of the destination image is higher than that of the imagery you're pasting, the Clipboard layer will become smaller when pasted. Conversely, if the resolution of the destination image is lower than the resolution of the Clipboard imagery, the Clipboard layer will be enlarged when pasted. You can use the Image Size dialog box to choose the same resolution (and dimensions, if desired) for both images (see page 42).

Use this copy and paste method if you want to copy only the visible portion of a layer (when displayed at 100% view) and not any Big Data beyond the layer's edge.

To copy and paste only the visible part of a layer to another image:

1. On the Layers palette, activate the layer you want to copy.

2. Choose Select menu > All (Control-A). The areas extending beyond the layer's edge won't be selected.

3. Choose Edit menu > Copy (Control-C).

4. Click in the destination image window.

5. Choose Edit menu > Paste (Control-V). A new layer will be created for the pasted pixels, and it can be restacked, like any other layer, using the Layers palette.

6. Click back in the original image window, then choose Select menu > None (Control-D) to deactivate the selection.

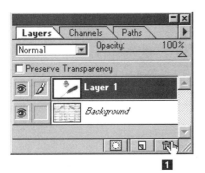

1

To delete a layer:

1. On the Layers palette, click the name of the layer you want to delete.

2. Click the Trash button, then click Yes.
   or
   Alt-click the Trash button **1**–**3**.

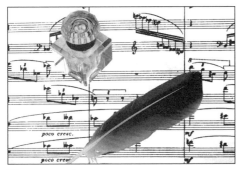

2 The original image.

3 After deleting Layer 1.

Copy and Paste a Layer; Delete a Layer

Merge Layers; Flatten Layers

Merging and flattening

Layers increase an image's file size, so when you've completely finished editing your image, you should merge or flatten it to conserve storage space. Learn the difference between the merge and flatten commands before you choose which one to use.

NOTE: Only the Photoshop file format supports multiple layers. To save your image in any other file format, you must first merge or flatten it down to one layer. To reserve the layered version for future editing, flatten a copy of it using File menu > Save a Copy. The layered version will remain open.

To merge two layers:

1. Activate the topmost layer of the two layers that you want to merge.

2. Choose Merge Down (Control-E) from the Layers palette command menu. The target layer will merge into the layer immediately below it.

The Merge Visible command merges all the currently visible layers into the bottommost displayed layer and **preserves** hidden layers.

To merge multiple layers:

1. Display only the layers you want to merge (all should have eye icons on the Layers palette), and hide the layers you *don't* want to merge. They don't have to be consecutive. Hide the Background if you don't want to merge layers into it.

2. Click on one of the layers to be merged.

3. Choose Merge Visible (Control-Shift-E) from the Layers palette menu.

The Flatten command merges currently displayed layers into the bottommost displayed layer and **discards** hidden layers.

To flatten layers:

1. Make sure all the layers you want to flatten are displayed (have eye icons).

2. Choose Flatten Image from the Layers palette command menu **1**–**2**.

3. Click OK. Any transparent areas in the bottommost layer will turn white.

To merge linked layers or a clipping group

■ To merge linked layers, choose **Merge Linked** from the Layers palette command menu or the Layer menu. The Merge Linked command **discards** hidden linked layers.

■ To merge layers in a clipping group, activate the underlined layer, then choose **Merge Group** from the Layers palette command menu or the Layer menu. The Merge Group command **discards** hidden grouped layers.

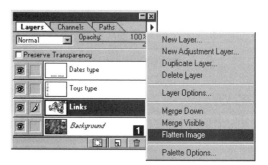

2 The Layers palette for the merged or flattened image.

LIGHTS & DARKS 8

A posterized image.

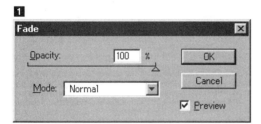

THIS CHAPTER covers the adjustment of light and dark values. For example, you can invert a layer to make it look like a film negative, posterize it to lower its luminosity levels to a specified number, or change all its pixels to black and white to make it high contrast. You can precisely adjust lightness or contrast in a layer's highlights, midtones, or shadows using features like Levels or Curves. To darken a large or small area of a layer by hand, drag across it with the Burn tool. To lighten an area, drag across it with the Dodge tool. All the commands discussed in this chapter can be applied to a color image, but try applying them to a grayscale image first to learn how they work.

TIP The Fade command (Filter menu > Fade or Control-Shift-F) **1** works for the Adjust commands, not just for filters!

Normally, the Adjust commands affect only the current target layer or a selection on the target layer. If you're using Photoshop version 4.0 or later, however, you can apply most Adjust submenu commands using a different method: via an adjustment layer. Unlike normal layers, the adjustment layer affects all the currently visible layers below it—not just the target layer. The beauty of the adjustment layer is that it won't actually change pixels until it's merged with the layer below it, so you can use it to try out various effects. And if you're not happy with the adjustment layer effect, you can just discard it. Instructions for creating an adjustment layer are on the next page.

TIP If you're really happy with an adjustment layer and you want to use it in another image, just drag-and-drop it from the Layers palette into the destination image window!

A few things to know before you begin...

■ To apply any of the commands discussed in this chapter to a selected area of a layer rather than to an entire layer, just create a **selection** before you choose the commmand.

■ Dialog boxes opened from the Adjust submenus (Image menu) have a **Preview** box. Changes preview on the entire screen with the Preview box unchecked; changes preview only in the image or in a selection with the Preview box checked. CMYK color displays more acccurately with the Preview option on.

■ To reset the settings in a dialog box, hold down Alt and click the **Reset** button.

■ To open a dialog box with its **last used settings**, hold down **Alt** while choosing the command from the menu bar or include Alt in the keyboard shortcut for that command.

The adjustment layer affects all the currently visible layers below it—not just the target layer, but it doesn't actually change pixels until it's merged with the layer below it. If you're not happy with an adjustment layer effect, just trash it. Read more about adjustment layers on pages 109–110.

To create an adjustment layer:

1. Activate the layer above which you want the adjustment layer to appear.

2. Control-click the Create New Layer button on the Layers palette **1**.
or
Choose New Adjustment Layer from the Layers palette command menu.

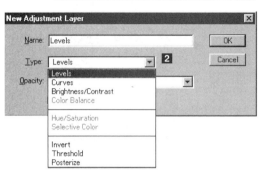

3. Choose an adjustment type from the Type drop down menu **2**.

4. *Optional:* Choose other layer options (Opacity, Mode, Group with Previous Layer, or rename the layer). You can change these options later on.

5. Click OK or press Enter.

6. Make the desired image adjustments, then click OK **3**. An adjustment layer can be modified at any time, until it's merged it with the layer directly below it (Control-E).

TIP To limit the adjustment layer effect to just the layer below it, group the two together: Alt-click the line between them on the Layers palette.

3 The adjustment layer icon.

The Equalize command redistributes the target layer's light and dark values. It may improve an image that lacks contrast or is too dark.

To equalize a layer:

Choose Image menu > Adjust > Equalize **4**.

TIP To limit the Equalize effect to part of a layer, select the area before choosing the command, then click Select Area Only in the Equalize dialog box. To equalize a whole layer based on the values within the selected area, click Entire Image Based on Area.

4 The original image.

After applying the **Equalize** command.

PHOTO: PAUL PETROFF

1 The original image.

2 The image **inverted**.

Choose the Invert command to make the target layer look like a film negative, or a negative look like a positive. Each pixel will be replaced with its opposite brightness and/or color value.

To invert a layer's lights and darks:

Choose a target layer, then choose Image menu > Adjust > Invert (Control-I) **1**–**2**.

or

To use an adjustment layer, Control-click the Create New Layer button at the bottom of the Layers palette, choose Type: Invert, then click OK.

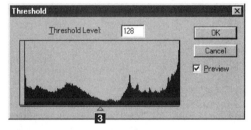
3

Use the Threshold dialog box to make the target layer high contrast by converting color or gray pixels into black and white pixels.

To make a layer high contrast:

1. Choose a target layer, then choose Image menu > Adjust > Threshold.

or

To use an adjustment layer, Control-click the Create New Layer button at the bottom of the Layers palette, choose Type: Threshold, then click OK.

4 The original image.

2. Move the slider to the right to increase the number of black pixels **3**.

or

Move the slider to the left to increase the number of white pixels.

or

Enter a number between 1 and 255 in the Threshold Level field. Shades above this number will become white, shades below become black.

5 After using the **Threshold** command.

3. Click OK or press Enter **4**–**5**.

Use the Posterize command to reduce the number of color or value levels in the target layer. This effortless command can produce beautiful results.

To posterize a layer:

1. Choose a target layer, then choose Image menu > Adjust > Posterize.
   or
   To use an adjustment layer, Control-click the Create New Layer button at the bottom of the Layers palette, choose Type: Posterize, then click OK.

2. Make sure the Preview box is checked, then enter a number between 2 and 255 in the Levels field **1**. To produce a dramatic effect, enter a number between 4 and 8.

3. Click OK or press Enter **2**–**4**.

TIP If the number of shades in an image is reduced using the Posterize command, or any other tonal adjustment command is made, and the image is saved, the original shade information will be permanently lost.

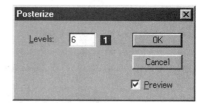

2 The original image.

3 Post **posterization**.

4 posterized image.

PHOTO: PAUL PETROFF

Posterize

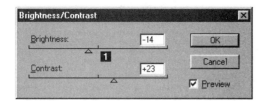

If you use the Levels dialog box to make tonal adjustments, you'll be able to adjust the shadows, midtones, and highlights individually, but the Brightness/Contrast command, discussed below, is simpler to use.

To adjust brightness and contrast (Brightness/Contrast):

1. Choose a target layer, then choose Image menu > Adjust > Brightness/Contrast.

or

To use an adjustment layer, Control-click the Create New Layer button at the bottom of the Layers palette, choose Type: Brightness/Contrast, then click OK.

2. To lighten the layer, move the brightness slider to the right **1**.

or

To darken the layer, move the Brightness slider to the left.

or

Enter a number between -100 and 100 in the Brightness field.

3. To intensify the contrast, move the Contrast slider to the right.

or

To lessen the contrast, move the Contrast slider to the left.

or

Enter a number between -100 and 100 in the Contrast field.

4. Click OK or press Enter **2**–**4**.

TIP When you move a slider in any of the Adjust submenu dialog boxes, note its position relative to the other sliders and how the layer changes.

2 The original image.

3 The Brightness slider moved to the right.

4 **Brightness** and **contrast** adjusted.

Adjust Brightness and Contrast

Use the Levels dialog box to make fine adjustments to a target layer's highlights, midtones, or shadows.

To adjust brightness and contrast using Levels:

1. Choose a target layer, then choose Image menu > Adjust > Levels (Control-L).

   or

   To use an adjustment layer, Control-click the Create New Layer button at the bottom of the Layers palette, choose Type: Levels, then click OK.

2. Do any of the following:

   To brighten the highlights and intensify contrast, move the Input highlights slider to the left 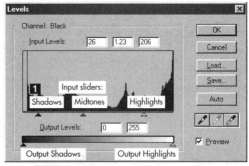. The midtones slider will move along with it. Readjust the midtones slider, if necessary.

   To darken the shadows, move the Input shadows slider to the right. The midtones slider will move along with it. Readjust the midtones slider, if necessary.

   To adjust the midtones independently, move the Input midtones slider.

   To decrease contrast and lighten the image, move the Output shadows slider to the right.

   To decrease contrast and darken the image, move the Output highlights slider to the left.

3. Click OK or press Enter **2**–**4**.

TIP To make a layer high contrast (black and white), move the Input shadows and highlights sliders very close together. Position them left of center to lighten the image, right of center to darken the image. You can use the Threshold command to produce the same effect.

TIP To adjust levels automatically, choose Image menu > Adjust > Auto Levels (Control-Shift-L) or click Auto in the Levels dialog box.

2 The original image.

3 After **Levels** adjustments.

PHOTO: PAUL PETROFF

4 To produce this image, an area of the image was selected before creating an adjustment layer (Type: Levels). The type was added in QuarkXPress.

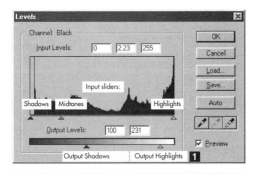

2 The original image.

3 The music layer screened back.

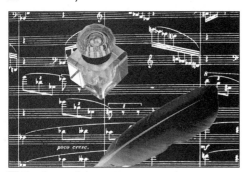

4 The Output slider positions reversed.

To screen back a layer:

1. Choose a target layer, then choose Image menu > Adjust > Levels (Control-L).
or
To use an adjustment layer, Control-click the New Layer button at the bottom of the Layers palette, choose Type: Levels, then click OK.

2. To reduce contrast, move the Output highlights slider slightly to the left **1**.
and
Move the Output shadows slider to the right.

3. To lighten the midtones, move the Input midtones slider to the left.

4. Click OK or press Enter **2**–**3**.

TIP To make a layer look like a film negative, reverse the position of the two Output sliders **4**. The farther apart the sliders are, the more each pixel's brightness and contrast attributes will be reversed. The Invert command produces a similar effect.

PHOTO: PAUL PETROFF

The original image.

The **screened back** version.

Use the Dodge tool to lighten pixels in small areas or use the Burn tool to darken pixels. You can choose different Brushes palette settings for each tool. The Dodge and Burn tools can't be used on a image in Bitmap or Indexed Color mode.

To lighten using the Dodge tool or darken using the Burn tool:

1. Choose a target layer.

2. Choose the Dodge ✎ or Burn ✋ tool. (Press O to toggle between the Dodge, Burn, and Sponge tools.)

3. On the Toning Tools Options palette **1**:

Position the Exposure slider between 1% (low intensity) and 100% (high intensity). Try a low exposure first (20%-30%) so the tool won't bleach or darken areas too quickly.

and

Choose Shadows, Midtones, or Highlights from the pop-up menu to Dodge or Burn only pixels in that value range.

4. Click the Brushes tab on the same palette, then click a hard-edged or soft-edged tip. A large, soft tip will produce the smoothest result.

5. Stroke on any area of the layer. Pause between strokes to allow the screen to redraw **2**–**3**.

TIP If you Dodge or Burn an area too much, choose Edit menu > Undo or choose File menu > Revert. Don't use the opposite tool to fix it—you'll get uneven results.

TIP To create a smooth, even highlight or shadow line, dodge or burn a path using the Dodge or Burn tool and the Stroke Path command (see page 173).

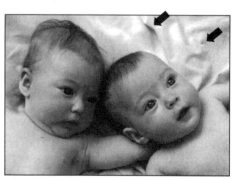

2 The Dodge tool with **Shadows** chosen from the Toning Tools Options palette was used to eliminate dark spots in the background of this image.

3 After dodging.

Dodge or Burn

The original image.

After applying Dodge and Burn strokes to the **neutral gray layer** to create stronger highlights and shadows on the crab.

The neutral gray layer, showing the Dodge and Burn strokes. They appear in shades of black when viewed on their own layer, but they accentuate lights and darks on the underlying layer.

In the following instructions, a new gray layer is created with its own mode, and then the Dodge and/or Burn tools are used to paint shades of gray on that layer, which has the effect of heightening or lessening contrast in the underlying layer. This technique works on a grayscale or color image and allows for unlimited undos.

To create a neutral gray, black, or white transition layer:

1. Choose a target layer in a grayscale or color image above which you want the transition layer to appear.

2. Alt-click the Create New Layer button on the Layers palette.

3. Enter a name for the layer.

4. Choose Overlay mode if you're going to use the Dodge or Burn tool.

5. Check the "Fill with Overlay-neutral color (50% gray)" box.

6. Click OK or press Enter.

7. Follow steps 2–5 on page 106 to create dodge or burn strokes. If you don't like the results, paint over areas with 50% gray (use this like multiple undos) or fill the entire layer again with 50% gray to remove all your changes and start over.

TIP The Sponge tool can't be used on the transition layer, even in a color image.

You can adjust lights and darks on a target layer by clicking on thumbnails in the Variations dialog box. (To adjust a color image using the Variations dialog box, see page 125.)

To adjust a grayscale image using thumbnail Variations:

1. Choose a target layer.

2. Choose Image menu > Adjust > Variations.

3. Position the Fine/Coarse slider right of center to make major adjustments or left of center to make minor adjustments **1**. Each notch to the right doubles the adjustment per click. Each notch to the left halves the adjustment per click.

4. Click the Lighter or Darker thumbnail in the Shadows, Midtones, or Highlights column. Compare the Current Pick thumbnail, which represents the modified image, with the Original thumbnail.

5. *Optional:* Check the Show Clipping box if you want to have highlighted the areas of the image that will be converted to white or black from the Variations adjustment.

6. *Optional:* Click the same thumbnail again to intensify the change, or click the opposite thumbnail to undo the modification.

7. Click OK or press Enter **2**–**3**.

TIP Click the Original thumbnail to undo all changes made using the Variations dialog box.

TIP Use the Levels or Brightness/Contrast dialog box to make more precise adjustments, and with the ability to preview adjustments in the image window.

Click the **Original** thumbnail to undo all adjustments.

The **Current Pick** represents the modified image.

The Variations dialog box. The following steps were taken to produce the image at the bottom of this page: The Fine/Coarse slider was moved to the right two notches, the Shadows-Darker box was clicked, the Highlights-Lighter box was clicked, the Fine/Coarse slider was moved to the left four notches, and finally, the Midtones-Darker box was clicked.

2 The original image.

3 After **Variations** adjustments.

Adjustment layer tips and tricks

- **Hide** an adjustment layer to temporarily remove its effect.

- Lower an adjustment layer's **opacity** in increments to progressively reduce its effect.

- Change an adjustment layer's **blending mode** to produce a variety of visual effects in relationship to its underlying layers. Overlay mode will heighten contrast, Multiply mode will darken the image, and Screen mode will lighten the image.

- If you don't want an underlying layer to be affected by the adjustment layer, **restack** it above the adjustment layer on the Layers palette.

- To limit the adjustment layer's effects to a section of its underlying layers, create a **selection** first. Or paint or fill with **black** on the adjustment layer to remove the adjustment effect or **white** to reveal the adjustment effect (instructions on the next page).

To use an adjustment layer to preview different settings for the same command

Create several of the same adjustment layer types, like Color Balance or Levels, hide the adjustment layers, and then show each one at a time to see how they affect the underlying image. You can restack adjustment layers among themselves, and you can place them at different locations within the overall layer stack. If you find using multiple adjustment layers to be confusing, you can adjust and readjust color or tonal values using a single adjustment layer.

More about adjustment layers

An adjustment layer is a special type of layer mask that is used to alter color and tonal characteristics in the layers below it, but those alterations don't permanently affect pixels in underlying layers until the adjustment layer is merged with them. The adjustment layer is really a method for previewing color and tonal adjustments, and it's a great way to experiment with effects before commiting to them.

Normally, an adjustment layer will affect all the currently visible layers below it, but you can use a clipping group to limit an adjustment layer's effect to only the layer or layers it's grouped with.

To edit an adjustment layer:

1. Double-click the adjustment layer name on the Layers palette.
or
Activate the adjustment layer, then choose Layer menu > Adjustment Options.

2. Change the dialog box settings.

3. Click OK.

When you merge down an adjustment layer, the adjustments become permanent for the image layer below it, so you should be certain you want the effect to become permanent before you perform another operation. If you change your mind, un-merge by choosing Edit menu > Undo right away.

To merge an adjustment layer:

1. Activate the adjustment layer.

2. Choose Merge Down from the Layers palette command menu (Control-E).

TIP To merge an adjustment layer with more than one other layer, see the sections on Merge Visible or Flatten Image on page 98. An adjustment layer cannot be merged with other adjustment layers; since they contain no real image pixels, there's nothing to merge.

Because an adjustment layer is a type of mask, when you activate an adjustment layer, the Color palette automatically resets to Grayscale and the Foreground and Background colors revert to black and white, or vice versa.

To restrict the area a new adjustment layer affects:

1. Create a selection on the layer above which the new adjustment layer will appear .

2. Create an adjustment layer. The adjustment layer thumbnail will be black, with an area of white to indicate where the selection was.

1 In this image, the adjustment layer contains a mask on the left side that is hiding the Threshold effect.

To restrict the area an existing adjustment layer affects:

1. Activate the adjustment layer.

2. Choose black as the Foreground color. (Click the Switch colors icon on the Toolbox to swap the Foreground and Background colors.)

3. To remove the adjustment layer effect:

Create a selection (or selections) and fill them with black.
or
Choose the Paintbrush tool, Normal mode, 100% opacity, then paint with black on the image. Choose a lower opacity to partially remove the adjustment layer effect.

4. *Optional:* To restore the adjustment layer effect, paint or fill with white.

TIP To reveal just a small area of the adjustment effect, fill the entire layer with black and then paint with white over specific areas. Fill the whole adjustment layer with white to display the adjustment effect over the whole image. To diminish the adjustment layer's effect over the whole layer by a percentage, lower its opacity via the Layers palette **2**.

2 In this image, the adjustment layer's opacity was lowered to 60%, which causes the Threshold effect to blend with the overall underlying image.

Layer mask shortcuts

- **Alt**-click the adjustment layer thumbnail to **view** the mask.

- **Shift**-click the adjustment layer thumbnail to temporarily **remove** any mask on the adjustment layer.

- **Control**-click the adjustment layer thumbnail to convert the non-masked area into a **selection**.

Restrict the Adjustment Layer Effect

CHOOSE COLORS 9

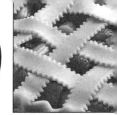

N THIS CHAPTER you will learn how to choose colors using the Color palette, and how to add, delete, save, append, and load colors using the Swatches palette.

What are the Foreground and Background colors?

When you use a painting tool or create type, the current Foreground color is applied.

When you use the Eraser tool, add a border to a picture using the Canvas Size dialog box, or move a selection on the Background using the Move tool, the hole that's left behind is automatically filled with the current Background color. The Gradient tool can produce blends using the Foreground and/or Background colors.

The Foreground and Background colors are displayed in the Foreground and Background color squares on the Toolbox **1** and on the Color palette **2**. (When written with an uppercase "F" or "B," these terms refer to colors, not the overall foreground or background areas of a picture.)

There are several ways to choose a Foreground or Background color, and they are described on the following pages:

- Enter values in fields or click on the big color square in the Color Picker.
- Choose premixed matching system colors using the Custom Colors dialog box.
- Pluck a color from an image using the Eyedropper tool.
- Enter values in fields or move sliders on the Color palette.
- Click a swatch on the Swatches palette.

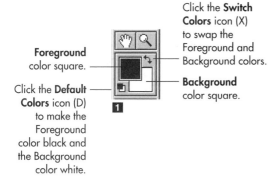

Foreground color square.

Click the **Switch Colors** icon (X) to swap the Foreground and Background colors.

Background color square.

Click the **Default Colors** icon (D) to make the Foreground color black and the Background color white.

1

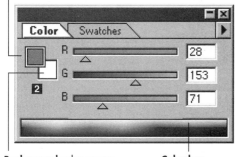

Foreground color square. The currently active square has a double frame.

R 28
G 153
B 71

2

Background color square.   **Color bar**

To choose a color using the Color Picker:

1. Click the Foreground or Background color square on the Toolbox **1**.

or

Click the Foreground or Background color square on the Color palette if it is already active.

or

Double-click the Foreground or Background color square on the Color palette if it is not active.

NOTE: If the color square you click on is a Custom color, the Custom Colors dialog box will open. Click Picker to open the Color Picker dialog box.

2. To choose from the Photoshop Color Picker:

Click a color on the vertical color bar to choose a hue, then click a variation of that hue in the large square **2**.

or

To choose a specific process color, enter percentages from a matching guide in the C, M, Y, and K fields. For an on-screen image, you can specify specific percentages in the R, G, and B fields. RGB colors range from 0 (black) to 255 (pure R, G,or B). You can also enter numbers in the HSB, or Lab fields.

3. Click OK or press Enter.

TIP To use the Photoshop Color Picker, Photoshop must be chosen from the Color Picker drop-down menu in the General Preferences dialog box (Control-K).

New color. Old color.

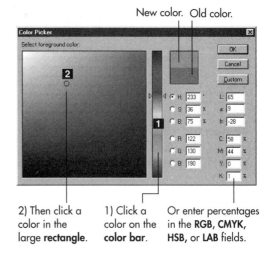

2) Then click a color in the large **rectangle**.

1) Click a color on the **color bar**.

Or enter percentages in the **RGB, CMYK, HSB,** or **LAB** fields.

Out of gamut?

An exclamation point indicates there is no ink equivalent for the color you chose—it is **out of printable gamut**. If you're planning to print your image, choose an in-gamut color or click the exclamation point to have Photoshop substitute the closest printable color (shown in the swatch below the exclamation point). When you convert your image to CMYK Color mode, the entire image will be brought into printable gamut. The out of gamut range is defined by the current settings in the Separation Setup and Printing Inks Setup dialog boxes.

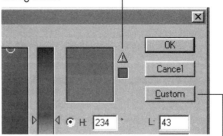

Click **Custom** to choose a predefined color.

All colors are printed as four-color from Photoshop, regardless of whether they are saved as spot or process colors. To save spot colors so they can be color separated from QuarkXPress, Illustrator, or FreeHand, use Pantone colors and also check the Short PANTONE Names box in General Preferences (Control-K).

Don't rely on your monitor to represent matching system colors accurately—you must choose them from a printed Pantone, Trumatch, Toyo, Focoltone, Anpa-Color, or DIC swatch book. And make sure those are the inks that your printer plans to use.

To choose a custom color using the Custom Colors dialog box:

1. Click the Foreground or Background color square on the Toolbox.
or
Click the Foreground or Background color square on the Color palette if it is already active.
or
Double-click the Foreground or Background color square on the Color palette if it is not active.

NOTE: If the color square you click on is not a Custom color, the Color Picker dialog box will open. Click Custom to open the Custom Colors dialog box.

2. Choose a matching guide system from the Book drop-down menu 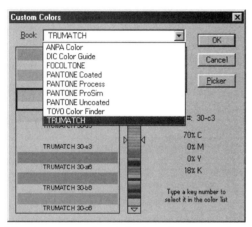.

3. Type a number (it will appear on the "Key #" line).
or
Click a color on the vertical color bar, then click a swatch.

4. *Optional:* Click Picker to return to the Color Picker.

5. Click OK or press Enter.

TIP To load a matching system palette onto the Swatches palette, see page 116.

TIP For the addresses of the various matching system companies (Pantone, Trumatch, etc.), see the Photoshop 4.0 User Guide.

1 In the Custom Colors dialog box, choose a matching system from the **Book** pop-up menu. Then type a number, or click a color on the vertical color bar and click a swatch.

Custom Colors

113

To choose a color from an image (Eyedropper):

1. On the Color palette, click the Foreground or Background color square if it is not already active.

2. Choose the Eyedropper tool (I). Hold down Alt to use the Eyedropper when the Paintbrush, Pencil, Line, Gradient, Paint Bucket, or Airbrush tool is selected.

3. Click on a color in any open image window **1**.

TIP Alt-click in the image window to choose a Background color when the Foreground color square is active, or to choose a Foreground color when the Background color square is active.

To choose a color using the Color palette:

1. Click the Foreground or Background color square if it isn't already active **2**.

2. Choose a color model for the sliders from the Color palette command menu **3**.

3. Move any of the sliders **4**.

or

Click on or press and drag on the color bar.

or

Enter values in the fields.

TIP In RGB mode, white (the presence of all colors) is produced when all the sliders are in their rightmost positions. Black (the absence of all colors) is produced when all the sliders are in their leftmost positions. Gray is produced when all the sliders are vertically aligned in any other position.

TIP The model you choose for the Color palette does not have to match the current image mode. For example, you can choose the CMYK Color model from the Color palette for a picture in RGB Color mode.

2 Click the Foreground or Background color square.

3 Choose a **model** for the sliders.

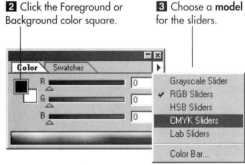

4 Click on the color bar or move any of the sliders. (Choose Color Bar from the command menu to choose a different **Spectrum style** or Shift-click the color bar to cycle through the styles.)

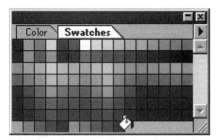

1 Click in the white area below the swatches.

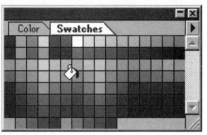

2 Or Alt-Shift-click between two swatches to insert a color between them.

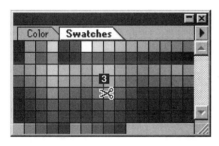

To choose a color from the Swatches palette:

To choose a Foreground color, just click on a color swatch.

To choose a Background color, Alt-click a color swatch.

To add a color to the Swatches palette:

1. Choose a Foreground color.

2. Click the Swatches tab to display the Swatches palette.

3. Position the cursor in the blank area below the swatches on the palette, and click with the paint bucket cursor **1**. The new color will appear next to the last swatch.

TIP To replace an existing swatch with the new color, Shift-click on the color to be replaced.

TIP To insert the new color between two swatches, Alt-Shift-click on either swatch **2**.

To delete a color from the Swatches palette:

Control-click on a swatch (scissors cursor) **3**.

TIP To restore the default Swatches palette, choose Reset Swatches from the Swatches palette command menu, then click OK.

NOTE: If you edit the Swatches palette, and then exit and re-launch Photoshop, your edited palette will reopen.

To save an edited swatches set:

1. Choose Save Swatches from the Swatches palette command menu.

2. Enter a name for the edited palette in the "Save swatches in" field **4**.

3. Choose a location in which to save the palette.

4. Click Save.

Choose, Add, Delete, Save Swatches

Nine preset color swatch palettes are supplied with Photoshop, and they can be loaded onto the Swatches palette. They include ANPA, Focoltone, Pantone (Coated, Process, ProSim, and Uncoated), System, Toyo, and Trumatch.

To replace a swatches set:

1. Choose Replace Swatches from the Swatches palette command menu.

2. Open the Palettes folder in the Photoshop application folder.

3. Double-click a palette ■. The loaded swatches will appear on the Swatches palette.
   or
   Highlight a palette, then click Open.

TIP Choose Reset Swatches from the Swatches palette command menu to restore the default palette.

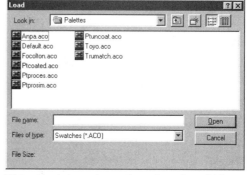

■ Double-click a palette in the Color Palettes folder.

You can append to an existing swatches set any swatches set that you've edited and saved or any of the palettes that are supplied with Photoshop.

To load a swatches set:

1. Choose Load Swatches from the Swatches palette command menu ■.

2. Open the Palettes or another palettes folder in the Photoshop application folder.

3. Double-click a palette (swatches set) ■.
   or
   Highlight a palette and click Open.

4. The appended swatches will appear below the existing swatches.

TIP To enlarge the palette to display the loaded swatches, drag the palette resize box or click the palette zoom box.

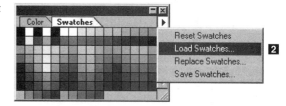

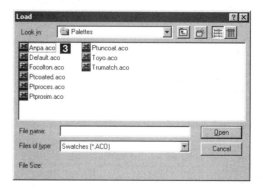

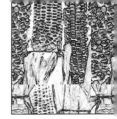

RECOLOR 10

The Preview option...

Image menu > Adjust submenu dialog boxes have a Preview box. If you're working on a normal layer—not an adjustment layer—changes affect the entire screen with the Preview box unchecked. Changes preview in just the image (or selection) with the Preview box checked. CMYK color displays more acccurately with Preview on.

...and a couple of very handy tips

- To display the **unmodified** image in the image window, uncheck the Preview box, and press and hold on the title bar of the dialog box.

- Use the **Save** command in the Levels, Curves, Replace Color, Hue/Saturation, Selective Color, or Variations dialog box to save color adjustment settings, and then apply them to another layer or to another image using the Load command. Or you can drag-copy an adjustment layer between images.

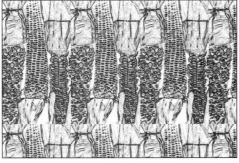

Pattern-making

Each new pattern you create using the **Define Pattern** command replaces the last one. You can, of course, save any image that contains a pattern that you want to reuse, and use the Define Pattern command any time you want to redefine it as a fill pattern.

IN THIS CHAPTER you will learn to fill a selection with color, imagery, or a pattern, color the edge of a selection, tint a Grayscale image, adjust a color image using the Hue/Saturation, Color Balance, Variations, Curves, and Levels commands, replace color using the Replace Color command, saturate or desaturate colors using the Sponge tool, and produce gradients.

All the Adjust submenu commands can be applied to a normal layer via the Image menu > Adjust submenu. Alternatively, many Adjust commands can be applied to an image via an adjustment layer. Unlike submenu commands, which affect only the current target layer, the adjustment layer affects all the currently visible layers below it. The adjustment layer, however, doesn't actually change pixels until it's merged with the layer below it. Adjustment layers are used in this chapter, but they're explained in Chapter 8.

To fill a selection or a layer with a color or a pattern:

1. Choose a target layer.

2. To fill the entire layer, proceed to step 3.

To fill only non-transparent areas on the layer, check the Preserve Transparency box on the Layers palette.

To limit the fill area, create a selection using any method described in Chapter 5.

To create a tiling pattern, select a rectangular or square area using the Rectangular Marquee tool, then choose Edit menu > Define Pattern.

3. To fill with the Foreground or Background color, choose that color now from the Color or Swatches palette.

(Continued on the following page)

4. Choose Edit menu > Fill (Shift-Backspace).

5. Choose one of the following: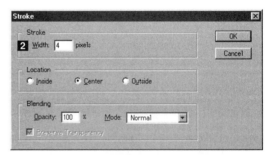

Use: Foreground Color, Background Color, Black, 50% Gray, or White.

Pattern to fill with the pattern you defined for step 2 on the previous page.

Saved to fill the selection or layer with the last saved version of the image. (Don't add or delete a layer from the image after saving.)

Snapshot to fill with imagery from the Take Snapshot or Take Merged Snapshot command buffer (see page 77).

6. Enter an Opacity percentage.

7. Choose a blending mode from the Mode drop-down menu.

8. *Optional:* If you forgot to check the Preserve Transparency box on the Layers palette, you can check it here.

9. Click OK or press Enter.

TIP If you dislike the new fill color, choose Edit menu > Undo now so it won't blend with your next color or mode choice.

1 In the Fill dialog box, choose a Fill color from the Use drop-down menu, enter an Opacity, and choose a Mode.

Fill shortcuts

Fill selection with Foreground color, 100% opacity	Alt-Backspace
Fill selection with Background color, 100% opacity	Backspace
Fill existing pixels (not transparent areas) with the Foreground color	Alt-Shift-Backspace
Fill existing pixels (not transparent areas) with the Background color	Control-Shift-Backspace

To color the edge of (stroke) a selection or a layer:

1. Choose a target layer, and check the Preserve Transparency box if you want to stroke the edges of existing pixels on the layer, but not transparent areas.

2. *Optional:* Select an area on the layer.

3. Choose a Foreground color.

4. Choose Edit menu > Stroke.

5. Enter a Width between 1 and 16 **2**.

6. Click Location: Inside, Center, or Outside (the position of the stroke on the selection or layer edge).

7. Enter a number in the Opacity field.

8. Choose a blending mode from the Mode drop-down menu.

9. Click OK or press Enter **3**.

TIP To stroke a path, see page 173.

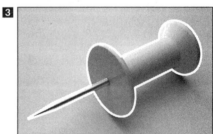

Stroke a Selection

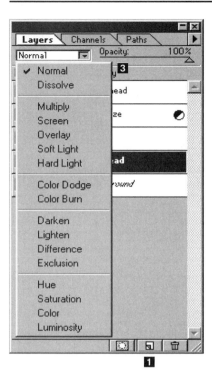

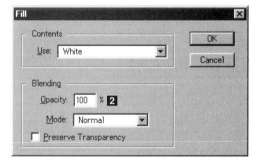

To fill a selection and preview fill modes and opacities:

1. Choose the target layer above which you want the fill layer to appear.

2. Click the Create New Layer button at the bottom of the Layers palette **1**. You will be filling on the new layer.

3. Select an area of the image you want to fill.

4. Uncheck the Preserve Transparency box on the Layers palette.

5. Choose a Foreground color.

6. Choose Edit menu > Fill.

7. Enter 100 in the Opacity field **2**.

8. Choose Normal from the Mode drop-down menu.

9. Click OK or press Enter.

10. To experiment with various color effects, choose an opacity and a mode from the Layers palette **3**.

11. Choose Select menu > None (Control-D).
or
Click the selection with the Marquee tool or the Lasso tool.

12. *Optional:* To merge the new layer with the layer below it, choose Merge Down from the Layers palette command menu (Control-E).

TIP To remove the color fill, use the Eraser tool before you merge the layer downward, or delete the layer altogether.

TIP You can continue to modify the new layer using the Layer Options dialog box, opened from the Layers palette, to try different options for blending the new layer with the layer below it (see page 148), or by painting on the new layer with any painting tool.

TIP Restack the layer to see how the color looks above or below different layers.

Preview Fill Modes and Opacities

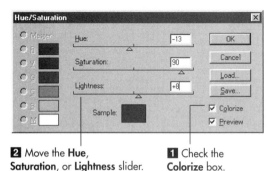

2 Move the **Hue**, **Saturation**, or **Lightness** slider. **1** Check the **Colorize** box.

To colorize a grayscale image using Hue/Saturation:

1. Open a Grayscale image.

2. Choose Image menu > Mode > RGB Color or CMYK Color.

3. Choose a target layer.

4. Choose Image menu > Adjust > Hue/Saturation (Control-U).
or
Create an adjustment layer by Control-clicking the Create New Layer button at the bottom of the Layers palette, choose Type: Hue/Saturation, then click OK.

5. Check the Colorize box, and check the Preview box. The image will be tinted red **1**.

6. Move the Hue slider left or right to apply a different tint **2**. Pause to preview.

7. Move the Saturation slider to reduce color intensity.

8. To lighten the image and colorize pure black, move the Lightness slider to the right. To darken the image and colorize pure white, move the Lightness slider to the left.

9. Click OK or press Enter.

TIP To restore the original dialog box settings, hold down Alt and click Reset.

TIP You can also tint a Grayscale image by converting it into a duotone.

TIP See page 146 for tips on painting color on a separate layer over gray layer.

Use the Desaturate command to strip color from a layer without actually changing image modes.

To strip color from a layer:

1. Choose a target layer.

2. Choose Image menu > Adjust > Desaturate (Control-Shift-U).

1 Click **Master** or click a color button (**R**, **Y**, **G**, **C**, **B**, or **M**).

2 Move the **Hue**, **Saturation**, or **Lightness** slider. In this figure, the B (Blue) button was clicked, and the Hue slider is moved to the left to add more C (Cyan) to the Blue.

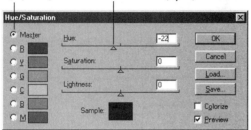

Color info

The Info palette displays before-adjustment and after-adjustment color breakdowns of the pixel or area of pixels currently under the cursor while an Adjust submenu dialog box is open **3**. The size of the sample area depends on the current Eyedropper Options palette **Sample Size** setting **4**.

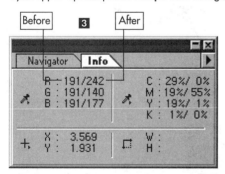

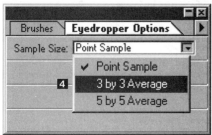

Color adjustments made using the Hue/Saturation command area easiest to discern in an image that has clearly defined color areas.

To adjust a color image using Hue/Saturation:

1. Choose a target layer.

2. Select an area of the layer to recolor only that area.

3. Choose Image menu > Adjust > Hue/Saturation (Control-U).

or

Create an adjustment layer by Control-clicking the Create New Layer button at the bottom of the Layers palette, choose Type: Hue/Saturation, then click OK.

4. Click Master to adjust all colors **1**.

or

Click a color button to adjust only that color.

5. Move the Hue slider left or right **2**. Pause to preview.

6. Move the Saturation slider to the left to decrease saturation or to the right to increase saturation.

7. To lighten the image and colorize pure black, move the Lightness slider to the right. To darken the image and colorize pure white, move the Lightness slider to the left.

8. Click OK or press Enter.

TIP To restore the original dialog box settings, hold down Alt and click Reset.

Adjust Color Image (Hue/Saturation)

Use the Replace Color command to change colors in an image without having to first select them.

To replace colors:

1. *Optional:* For an RGB image, choose View menu > CMYK Preview (Control-Y) to see a preview of the actual image and modifications to it in CMYK color. (The Sample swatch in the Replace Color dialog box will continue to display in RGB.)

2. Choose a target layer.

3. *Optional:* Create a selection to restrict color replacement to that area.

4. Choose Image menu > Adjust > Replace Color.

5. Click on the color you want to replace in the preview window in the Replace Color dialog box or in the image window **1**.

6. *Optional:*
Move the Fuzziness slider to the right to add related colors to the selection **2**.
or
Shift-click in the preview window or on the image to add other colors areas to the selection (or just choose the **+** eyedropper icon before you click).
or
Alt-click in the preview window or on the image to subtract color areas from the selection (or just choose the **–** eyedropper icon before you click).

7. Move the Hue, Saturation, or Lightness Transform sliders to change the selected colors. (Only the Lightness slider will be available for a Grayscale image.) The Sample swatch will change as you move the sliders **3**.

The Transform sliders will stay in their current position even if you click on a different area of the image.

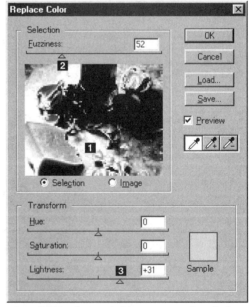

Most of the background of the image is selected. The white areas in the preview window are the **active** areas that will be modified.

Replace Color

8. Click OK or press Enter **1**–**2**.

TIP To restore the original dialog box settings, hold down Alt and click Reset.

TIP Choose Edit menu > Undo (Control-Z) to restore the previous selection in the preview window.

TIP The Sample swatch color from the Replace Color dialog box will display in the currently active square on the Color palette, and the Color palette sliders will reflect its individual components. If the gamut alarm displays, you have produced a non-printable color using the Transform sliders. The Transform sliders won't change the amount of Black (K) in a CMYK color—this component is set by Photoshop's Black Generation function.

TIP Click the Selection button to preview the selection in the preview window or click the Image button to display the entire image. Use the Control key to toggle between the two. If your image extends beyond the edges of your monitor, turn the Image preview option on so you'll be able to sample from the entire image with the eyedropper.

1 The original image.

2 After a **Lightness** adjustment to the background.

Replace Color

Use the Color Balance dialog box to apply a warm or cool cast to a layer's highlights, midtones, or shadows. Color adjustments are easiest to see in an image that has a wide tonal range.

To colorize or color correct using Color Balance:

1. To colorize a Grayscale image, choose an image mode from the Image menu > Mode submenu.

2. Choose a target layer.

3. Choose Image menu > Adjust > Color Balance (Control-B).

or

Create an adjustment layer by Control-clicking the Create New Layer button at the bottom of the Layers palette, choose Type: Color Balance, then click OK.

4. Click Shadows, Midtones, or Highlights **1**.

5. *Optional:* Check the Preserve Luminosity box to preserve brightness values.

6. Move any slider toward a color you want to add more of. Cool and warm colors are paired opposite each other.

Move sliders toward related colors to make an image warmer or cooler. For example, move sliders toward Cyan and Blue to produce a cool cast. Pause to preview.

7. *Optional:* Repeat step 6 with any other button selected for step 4.

8. Click OK or press Enter.

TIP Use a Paintbrush with a light opacity to recolor small areas manually.

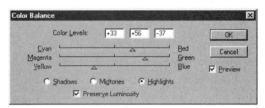

1 Click **Shadows**, **Midtones**, or **Highlights**, then move any of the sliders.

Colorize or Color Balance

Thumbnail previews in the Variations dialog box represent how an image will look with various color adjustments. To make more precise adjustments and preview changes in the document window, use the Color Balance dialog box.

To adjust color using thumbnail Variations:

1. Choose a target layer.

2. Choose Image menu > Adjust > Variations.

3. Click Shadows, Midtones, or Highlights to modify only those areas **1**.
or
Click Saturation to adjust only saturation.

4. Position the Fine/Coarse slider to the right of center to make major adjustments or to the left of center to make minor adjustments **2**. Each notch to the right doubles the adjustment per click. Each notch to the left halves the adjustment per click.

5. Click any "More..." thumbnail to add more of that color to the layer **3**. Pause to preview. The Current Pick thumbnail represents the modified layer.

6. *Optional:* Click Lighter or Darker to modify the luminosity without modifying the hue **4**.

7. *Optional:* Check the Show Clipping box to display neon highlights in areas of nonprintable, out-of-gamut color.

8. *Optional:* Repeat steps 3–6.

9. Click OK or press Enter.

1 First click **Shadows, Midtones, Highlights,** or **Saturation**.

2 Move the **Fine/Coarse** slider to choose the degree of adjustment.

Click the **Original** thumbnail to restore the unmodified layer.

The **Current Pick** thumbnail represents the modified layer.

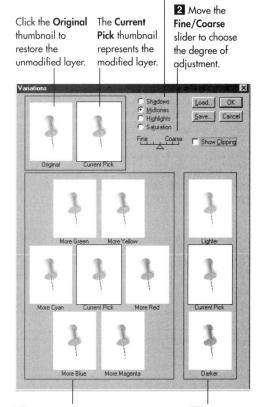

3 Click any "**More...**" thumbnail to add more of that color to the layer. Click the diagonally opposite thumbnail to undo the modification.

4 Click **Lighter** or **Darker** to modify the luminosity without modifying the hue.

Curves and Levels

If you use the Curves or Levels command to make color or tonal adjustments, you should adjust the overall image tone first (the composite channel), and then adjust the individual color channels, if necessary (a bit more cyan, a bit less magenta, etc.).

If you adjust an individual color channel, keep in mind that color opposites (cyan and red, magenta and green, yellow and blue) work in tandem. Lowering, cyan, for example, adds more red; lowering red adds more cyan; adding more magenta and yellow decreases the amount of cyan. The moral of the story: you'll probably have to adjust more than one channel to remove an undesirable color cast. If you overzealously adjust only one channel, you'll throw off the color balance of the whole image.

Using the Curves command, you can correct a picture's highlights, quarter tones, midtones, three-quarter tones, or shadows separately. You can use several adjustment layers for color adjustments: use one for the composite channel first and then use one for each individual channel to tweak the color. And you can experiment with the layer opacity or layer mask to remove or lessen the effect in target areas.

To adjust color or values using the Curves command:

1. Choose Image menu > Adjust > Curves (Control-M).
   or
   Create an adjustment layer by Control-clicking the Create New Layer button at the bottom of the Layers palette, choose Type: Curves, then click OK.

2. The Input and Output readouts indicate either brightness values for RGB Color mode or percentage values for CMYK Color mode (light to dark, from left to right). Click on the gradation bar to switch between the two.

3. *Optional:* Choose a channel name to adjust that color separately.

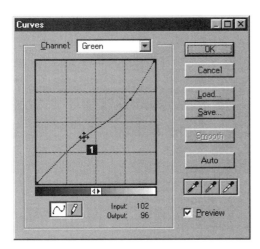

4. Noting where the grid lines meet the gradation bar, drag the part of the curve you want to adjust straight upward to darken or downward to lighten (when in percentage mode) **1**.
and/or
For more precise adjustments, click on the curve to create points to force the curve to remain fixed, then drag between points to produce more subtle adjustments (To remove a point, drag it to the end of the curve or over an adjacent point.)
and/or
Move the extreme end of the curve to reduce absolute black to below 100%, or absolute white to above 0%.

5. Click OK or press Enter **2**–**3**.

TIP We don't recommend using the Curves Pencil tool to draw a curve—it tends to produce a bumpy curve, which in turn produces sharp color transition jumps.

TIP For an image in RGB Color mode, click on the image to see that pixel value placement on the curve. You can then accurately adjust that pixel point. The pixel value will show on individual C, M, Y, and K channels, but not on the composite CMYK channel.

Curves

2 Before Curves adjustment.

3 After Curves adjustment.

To adjust individual color channels using Levels:

1. Make sure the Info palette is open.

2. Choose Image menu > Adjust > Levels (Control-L).

or

Create an adjustment layer by Control-clicking the Create New Layer button at the bottom of the Layers palette, choose Type: Levels, then click OK.

3. Check the Preview box.

4. If there's an obvious predominance of one color in the image (like too much red or green), choose that channel name from the Channel drop-down menu **1**.

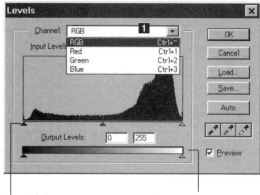

Input sliders   **Output** sliders

Follow any of these steps for a **CMYK** Color image (the sliders have the **opposite** effect in an **RGB** image):

To increase the amount of that particular color, move the black or gray input slider to the right. The black triangle affects the shadows in the image, the gray triangle affects the midtones.

or

To decrease the amount of that color, move the gray or white Input slider to the left. The white slider affects the highlights. The Output sliders are particularly effective for adjusting skin tones in a photograph.

or

To tint the image with the chosen channel color, move the output white slider to the left. To lessen the chosen channel color, move the Black output slider to the right.

Repeat these steps for any other channels that need adjusting, bearing in mind that one channel adjustment may affect another.

5. Click OK or press Enter.

TIP Hold Alt and click Reset to restore the original the dialog box settings.

In this exercise, you'll be painting shades of gray on a neutral black or white layer with the Color Dodge or Color Burn mode setting to heighten or lessen color in the underlying layer. Though this exercise uses the Color Dodge and Color Burn modes, you can use the neutral color layer option with other layer modes.

To silhouette color areas on black:

1. Activate the layer above which you want the new layer to appear.
2. Choose Layer menu > New > Layer.
   or
   Alt-click the Create New Layer button on the Layers palette.
3. Type a name for the layer.
4. We chose Color Dodge mode for our illustration **1**, but you can choose any mode other than Normal, Dissolve, Hue, Saturation, Color, or Luminosity.
5. Check the "Fill with [mode name]-neutral color" box **2**.
6. Click OK. Our layer was filled with black.
7. Choose the Paintbrush tool. ✏
8. Paint with 60-88% gray. You'll actually be changing the neutral black on the layer. Areas you stroke over will become much lighter.

   If you're displeased with the results, paint over areas or fill the entire layer again with black to remove all the changes, and start over. Repainting or refilling with black will remove any existing editing effects while preserving pixels in the underlying layers.
9. To heighten the color effect, you can choose another mode from the Layers palette. We chose Color Burn mode. Your image strokes will be silhouetted against black **3**–**4**. Paint with a medium gray to restore more original color.

3 The original image.

4 After painting on the Color Dodge mode layer, setting the layer mode to Color Burn, and then painting medium gray strokes on the Color Burn mode layer to heighten contrast between the figures and the black background of the Color Burn mode.

Use the Sponge tool to make color areas on a target layer more or less saturated. (The Sponge tool is also discussed on page 254, where it's used to bring colors into printable gamut.) This tool can't be used on a Bitmap or Indexed Color image.

To saturate or desaturate colors using the Sponge tool:

1. Double-click the Sponge tool.

2. On the Toning Tools Options palette, position the Pressure slider between 1% (low intensity) and 100% (high intensity) **1**. Try a low Pressure first (20%-30%) so the tool won't saturate or desaturate areas too quickly.
and
Choose Desaturate or Saturate from the drop-down menu **2**.

3. Click the Brushes tab on the same palette, then click a hard-edged or soft-edged tip. A soft tip will produce the smoothest result.

4. Choose a target layer.

5. Stroke on any area of the layer, pausing to allow the screen to redraw. Stroke again to intensify the effect.

TIP If you Saturate or Desaturate an area too much, choose Edit menu > Undo or File menu > Revert. Don't try to use the tool with its opposite setting to fix it—you'll get uneven results.

TIP You can also adjust saturation in an image using the Image menu > Adjust > Hue/Saturation or Replace Color command.

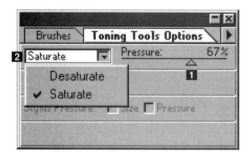

Saturate or Desaturate (Sponge Tool)

Gradients

A gradient is a gradual blend between two or more colors.

The Gradient tool can't be used on an image in Bitmap or Indexed Color mode.

To create a linear or radial gradient:

1. Choose a target layer.

2. *Optional:* Select an area of a layer. Otherwise, the gradient will fill the entire layer.

3. Choose the Gradient tool (G). ▣

4. On the Gradient Tool Options palette, Choose Linear or Radial from the Type drop-down menu **1**.
   and
   Choose an Opacity.
   and
   Choose an existing gradient from the Gradient drop-down menu.
   and
   Choose a mode.

5. *Optional:* Check the Dither box to minimize banding (stripes) in the gradient.

6. *Optional:* Uncheck the Mask box to disable any transparency in the gradient.

7. Choose Foreground and/or Background colors if the gradient Style you chose uses them.

8. For a linear gradient, drag from one side of the image or selection to the other. Drag a long distance to produce a subtle transition area **2**; drag a short distance to produce an abrupt transition **3**. Hold down Shift while dragging to constrain the gradient to the nearest 45° angle. To produce a diagonal gradient, drag from corner to corner **4**.

   For a radial gradient, press to establish a center point, then drag outward **5**–**6**.

TIP To delete a gradient fill, choose Edit menu > Undo immediately.

2 The Gradient tool dragged from the middle to the right.

3 The Gradient tool dragged a short distance in the middle using the same colors.

4 The Gradient tool dragged from lower right to upper left.

PHOTO: NADINE MARKOVA

5 The original image.

6 A **radial** gradient in the background. The arrow shows where the mouse was dragged.

(Continued on the following page)

Linear or Radial Gradient

TIP To reverse the order of colors for a Foreground to Background gradient, drag in the opposite direction. Or, click the Switch colors button on the Toolbox before dragging. ↰

TIP To produce more of the Foreground color than the Background color in a gradient, click Edit on the Gradient tool Options palette, then move the little Midpoint diamond or click the diamond and enter a percentage above 50 in the Location field **1**.

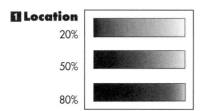

1 Location

20%

50%

80%

To create your own gradient:

1. Choose the Gradient tool (G). ▨ Open the Swatches palette if you're going to use it to choose colors for the gradient.

2. Click Edit on the Options palette.

3. Click New (Control-N).

4. Type a name for the gradient, then click OK **2**.

5. Click on the leftmost square under the gradient bar to set the starting color **3**.

6. Click a color on the Swatches palette or click in any open image window.
or
Click the color swatch in the Gradient Editor **4**, then choose a color from the Color Picker.
or
To create a gradient that will use the current Foreground color, click the Foreground selection box **5**.
or
To create a gradient that will use the current Background color, click the Background selection box **6**. (Click the plain icon **7** to choose a fixed color.)

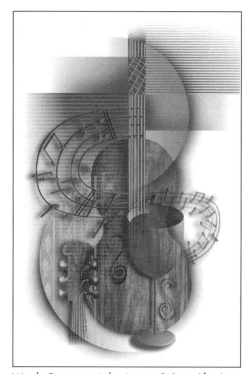

Wendy Grossman, in her image, **Guitar with wine**, used gradients, as well as patterns, from Illustrator.

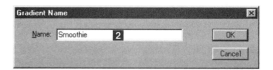

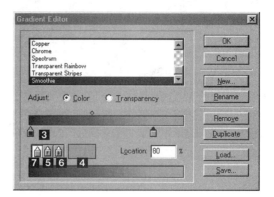

Create a Gradient

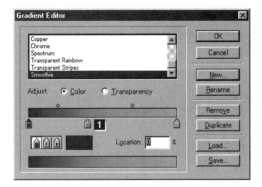

Click **Save** in the Gradient Editor dialog box to save all the gradients currently on the list to a separate file. This is a good way to organize a bunch of gradients so you can access them easily. Click **Load** to load a previously saved gradient file.

Control-Alt-click Save to save the currently highlighted gradient as a **Curves map**. In the Curves dialog box, load in the gradient file to have the gradient colors replace colors in the image according to their respective luminosity levels.

7. Click the rightmost square under the gradient bar to set the ending color, then repeat step 6.

8. *Do any of these optional steps:*

To add intermediate colors to the gradient, click below the gradient bar to create a new square **1**, then choose a color (step 6 on the previous page). Reposition it by dragging.

To reposition a midpoint diamond, which controls where the colors to the left and right of the diamond are 50% each, drag it to a new position or click on it, then enter a percentage in the Location field.

Move the starting or ending square, or enter a new value in the Location field for either square. Moving a square inward will produce more solid color at that edge of the gradient fill. 0% is at the left, 100% is at the right.

To remove an intermediate color, drag its square downward off the bar. You can't remove a starting or ending color.

9. Click OK or press Enter.

TIP Leave the Mask box checked on the Options palette to preserve transparent areas when you fill with a gradient.

To edit an existing gradient:

1. Choose the Gradient tool (G). ▢

2. Click Edit on the Options palette.

3. Highlight the name of gradient you want to edit on the scroll list.

4. Follow steps 5–12 in the previous set of instructions.

TIP To remove a gradient, follow steps 1–3, above, click Remove, then click OK.

TIP To duplicate a gradient, follow steps 1–3, above, click Duplicate, enter a name, then click OK. Use this command if you want to edit a gradient and preserve the original.

Edit a Gradient

To change the opacity of gradient colors:

1. Choose the Gradient tool (G).

2. Click Edit on the Options palette.

3. Highlight the name of the gradient you want to edit.

4. Click Adjust: Transparency **1**.

5. Click the leftmost or rightmost square under the transparency bar.

6. Enter an Opacity percentage. Note how transparent that color is in the color bar at the bottom of the dialog box **2**.

7. To add other opacity levels, click just below the transparency bar to produce a new square, then enter an opacity percentage. To delete an intermediate square, drag it downward off the bar. To move a square, drag it or change its Location percentage.

8. To adjust the location of the midpoint opacity, drag the diamond above the transparency bar, or click on it, then enter a Location percentage.

9. Click OK or press Enter.

To create a multicolor wash:

1. Choose a target layer (not the Background).

2. *Optional:* Select an area of a layer.

3. Choose the Gradient tool (G).

4. On the Gradient Tool Options palette, choose an Opacity.
   and
   Choose Foreground to Transparent from the Gradient drop-down menu, or choose a gradient that you've created that finishes with transparency.

5. Drag from left to right on the image.

6. Choose another target layer or create a new layer, then repeat step 4.

7. Drag from right to left on the image **3**.

8. *Optional:* Using the Layers palette, change the opacity or mode for, or restack, the gradient layers.

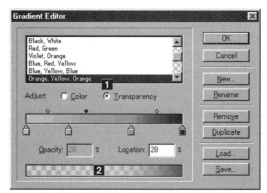

Two gradients, on separate layers, were applied to this image. The middle of the gradients have a 20% opacity, to allow the balloons to peek through. Looks like diddly squat in black and white. Looks nice in color.

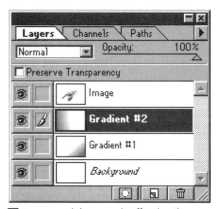

3 Create a subtle painterly effect by placing translucent gradient washes on separate layers.

PAINT 11

IN THIS CHAPTER you will learn to use Photoshop's Line, Airbrush, Pencil and Paintbrush tools. You can paint on a scanned image or you can paint a picture from scratch. You will learn how to create custom brush tips for the painting tools using the Brushes palette, how to save and load brush palettes, and about the Options palette options, like mode and opacity. The Paint Bucket, Smudge, and Eraser tools are also covered in this chapter. Gradients are covered in Chapter 16.

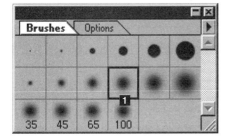

Paintbrush

Airbrush

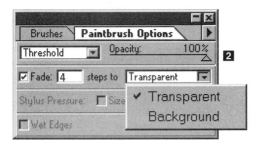

To use the Paintbrush or Airbrush tool:

1. Choose a target layer. Create a selection on the target layer if you want to paint in a restricted area.

2. Click the Paintbrush (B) 𝒷 or Airbrush (A) tool. 𝒵

3. Choose a Foreground color (see pages 111–115).

4. Click a hard-edged tip in the first row of the Brushes palette or a soft-edged tip in the second or third row **1**. If a tip is too large to be displayed, its width in pixels will be indicated by a number.

5. Click the Options tab on the palette.

6. On the Options palette, move the Opacity/Pressure slider **2**. At 100%, the stroke will completely cover the underlying pixels.
and
Choose from the mode drop-down menu (see "Blending modes" on pages 26–28).

7. *Optional:* To create a stroke that fades

(Continued on the following page)

135

as it finishes, check the Fade box and enter a number of steps. The higher the Fade amount, the longer the stroke will be before it fades. Choose Transparent from the "steps to" pull-down menu to fade from the Foreground color to no color, or choose Background to fade from the Foreground color to the Background color.

8. *Optional:* Check the Wet Edges box for the Paintbrush tool to produce a stroke with a higher concentration of color at the edges, like the pooling effect in traditional watercoloring. Use a soft-edged brush tip with this option **1**–**3**.

9. Drag across any area of the picture. If you press and hold on an area with the Airbrush tool without dragging, the paintdrop will gradually widen and become more saturated.

TIP If you have a stylus hooked up but you're not using it, uncheck all the Stylus Pressure boxes on the Options palette so the Paintbrush tool will work properly with a mouse.

TIP To undo the last stroke, choose Edit menu > Undo immediately. Only the last stroke can be undone.

TIP To draw a straight stroke, click once to begin the stroke, then hold down Shift and click in a different location to complete the stroke.

TIP Alt-click on any open image to sample a color while a painting tool is chosen.

TIP With the Preserve Transparency box checked on the Layers palette, paint strokes will recolor only existing pixels—not transparent areas.

TIP To choose an Opacity level via the keyboard, press any number from 0 through 9 (0 equals 100 percent). You can also enter the actual value numerically (38, 05, etc.), but type it quickly.

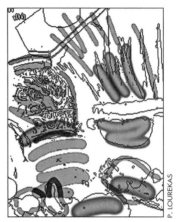

1 Strokes created with the Paintbrush tool with the **Wet Edges** box checked on the Paintbrush Options palette.

2 More Wet Edges.

3 The stroke on top was created with the Paintbrush tool, Wet Edges box unchecked. The stroke on the bottom was created with the Wet Edges box checked.

Are you using a stylus?

If you're using a pressure-sensitive tablet and the Control Panel software for the particular tablet you're using is installed, you can choose settings for your stylus for the Airbrush, Paintbrush, Pencil, Blur, Sharpen, Eraser, Rubber Stamp, Smudge, Dodge, Burn, or Sponge tool. Double-click the tool, then click one of the following on the Options palette:

- **Size:** The heavier the pressure, the wider the stroke.

- **Color**: Light pressure applies the Background color, heavy pressure applies the Foreground color, and medium pressure applies a combination of the two.

- **Opacity/Pressure/Exposure**: The heavier the pressure, the more paint is applied.

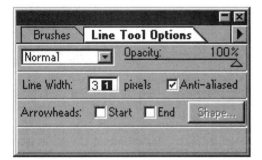

To draw straight lines:

1. Choose the Line tool (N). \

2. On the Line Tool Options palette **1**:

Enter a number between 1 and 1000 in the Line Width field.
and
Choose a blending mode from the mode drop-down menu.
and
Choose an Opacity.

3. Choose a Foreground color.

4. Draw a line. The line will fill with the Foreground color when the mouse is released **2**–**3**.

TIP Hold down Shift while dragging to constrain the line to the nearest 45° angle.

TIP To create an arrow, click the Start and/or End box on the Line Tool Options palette. Click Shape, enter numbers in the Width, Length, and Concavity fields in the Arrowhead Shape dialog box **4**, click OK, then draw a line (hold down Shift to constrain the angle).

2 A border created with the Pencil tool (Dissolve mode at 85% opacity), and then the Diffuse filter applied to the border.

3 Straight lines added to an image using the Line tool.

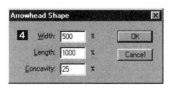

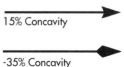

15% Concavity

-35% Concavity

Draw Straight Lines

To modify a brush tip:

1. Double-click a brush tip on the Brushes palette **1**.

   or

   Click a tip, then choose Brush Options from the palette command menu.

2. Move the Diameter slider **2**.

   or

   Enter a number between 1 and 999 in the Diameter field.

3. Move the Hardness slider.

   or

   Enter a number between 0 and 100 in the Hardness field (the percentage of the diameter of the stroke that's opaque).

4. Move the Spacing slider.

   or

   Enter a number between 0 and 999 in the Spacing field. The higher the Spacing, the farther apart each paint-drop will be.

   or

   Uncheck the Spacing box to have the brush respond to mouse or stylus speed. The faster the mouse or stylus is dragged, the more paintdrops will skip.

5. Enter a number between 0 to 100 in the Roundness field. The higher the number, the rounder the tip.

   or

   Reshape the tip by dragging either black dot up or down in the left preview box.

6. Enter a number between -180 and 180 in the Angle field.

   or

   Move the gray arrow in a circular direction in the left preview box.

7. Click OK or press Enter **3**.

TIP Only the Spacing percentage can be changed for the Assorted brushes and most of the Drop Shadow brushes.

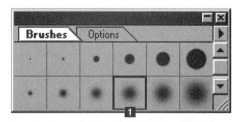

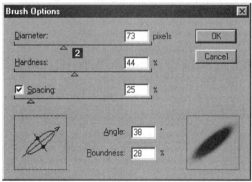

Choose **Diameter**, **Hardness**, **Spacing**, **Angle**, and **Roundness** values in the Brush Options dialog box.

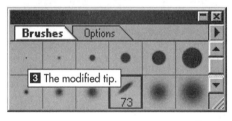

3 The modified tip.

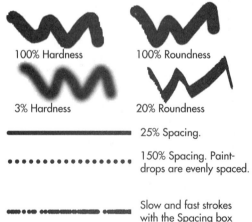

100% Hardness

100% Roundness

3% Hardness

20% Roundness

25% Spacing.

150% Spacing. Paint-drops are evenly spaced.

Slow and fast strokes with the Spacing box unchecked. Paintdrops are unevenly spaced.

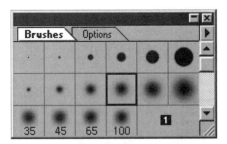

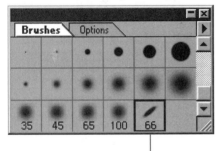

2 The new tip appears after the last tip.

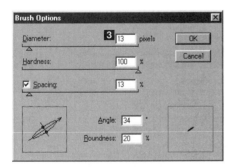

4 A **calligraphic** line added to an image.

To create a new brush tip:

1. Click on the blank area at the bottom of the Brushes palette **1**.
or
Choose New Brush from the palette command menu.

2. Follow steps 2–7 on the previous page to customize the tip. The new tip will appear after the last tip on the palette **2**.

To delete a brush tip:

Control-click the brush tip that you want to delete.
or
Click the brush tip on the Brushes palette, then choose Delete Brush from the palette command menu.

You can use the Pencil, Airbrush, or Paintbrush tool to create a linear element, such as a squiggly or a calligraphic line. Use different Angle and Roundness values to create your own line shapes.

To draw a calligraphic line:

1. Click the Pencil, Airbrush, or Paintbrush tool.

2. Choose a Foreground color.

3. On the Brushes palette, double-click a hard-edged brush tip or click on the blank area at the bottom of the palette to create a new tip.

4. The brush will preview in the dialog box as you choose these settings **3**:

Choose a Diameter between 10 and 15.

Choose a Spacing value between 1 and 25.

Position the Hardness slider at 100%.

Enter 34 in the Angle field.

Enter 20 in the Roundness field.

5. Click OK or press Enter.

6. *Optional:* Move the Pressure/Opacity slider on the Options palette.

7. Draw shapes or letters **4**.

Monochromatic shades of the Foreground color are applied when you use a brush tip created from an area of a picture.

To create a brush tip from an image:

1. Choose the Rectangular Marquee tool. ⬚

2. Marquee an area of a picture. The selection cannot exceed 1,000 by 1,000 pixels **1**.

3. Choose Define Brush from the Brushes palette command menu. The new tip will appear after the last tip on the palette **2**.

TIP Use the tip with the Paintbrush or Airbrush tool. Click on a white or monochromatic area if you want to see the brush image clearly.

TIP To smooth the edges of the stroke, double-click the custom brush tip, then check the Anti-aliased box. This option is not available for a large brush. You can also specify a Spacing value in the same dialog box. The higher the Spacing percentage, the larger the gap between paintdrops. You can enter a Spacing percentage over 100%.

1 Select an area of an image.

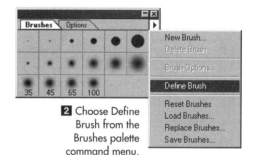

2 Choose Define Brush from the Brushes palette command menu.

A custom brush tip, taken from the necklace of the statue, and used as a brushed-on texture.

A custom brush tip, used like a stamp (various opacities).

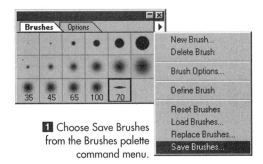

■1 Choose Save Brushes from the Brushes palette command menu.

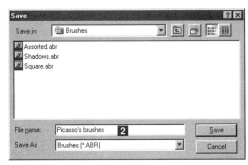

To save a brush set:

1. Choose Save Brushes from the palette command menu **■1**.

2. Enter a name in the "File name" field **■2**.

3. Choose a location in which to save the palette.

4. Click Save or press Enter.

Three Brushes palettes are supplied with Photoshop in addition to the Default Brushes: Assorted Brushes, which are special shapes and symbols, Drop Shadow Brushes, which are brush tips with soft edges that you can use to make drop shadows, and hard-edged Square Brushes.

To load a brush set:

1. To append a brush set to the existing set, choose Load Brushes from the palette command menu **■3**.

or

To have the new brush set replace the currently displayed set, choose Replace Brushes.

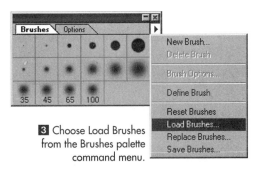

■3 Choose Load Brushes from the Brushes palette command menu.

2. Open the Brushes & Patterns folder, which is in the Goodies folder in the Photoshop application folder.

3. Double-click a palette name **■4**. The brushes will be added to the existing brush set.

or

Click a palette name, then click Open.

TIP The brushes that were on the Brushes palette when you last quit Photoshop will still be there next time you launch Photoshop. To restore the default Brushes palette, choose Reset Brushes from the palette command menu, then click OK.

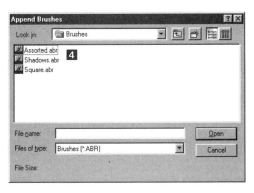

Save Brush Set; Load Brush Set

To create a drop shadow for imagery on a layer:

1. Make sure the object you want to create the shadow for is silhouetted on its own layer **1**, and activate that layer now. (Silhouetting instructions are on page 60).

2. Choose Duplicate Layer from the Layers palette command menu or from the Layer menu, and name it "Image."

3. Double-click the original layer name on the Layers palette, and name it "Shadow" **2**.

4. Choose the Move tool. ⊹

5. Make sure the Shadow layer is still active, then drag its layer downward and slightly to the right in the image window to reveal some of the shadow.

6. Check the Preserve Transparency box for the Shadow layer.

7. Choose a dark Foreground color.

8. Choose Edit menu > Fill, choose Foreground Color, 80–100% Opacity, Normal mode, then click OK.

9. Uncheck the Preserve Transparency box for the Shadow layer.

10. Choose Filter menu > Blur > Gaussian Blur.

11. Enter a Radius between 4 and 8 pixels.

12. Click OK or press Enter **3**.

13. *Optional:* Choose Multiply mode for the Shadow layer to reveal texture, if any, below it.

14. To tweak the shadow layer's position, make sure it's the target layer, then drag it using the Move tool or by pressing an arrow key.

TIP If the entire shadow isn't visible in the image window, use the Image menu > Canvas Size command to expand the canvas to display the shadow fully.

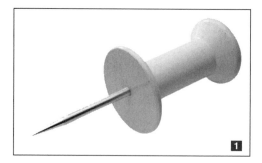

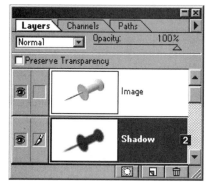

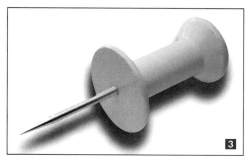

Create a shadow effect via Levels

Create a selection for the shadow shape, and feather its edge. Control-click a silhouetted object's layer if you want to use that shape for the selection. Select the layer to be shadowed, then move the selection marquee. Control-click the Create New Layer button to create an adjustment layer with a mask derived from the selection. Choose Type: Levels, then click OK. Move the black and/or gray Input sliders to the right to darken that part of the layer, choose an individual channel (Channel drop-down menu), move Input sliders to colorize the shadow area, then click OK. Choose Multiply mode for the adjustment layer to reveal more texture or detail from the original layer.

Create a Drop Shadow

The Paint Bucket tool replaces pixels with the Foreground color or a pattern, and fills areas of similar shade or color within a specified Tolerance range. Unlike the Edit menu > Fill command, you can use the Paint Bucket without creating a selection.

NOTE: The Paint Bucket tool won't work on an image in Bitmap color mode.

To fill an area using the Paint Bucket tool:

1. Choose a target layer. If you don't want to fill transparent areas on the layer, check the Preserve Transparency box.

2. Choose the Paint Bucket tool (K). ✑

3. On the Paint Bucket Options palette **1**:

Enter a number up to 255 in the Tolerance field. The higher the Tolerance value, the wider the range of colors the Paint Bucket will fill. Try a low number first.

and

Choose Foreground or Pattern from the Contents drop-down menu.

and

Choose a blending mode from the mode drop-down menu. Experiment with Soft Light, Multiply, or Color Burn mode.

and

Choose an Opacity.

and

Check the Anti-aliased box to smooth the edges of the filled area.

and

Check the Sample Merged box if you want the Paint Bucket to sample from colors on all the currently visible layers.

4. Choose a Foreground color or define a pattern.

5. Click on the image **2**–**3**.

TIP To undo the fill, choose Edit menu > Undo (Control-Z) immediately.

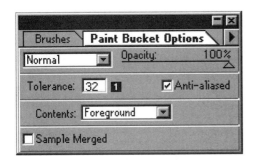

2 The original image.

PHOTO: PAUL PETROFF

3 After clicking with the **Paint Bucket** tool.

NOTE: If you use the Eraser tool on a layer with the Preserve Transparency box checked, or on the Background of an image, the erased area will be replaced with the current Background color. If you use the Eraser on a layer with Preserve Transparency unchecked, the erased area will be transparent.

To erase part of a layer:

1. Choose a target layer.

2. Choose the Eraser tool (E). ✐

3. Choose Paintbrush, Airbrush, Pencil, or Block from the drop-down menu on the Eraser Options palette **1**. Or press "E" to cycle through the tools.

4. Choose an Opacity/Pressure percentage.

5. Click a brush tip on the Brushes palette. (Don't bother to choose a tip for the Block option; its size won't change.)

6. If you're going to erase the Background of the image or if Preserve Transparency is checked on the Layers palette, choose a Background color.

7. Click on or drag across any pixels on the layer **2**–**4**.

TIP To restore areas from the last saved version of an image, use the Eraser tool with the Erase to Saved box checked on the Eraser Options palette or use the Rubber Stamp tool with its From Saved option. Neither method will work if you changed the mode, dimensions, or resolution of the image or added or deleted a layer or layer mask from it since it was last saved.

TIP To erase a whole image if it doesn't contain layers, click Erase Image on the Options palette. To erase only the entire target layer, click Erase Layer. Bug fix: If either option is dimmed, force the palette to redraw: Click another tool or hide, then redisplay the palette.

TIP To produce a wet-edged eraser effect, choose Paintbrush from the drop-down menu and check the Wet Edges box.

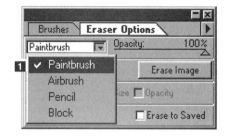

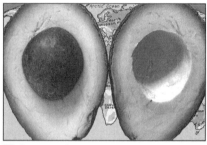

2 The original image.

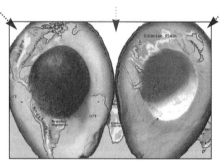

3 After erasing part of the avocados layer to reveal the map underneath it (Airbrush option, 55% opacity), and erasing part of the map layer to white (Paintbrush option, 100% opacity).

4 A detail of the partially **erased** map layer.

Erase Part of a Layer

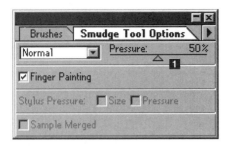

2 Smudge—
Normal mode.

3 Smudge—
Darken mode.

4 Smudge—
Lighten mode.

The Smudge tool can't be used on a image in Bitmap or Indexed Color mode.

To smudge colors:

1. Choose the Smudge tool (U). 🖉

2. On the Smudge Tool Options palette **1**, move the Pressure slider below 100%.
and
Choose a blending mode (see page xx), such as Normal to smudge all shades or colors, or Darken to push dark colors into lighter colors, or Lighten to push light colors into darker colors.

3. *Optional:* To start the Smudge with the Foreground color, check the Finger Painting box on the Smudge Tool Options palette. Otherwise, the smudge will start with the color under the cursor where the stroke begins. The higher the Pressure percentage, the more Foreground color is applied.

Hold down Alt to temporarily turn on the Finger Painting option if the Finger Painting box is unchecked.

4. *Optional:* Check the Sample Merged box on the Options palette to start the smudge with colors from all the currently visible layers in the image (uncheck Finger Painting if you use this option). Uncheck Sample Merged to smudge only with colors from the target layer. In either case, of course, pixels will only smudge on the currently active layer.

5. Click the Brushes tab on the palette, then click a hard-edged or soft-edged tip.

6. Drag across an area of the image **2**–**4**. Pause to allow the screen to redraw.

By drawing colored strokes on a separate layer to apply tints to a grayscale image, you'll have a lot of flexibility: You can change the blending mode or opacity for the Paintbrush or Airbrush tool or the color layer, and erase or dodge tints here or there without affecting the underlying gray image.

To apply tints to a grayscale image:

1. Open a Grayscale mode image, and convert it to RGB Color mode (Image menu > Mode > RGB Color).

2. Alt-click the Create New Layer button on the Layers palette to create a new layer above the grayscale image, and select Color mode for the new layer.

3. Choose the Paintbrush or Airbrush tool.

4. Choose a Foreground color.

5. Choose an Opacity/Pressure percentage below 100% from the Options palette. Choose a low-ish opacity for a subtle tint. You can change opacities between strokes. And remember, you can lower the opacity of the whole layer via the Layers palette.

6. Paint strokes on the new layer.

7. *Optional:* Use the Eraser tool to remove areas of unwanted color (uncheck the Preserve Transparency box for this), then repaint, if desired. Or use the Dodge tool at a low Exposure percentage to gently lighten the tints by hand.

8. *Optional:* Choose a different blending mode for the color layer. Soft Light, Color Burn, and Multiply can produce exquisite effects.

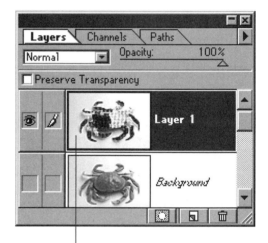

This layer contains the **color tints**.

Apply Tints to a Grayscale Image

MORE LAYERS 12

IN THIS CHAPTER you will learn to blend between layers using the Layers palette opacity and mode controls and the Layer Options dialog box. You will also learn how to create, modify, and move layer masks, link layers to move them as a unit, save a copy of a layer in a separate document, use layers as a clipping group, merge layers, and flatten layers. (Basic layer operations are covered in Chapter 7, Layers)

Change a Layer's Opacity

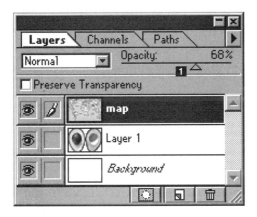

To change the opacity of a layer (or a floating selection):

Move the Opacity slider on the Layers palette **1**. The lower the opacity, the more pixels from the layer below will show through the target layer **2**–**3**.

TIP You can also choose an opacity for a layer using the Layer Options dialog box (see the following page).

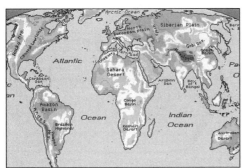

2 The map layer, 100% Opacity, on top of the avocados layer.

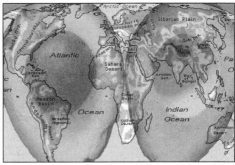

3 The map layer **opacity** reduced to 68%.

You can control which pixels in a pair of layers will be visible using the Underlying sliders in the Layer Options dialog box.

To blend pixels between two layers:

1. Double click a layer name on the Layers palette **1**.

   or

   Choose a target layer, then choose Layer Options from the Layers palette command menu.

2. Make sure the Preview box is checked **2**, then move the black Blend If: This Layer slider to the right to remove shadow areas from the target layer **3**.

   and/or

   Move the white This Layer slider to the left to remove highlights from the target layer.

   and/or

   Move the black Underlying slider to the right to restore shadow areas from the layer below the target layer **4**.

   and/or

   Move the white Underlying slider to the left to restore highlights from the layer below the target layer.

3. Click OK or press Enter **5**–**6**.

TIP To eliminate white in the topmost of the two layers, move the white This Layer slider to about 245.

TIP To blend or restore colors from one channel at a time, choose from the Blend If drop-down menu before moving the sliders.

TIP To adjust the midtones independently of the shadows, Alt-drag the right part of the black slider (it will divide in two). To adjust the midtones independently of the highlights, Alt-drag the left part of the white slider.

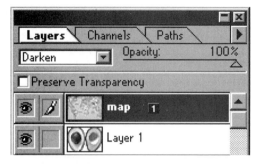

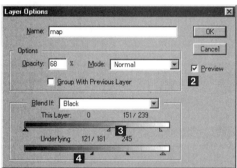

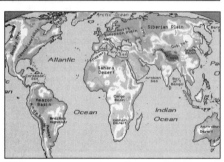

5 The map layer is above the avocados layer.

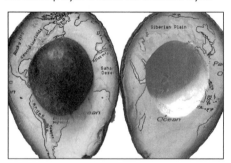

6 The same image after dividing and moving the white **This Layer** slider and the black **Underlying** slider in the Layer Options dialog box.

Blend Between Layers

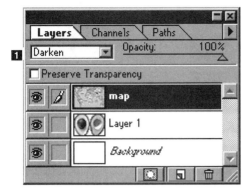

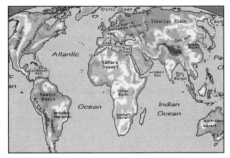

2 The map layer above the avocados layer.

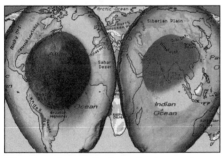

3 With Darken mode chosen for the map layer.

Layer blending modes

The layer blending mode you choose for a target layer affect how that layer's pixels blend with the pixels in the layer directly below it. Some modes produce subtle effects (Soft Light mode, for example); others produce dramatic color shifts (try Difference mode). Normal, of course, is the default mode.

The easiest way to choose a blending mode for a layer is from the mode drop-down menu on the Layers palette **1**–**4**. The modes are discussed in detail on pages 26–28. You can also choose a mode for a layer in the Layer Options dialog box (double-click a layer name to open it).

TIP For the Paintbrush, Airbrush, Paint Bucket, Pencil, and Line tool, you can choose an additional mode, called Behind, that you can't choose for a layer. Behind mode creates the effect of painting on the back of the current layer. For the Line and Paint Bucket tool, you can also choose Clear mode, which works like an eraser. Uncheck Preserve Transparency to access either mode.

4 The layer **blending modes**

Layer Blending Modes

149

Layer masks

A layer mask is simply an 8-bit grayscale channel that has White or Black as its Background color. By default, white areas on a layer mask permit pixels to be seen, black areas hide pixels, and gray areas partially mask pixels. You can use a mask to temporarily hide pixels on a layer so you can view the rest of the composite picture without them. Later, you can modify the mask, remove the mask and make the effect permanent, or discard the mask altogether.

An advantage of using a layer mask is that you can access it from both the Layers palette and the Channels palette. You'll see a thumbnail for the layer mask on the Layers palette and on the Channels palette when a layer that contains a mask is highlighted. Unlike an alpha channel selection, however, which can be loaded onto any layer, a layer mask can only be turned on or off for the layer or clipping group (group of layers) it's associated with.

To create a layer mask:

1. On the Layers palette, click on the name of the layer to which you want to add a mask.

2. If you want to create a mask in the shape of a selection, leave the selection active.

3. To create a white mask in which all the layer pixels are visible, choose Layer menu > Add Layer Mask > Reveal All or click the Add Layer Mask button at the bottom of the Layers palette **1**.
or
To create a black mask in which all the image layer pixels are hidden, choose Layer menu > Add Layer Mask > Hide All or Alt-click the Add Layer Mask button at the bottom of the Layers palette.
or
To reveal only layer pixels within an active selection, choose Layer menu > Add Layer Mask > Reveal Selection or

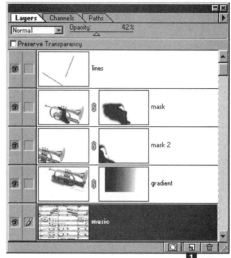

The Layers palette showing the three trumpet layers, each with its own layer mask. Portions of the middle and bottom trumpets are hidden by a black/white layer mask. The topmost trumpet fades out via a gradient in its layer mask.

The trumpets **without layer masks**.

The trumpets **with layer masks**.

Create a Layer Mask

click the Add Layer Mask button at the bottom of the Layers palette.

To hide layer pixels within the selection, choose Layer menu > Add Layer Mask > Hide Selection or Alt-click the Add Layer Mask button at the bottom of the Layers palette.

TIP To turn the mask and layer thumbnail display on or off or change the thumbnail size, choose Palette Options from the Layers palette command menu.

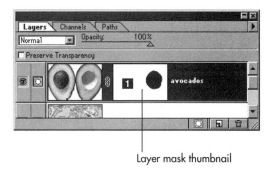

Layer mask thumbnail

To reshape a layer mask:

1. Choose the Paintbrush tool (B). *✐*

2. On the Options palette, choose 100% Opacity and Normal mode. (Or choose an opacity below 100% to partially hide layer pixels.)

3. Click a brush tip on the Brushes palette.

4. To reshape the layer mask while viewing the layer pixels, click the layer mask thumbnail on the Layers palette **1** (not on the layer name). The selected thumbnail will have a dark border and a mask icon will appear next to the layer thumbnail.
or
To display the mask channel by itself in the image window, Alt-click the layer mask thumbnail. (Alt-Shift-click the layer mask thumbnail to redisplay the mask over the image layer.)

5. Paint on the picture with black as the Foreground color to enlarge the mask and hide pixels on the layer. (D is the default colors shortcut.)
and/or
Paint with white as the Foreground color to reduce the mask and restore pixels on the layer.
and/or
Paint with gray as the Foreground color to partially hide pixels on the layer.

6. When you're finished modifying the layer mask, click the layer thumbnail to reselect the pixels on that layer **2**.

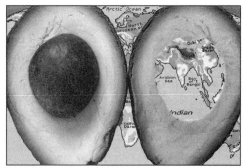

2 The center of the avocado on the right is blocked by a **layer mask**.

By default, a layer and layer mask move together. Follow these steps to move a layer mask independently.

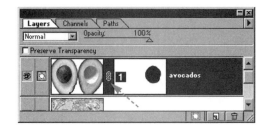

To move a mask without moving its layer:

1. On the Layers palette, click the link icon ⊗ between the layer and the layer mask thumbnails **1**.

2. Click on the layer mask icon.

3. Choose the Move tool (V). ▶⊕

4. Drag the layer mask in the image window.

5. Click again between the layer and layer mask thumbnails to re-link them.

To fill type with imagery using a layer mask:

1. Activate a layer (not the Background).

2. Choose Layer menu > Add Layer Mask > Hide All.

3. Choose the Type Mask tool. ▔T▔

4. Click on the image, type the letters you want to appear on the image, choose a font and other type specifications, then click OK.

5. Reposition the type selection, if desired, by placing the pointer inside the selection and dragging.

6. Choose Edit menu > Fill.

7. Choose Use: White, 100% Opacity, Normal mode, then click OK.

8. Choose Select menu > None.

9. Reselect the Layer thumbnail **2**–**3**.

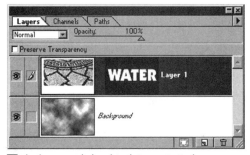

2 The layer mask thumbnail. Layer 1 pixels are revealed through the **white** type in the layer mask.

3 In this image, the water layer is visible only through the letter shapes of the layer mask.

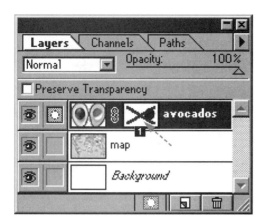

To temporarily remove the effects of a layer mask:

Shift-click the layer mask thumbnail on the Layers palette. A red "X" will appear over the thumbnail and the entire layer will be displayed **1**.

(Shift-click the layer mask thumbnail again to remove the "X" and restore the mask effect.)

TIP For this effect to work, make sure the mask channel is hidden—that no eye icon is showing for the mask on the Channels palette.

TIP To invert the effect of a layer mask, highlight the layer mask icon, then choose Image menu > Adjust > Invert (Control-I). Hidden areas will be revealed, and vice versa.

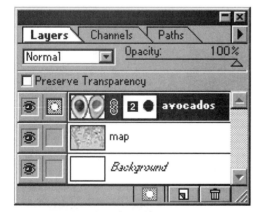

Layer masks that are no longer needed should be discarded, because they occupy storage space.

To apply or discard the effects of a layer mask:

1. On the Layers palette, click on the thumbnail of the mask that you want to remove **2**.

2. Click the Trash icon.
or
Choose Layer menu > Remove Layer Mask.

3. To make the mask effect permanent, click Apply **3**.
or
To remove the mask without applying its effect, click Discard.

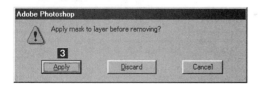

Once layers are linked together, they can be moved as a unit in the image window or drag-copied to another image. Linking is especially useful when the position of the layers in relationship to each other is critical. You can also apply the Transform or Free Transform command to linked layers. In fact, you'll minimize image distortion due to resampling by transforming multiple layers all at once instead of individually.

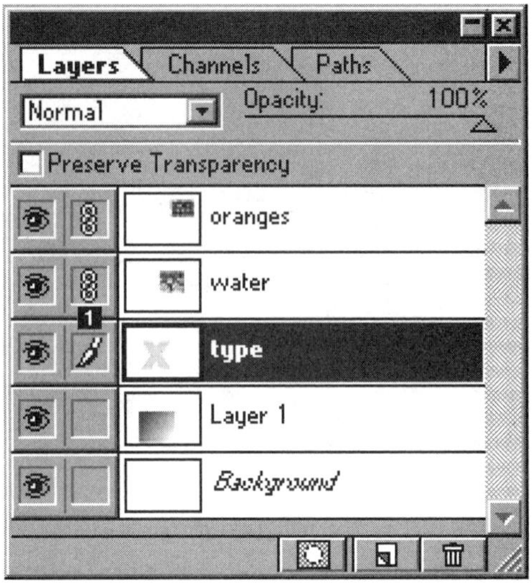

Click to display the **link** icon in the second column on the Layers palette for any layers you want to link to the active layer. In this illustration, the first three layers are linked.

To link layers and move them as a unit:

1. On the Layers palette, click on one of the layers that you want to move.
2. Click in the second column for any other layer you want to link to the layer you chose in step 1. The layers you link don't have be consecutive. The link icon will appear next to any non-active linked layers **1**.
3. Choose the Move tool (V).
4. Press and drag the linked layers in the image window.

TIP To unlink a layer, click the link icon.

The bottommost layer of a clipping group of layers (the base layer) clips (limits) the display of pixels and controls the mode and opacity of the layers above it. Only pixels that overlap pixels on the base layer are visible.

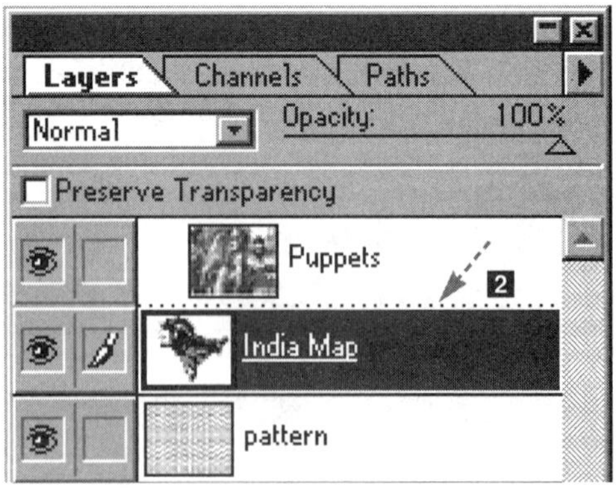

Click between two layers to join them in a **clipping group**. A dotted line will appear, and the **base** layer will be underlined.

To create a clipping group of layers:

1. Click on a layer name.
2. Alt-click on the line between that layer name and the name just above it (the cursor will be two overlapping circles). A dotted line will appear between clipping group layer names, the base layer name will be underlined, and the thumbnail for the topmost layer will be indented **2**. (The layers you choose for a clipping group must be listed consecutively on the Layers palette.)

1 The map of India is clipping (limiting) the view of the puppets.

3. *Optional:* Repeat step 2 to add more layers to the clipping group **1**.

TIP To remove a layer from a clipping group, Alt-click on the dotted line on the Layers palette. The solid line will reappear.

TIP To create a clipping group using the Layer Options dialog box, double-click the layer name on the Layers palette just above the layer you want to be the base (bottommost) layer, then check the Group With Previous Layer box.

TIP To fill type with imagery using a clipping group, see the instructions on page 183.

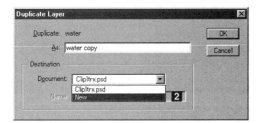

To drag-copy a layer from one image to another

Drag the name of the layer you want to copy from the **Layers palette** into the destination **image window**. It will appear where you release the mouse. Hold down **Shift** while dragging to center the layer in the destination image window.

Use the following technique to save an individual layer in a new document or in an existing, open document. You might want to do this before you perform an operation that requires flattening, such as converting to Indexed Color mode (which does not support multiple layers) or saving your document in a file format other than Photoshop, if you only need to preserve one or two individual layers.

To save a copy of a layer in a separate file:

1. Activate the layer you want to save a copy of.

2. Choose Duplicate Layer from the Layers palette command menu.

3. Choose Destination Document: New **2**.

4. Enter a name for the new document in the As field.

5. Click OK or press Enter.

6. Save the new document.

In these instructions, a filter is applied to a duplicate layer and then the original and duplicate layers are blended using Layers palette opacity and mode controls. Use this technique to soften the effect of an image editing command, like a filter, or to experiment with various blending modes or adjust commands. You can also use a layer mask to limit the area of the effect, a technique that can't be done using the Fade command. If you don't like an effect, you can just delete the new layer and start over.

To blend a modified layer with the original layer:

1. Choose a target layer **1**.

2. Choose Duplicate Layer from the Layers palette command menu.

3. Click OK.

4. Modify the duplicate layer. (Apply a filter or other image editing command.)

5. On the Layers palette, move the Opacity slider to achieve the desired degree of transparency between the original layer and the modified, duplicate layer **2**–**3**.
and/or
Choose a different mode.

6. *Optional:* Create a layer mask to limit the area of effect.

TIP For a beautiful textural effect, duplicate the Background in a color image (preferably, a Background that isn't solid white), highlight the new layer, then choose Image menu > Adjust submenu > Desaturate (Control-Shift-U) to make it grayscale. Next, apply the Add Noise filter or the Pointillize filter **4**. Finally, lower the opacity and choose different modes for the new layer from the Layers palette.

TIP See pages 206–207 of the Filters chapter to learn how to create textures via a layer mask.

1 The original image.

2 To produce the figure below, we applied the Mezzotint filter.

3 After applying the Mezzotint filter to the duplicate layer, then lowering the opacity of the duplicate layer.

4 A blended layer effect using the Pointillize filter.

Blend Layers

THIS CHAPTER COVERS two special selection techniques: saving a selection to an alpha channel and working in Quick Mask mode.

If you save a selection to a specially created grayscale channel, called an **alpha channel,** you can load the selection onto the image at any time. If you have, for example, a selection with an irregular shape that would be difficult to reselect, you can save it to an alpha channel. A file can contain up to 24 channels, though from a practical point of view, since each channel increases a picture's storage size, (depending on the size of the selection area), you should be judicious when adding alpha channels. Alpha channels are accessed via the Channels palette **1**, and saved or loaded onto a picture via Select menu commands or the Channels palette. (See our "Tip" on page 166 for converting an alpha channel to a path to conserve file storage space.)

Using Photoshop's **Quick Mask** mode, the selected or unselected areas of an image can be covered with a semi-transparent colored mask, which can then be reshaped using any editing or painting tool. Masked areas are protected from editing. Unlike an alpha channel, a Quick Mask cannot be saved, but the new selection can be saved when you return to Standard (non-Quick Mask) mode.

NOTE: If you're unfamiliar with Photoshop's basic selection tools, read Chapter 5 before reading this chapter.

(Layer masks are covered in Chapter 12.)

Only highlighted channels can be edited.

1

An **eye** icon indicates that channel is displayed.

Non-color channels are called **alpha channels.**

Layers	**Channels**	Paths
👁	RGB	Ctrl+~
👁	Red	Ctrl+1
👁	Green	Ctrl+2
👁	Blue	Ctrl+3
	#4	Ctrl+4

Load channel as selection Save selection as channel Create new channel Delete channel

Masks

157

A selection that is saved in an alpha channel can be loaded onto any image whenever it's needed.

To save a selection to a channel:

1. Select an area of a target layer .

2. Choose Select menu > Save Selection, then click OK.

or

Click the Save Selection as Channel button on the Channels palette **2** (the second icon at the bottom of the palette).

Both alpha channels and Quick Masks are converted to 8-bit grayscale on the Channels palette.

TIP Choose New from the Document drop-down menu in the Save Selection dialog box to save a selection to an alpha channel in a new, separate document **3**.

TIP Choose an Operation option in the Save Selection dialog box to combine a current selection with an existing alpha channel that you choose from the Channel drop-down menu. (Operation options are discussed on page 160.)

TIP You can save an alpha channel with an image only in the Photoshop, TIFF, Pixar, PNG, Targa, or PICT (RGB) file format. To save a copy of a file without alpha channels, check the Don't Include Alpha Channels box, if available.

TIP If you save a floating selection to a channel, the selection will remain floating (it won't replace underlying pixels).

TIP Choose "......Mask" from the Channel drop-down menu in the Save Selection dialog box to turn the selection into a layer mask for the target layer. The layer image will be revealed only where the selection was.

1 Select an area on a layer.

2 Save selection as channel

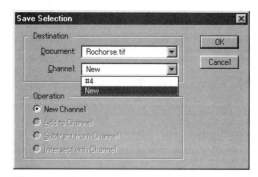

3 Choose Channel: **New** in the Save Selection dialog box. If you are saving to an existing channel, choose an **Operation** option to add to or subtract from white areas on the channel.

1 Click an alpha channel name on the Channels palette.

2 An alpha channel. The **selected** area is **white**, the **protected** area is **black**.

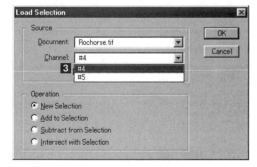

Load selection shortcuts
To load an alpha channel as a selection using the Load Selection dialog box, Alt-click the Load Channel as Selection button on the Channels palette. To bypass the Load Selection dialog box, drag the name of the alpha channel you want to load over the Load Channel as Selection button.

An alpha channel can be displayed without loading it onto the image as a selection.

To display a channel selection:

1. Click an alpha channel name on the Channels palette **1**. The selected area will be white, the protected area black **2**.

2. To restore the normal image display, click the top channel name on the palette (Control- ~).

TIP If the selection has a Feather radius, the faded area will be gray and will only be partially affected by editing.

TIP Reshape the mask with any painting tool using black, gray, or white "paint."

To load a channel selection onto an image:

1. If the composite image isn't displayed, click the top channel name on the Channels palette. You can combine the channel selection with an existing selection in the image (see the next page).

2. Choose Select menu > Load Selection.

3. Choose the channel name from the Channel drop-down menu **3**.

4. To load a channel while there's an existing selection in the image, choose an Operation option (see the next page).

5. *Optional:* Check the Invert box to switch what will be the selected and unselected areas in the loaded selection.

6. Click OK or press Enter.

TIP To select only pixels on a layer, and not transparent areas, choose Channel: "[ ] Transparency" or Control-click the layer name.

TIP To load a channel selection onto a different image, make sure the source and destination images have the same dimensions and resolution, activate the destination image, then follow steps 2–6, above, choosing the source image name in the Load Selection dialog box. To load a layer mask selection, activate that layer first in the source image.

159

Save Selection Operations

When saving a selection to an existing channel, you can choose from these Operation options in the **Save Selection** dialog box:

Channel and
Selection to be Saved

Resulting Channel

ADD

New Channel saves the current selection in a new channel.

Shortcut: Click the Save Selection as Channel button on the Channels palette.

Add to Channel adds the new selection to the channel.

Channel and
Selection to be Saved

Resulting Channel

SUBTRACT

INTERSECT

Subtract from Channel removes white or gray areas that overlap the new selection.

Intersect with Channel preserves only white or gray areas that overlap the new selection.

Load Selection Operations

If a channel is loaded while an area of a layer is selected, you can choose from these Operation options in the **Load Selection** dialog box:

Selection and
Channel to be Loaded

Resulting Selection

ADD

New Selection—the channel becomes the current selection.

Shortcut: Control-click the channel name or drag the channel name over the Load Channel as Selection button. :⃝

Add to Selection adds the channel selection to the current selection.

Shortcut: Control-Shift-click the channel name.

Selection and
Channel to be Loaded

Resulting Selection

SUBTRACT

INTERSECT

Subtract from Selection removes areas of the current selection that overlap the channel selection.

Shortcut: Control-Alt-click the channel name.

Intersect with Selection preserves only areas of the current selection that overlap the channel selection.

Shortcut: Control-Alt-Shift click the channel name.

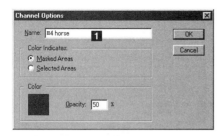

To rename a channel:

1. Double-click a channel name on the Channels palette.

or

Click a channel name, then choose Channel Options from the palette command menu.

2. Type a new name in the Name field **1**.

3. Click OK or press Enter.

TIP Normally, the selected areas of an alpha channel are white and the protected areas are black or colored. To reverse these colors without changing which area is selected, double-click an alpha channel name on the Channels palette, then click Color Indicates: Selected Areas **2**–**3**.

2 The horse is the selected area.

3 The horse is still the selected area, but it is now black instead of white.

To delete a channel:

1. Click the name of the channel that you want to delete on the Channels palette.

2. Click the Trash icon at the bottom of the palette **4**, then click Yes.

or

Alt-Click the Trash icon.

or

Choose Delete Channel from the Channels palette command menu.

To duplicate a channel:

Drag the name of the channel that you want to duplicate over the Create new channel icon **5**.

or

Highlight the channel name, choose Duplicate Channel from the Channels palette command menu, then click OK.

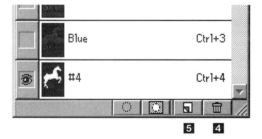

5   **4**

You can superimpose an alpha channel selection as a colored mask over an image, and then reshape the mask.

To reshape an alpha channel mask:

1. Make sure there is no selection on the image.

2. Click an alpha channel name on the Channels palette. An eye icon will appear next to it **1**.

3. Click in the leftmost column at the top of the palette. An eye icon will appear. There should be only one highlighted channel—the alpha channel name **2**.

4. Choose the Pencil ℓ or Paintbrush tool. 🖌

5. On the Options palette, choose Normal mode.
and
Choose 100% Opacity to create a full mask, or a lower Opacity to create a partial mask.

6. To enlarge the masked (protected) area, stroke on the cutout with black as the Foreground color **3**. (Click the Switch colors icon on the Toolbox to switch the Foreground color between black and white (X) **4**.)
or
To enlarge the unmasked area, stroke on the mask with white as the Foreground color **5**.

7. To hide the mask, click the alpha channel's eye icon.
or
Click the Layers tab, then choose a target layer.

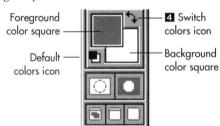

Foreground color square — **4** Switch colors icon
Default colors icon — Background color square

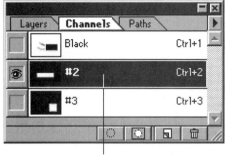

1 Click the alpha channel name on the Channels palette.

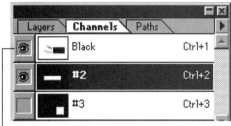

2 Click in the leftmost column at the top of the palette. Make sure the alpha channel name stays highlighted.

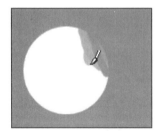

3 Enlarge the **masked** area by stroking on the cutout with **black** as the Foreground color.

5 Enlarge the **unmasked** area by stroking on the mask with **white** as the Foreground color.

Reshape an Alpha Channel Mask

PHOTO: CARA WOOD

1 Select an area on a layer.

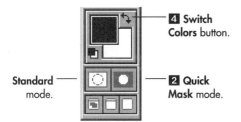

Standard mode.

4 Switch Colors button.

2 Quick Mask mode.

3 The unselected area is covered with a mask.

If you choose Quick Mask mode when an area of a target layer is selected, a semi-transparent tinted mask will cover the unselected areas, and the selected areas will be revealed in a cutout. You'll still be able to see the image through the mask. The cutout or mask can be reshaped using the Pencil, Airbrush, or Paintbrush tool.

NOTE: You can't save a Quick Mask via Save Selection while your image is in Quick Mask mode, but you can save your selection to a channel when you return to standard screen display mode.

To create a Quick Mask:

1. Select an area of a target layer **1**.

2. Click the Quick Mask mode icon on the Toolbox (Q) **2**. A mask will cover part of the picture **3**.

3. Choose the Pencil *✏* or Paintbrush tool. *🖌*

4. On the Options palette, move the Opacity slider to 100%.
and
Choose Normal from the mode drop-down menu.
and
Make sure all check boxes on the palette are unchecked.

5. Click the Brushes tab, then click a tip on the Brushes palette.

6. Stroke on the cutout with black as the Foreground color to enlarge the masked (protected) area. (Press D to reset the default colors to black and white.)
or
Stroke on the mask with white as the Foreground color to enlarge the cutout (unmasked area). (Click the Switch Colors icon on the Toolbox to switch the Foreground and Background colors (X) **4**.)
or
Stroke with gray or a brush with an opacity below 100% (Options palette) to create a partial mask.

(Continued on the following page)

Create a Quick Mask

7. Click the Standard mode icon (Q) to turn off Quick Mask. The selection will remain active.

8. Modify the layer. Only the unmasked (selected) area will be affected.

9. *Optional:* Save the selection (the areas that were previously unprotected) to a channel so you can use it later (see page 158).

TIP To create a Quick Mask without first creating a selection, click the Pencil or Paintbrush tool, double-click the Quick Mask icon on the Toolbox, click Selected Areas ■, click OK, then stroke with black on the layer. The selected areas will be covered with a mask—not the protected areas—so you'll be creating what will be the selected area.

TIP To quickly switch the mask color between the selected and masked areas, Alt-click the Quick Mask icon on the Toolbox.

TIP In the Quick Mask Options dialog box, you can also click the Color box and choose a new mask color, and you can change the opacity of the mask color (both affect display only).

TIP "Quick Mask" will be listed on the Channels palette and on the document window title bar while Quick Mask mode is on ■.

TIP If you modify a Quick Mask using a tool with a low opacity, that area will be partially affected by modifications.

■ In the Mask Options dialog box, choose whether Color Indicates: **Masked Areas** or **Selected Areas**. Click the **Color** square to choose a different mask color.

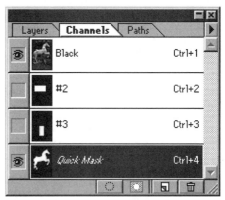

■ "Quick Mask" appears on the Channels palette. To open the Quick Mask Options dialog box, double-click "Quick Mask" or double-click the Quick Mask icon on the Toolbox.

The **Quick Mask** icons on the Toolbox.

 Color Indicates: **Masked areas**

 Color Indicates: Selected **Areas**

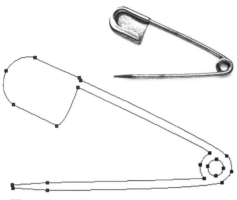

1 A path with all its anchor points **selected**.

LIKE THE PEN tool in Adobe Illustrator, the Pen tool in Photoshop creates outline shapes, called paths, consisting of anchor points connected by curved or straight line segments **1**. A path can be precisely reshaped by adding, deleting, or moving its anchor points. A curved line segment can also be reshaped by adjusting its Bézier direction lines. A path can be used on any layer. If you stroke or fill a path, the color pixels will appear on the currently active layer.

You can convert a selection into a path, reshape it, and then convert it back into a selection. This is a good method for creating a selection with a very exacting fit, which, for certain kinds of shapes, works better than using the Lasso tool or Quick Mask mode. And there's an added bonus: Paths occupy much less storage space than channels.

Paths are displayed, selected, activated, restacked, and deleted using the Paths palette **2**. The Toolbox contains five path-making and reshaping tools **3**.

You can also export a path to Illustrator, where it can also be used as a path, and you can silhouette part of an image using a clipping path in the EPS format to place in an illustration or page layout program.

2 The **Paths** palette.

A **saved** path.

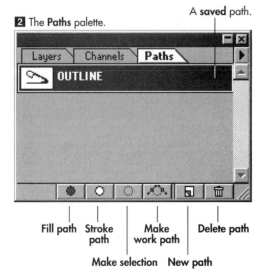

Fill path | Stroke path | Make work path | Delete path

Make selection | New path

3 The Pen tool and its related tools. Press **P** to cycle through them.

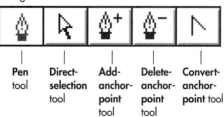

Pen tool | Direct-selection tool | Add-anchor-point tool | Delete-anchor-point tool | Convert-anchor-point tool

Paths

If you convert a selection into a path, you can precisely reshape it and then use it as a path or convert it back into a selection.

To convert a selection into a path:

1. Select an area of an image **1**.

2. Alt-click the Make Work Path button at the bottom of the Paths palette **2**.
or
Choose Make Work Path from the Paths palette command menu.

3. Enter 3, 4, or 5 in the Tolerance field **3**. The minimum is 0.5; the maximum is 10. At a low Tolerance value, many anchor points will be created and the path will conform precisely to the selection marquee. At a high Tolerance value, fewer anchor points will be created and the path will be smoother, but it will conform less precisely to the selection.

4. Click OK or press Enter **4**. The new work path name will appear on the Paths palette. Don't leave the path as a work path, though—save it by following the steps on page 168.

TIP To quickly convert a selection into a path using the current Make Work Path Tolerance setting, click the Make Work Path button at the bottom of the Paths palette.

TIP To reclaim storage space occupied by an alpha channel, convert it into a selection and then into a path, save the path, delete the alpha channel, then save the image. Follow the instructions on page 159 to load an alpha channel selection; follow steps 2–4 on this page and then the steps on page 168 to save the path; delete the alpha channel (choose Delete Channel from the Channels palette command menu); then save the image. Later on you can convert the path back into a selection (see page 172) and save the selection to a new alpha channel.

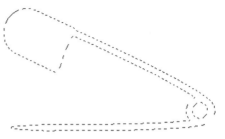

1 A **selection**.

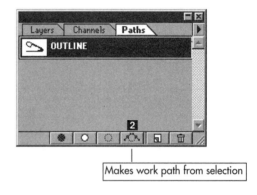

Makes work path from selection

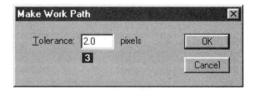

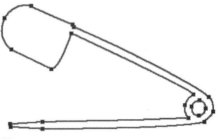

4 A **selection** converted into a **path**.

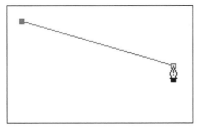

1 Click to create **straight** sides.

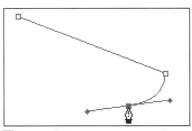

2 Press and drag to create a **curved** segment.

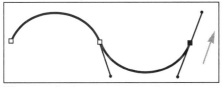

3 Drag in the direction you want the curve to follow. Place anchor points at the ends of the curve, not at the height of the curve. The fewer the anchor points, the more graceful the curves.

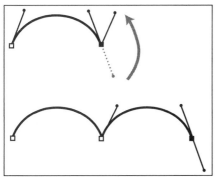

4 To draw **non-continuous** curves, **Alt**-drag from the last anchor point in the direction you want the next curve to follow. Both direction lines will be on the same side of the curve segment.

To create a path (Pen tool):

1. Choose the Pen tool. ✒ **NOTE:** If a path name is currently active, the new path will save under that name.

2. *Optional:* To list the path on the Paths palette before you draw it, click the New Path button at the bottom of the Paths palette. ▣ To name the path before you draw it, Alt-click the New Path button.

3. Check the Rubber Band box on the Pen Tool Options palette to preview the line segments as you draw.

4. Click, move the mouse, then click again to create a straight segment **1**. Hold down Shift while clicking to draw the line to the nearest 45° angle.
or
Press and drag to create a curved segment, then release the mouse. Direction lines will appear **2**–**3**.
or
To create a non-continuous curve, Alt-drag from the last anchor point in the direction you want the next curve to follow, release Alt and the mouse, then drag in the direction of the new curve **4**.

5. Repeat step 3 as many times as necessary to complete the shape.

6. To leave the path open, click the Direct-selection or Pen tool. If you don't deselect the path name or end the path—closed or open—any additional paths you draw will be saved under the same name.
or
To close the path, click on the starting point (a small circle icon will appear next to the pointer).

7. The path will be a Work Path. To save it, follow the instructions on page 168.

TIP Press Backspace to erase the last created anchor point. Press Backspace twice to delete the entire path.

To move a path:

1. On the Paths palette, activate the name of the path you want to move.

2. Choose the Direct-selection tool. ⬦

3. Alt-click the path in the image window to select all its points.

4. Drag the path in the image window.

To copy a path in the same image:

To copy the path and name it, on the Paths palette, Alt-drag the path name over the New Path button at the bottom of the palette **1**, enter a name **2**, then click OK or press Enter. (To copy the path without naming it, drag the path name without holding down Alt.)

To drag-and-drop a path to another image:

1. Open the source and destination images.

2. Choose the Direct-selection tool. ⬦

3. Drag the path name from the Paths palette into the destination image. If there is already an active path in the destination image, the path you drag will be added to its name.

A new path created with the Pen tool will be automatically labeled "Work Path," and it will save with the file, but the next path you create will replace it; the new replaces the old. Follow these instructions to save a path so it won't be deleted by a new path. Once a path is saved, it is resaved automatically each time it's modified.

To save a work path:

1. With the Work Path active, choose Save Path from the Paths palette command menu.
or
Double-click the path name.

2. Enter a name **3**.

3. Click OK or press Enter.

How to scale or rotate a path

You can't scale a path by itself, but here's a workaround: Drag the path you want to scale or rotate to a new document, use the Image menu > Image Size command to resize the document or an Image menu > Rotate Canvas command to rotate it (the path will scale or rotate along with it), and then drag the scaled or rotated path back to the original document.

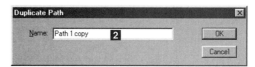

3 Type a Name in the Save Path dialog box.

To quickly save a work path under the default name

Drag the path name over the New Path button ⬚ at the bottom of the Paths palette **1**. To rename it, double-click the path name, then type a new name.

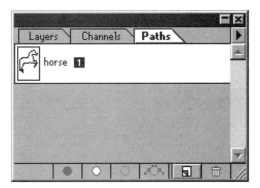

To display a path, simply click its name on the Paths palette.

To display a path:

Click the path name on the Paths palette **1**.

To hide a path:

Shift-click the path name on the Paths palette.
or
Click below the path names on the Paths palette.
or
Activate the name of the path you want to hide on the Paths palette, then choose View menu > Hide Path (Control-Shift-H). If you choose this option, you'll have to choose View menu > Show Path to redisplay all the paths.
or
Activate the name of the path you want to hide on the Paths palette, then choose Turn Off Path from the Paths palette command menu.

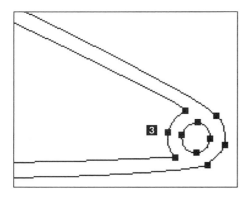

To select anchor points on a path:

1. Click a path name on the Paths palette.
2. Choose the Direct-selection tool. ▶
3. Click on the path to select one anchor point.
   or
   Shift-click to select additional anchor points **2**.
   or
   Alt-click the path to select all its anchor points **3**. An entire path can be moved when all its points are selected.

TIP To change the stacking position of a path, just drag the path name up or down on the Paths palette.

TIP Hold down Control to use the Direct-selection tool while any Pen tool is selected.

To reshape a path, you can drag, add, or delete an anchor point or move a segment. To modify the shape of a curved line segment, move a direction line toward or away from its anchor point or rotate it around its anchor point.

To reshape a path:

1. On the Paths palette, click on the name of the path you want to reshape.

2. Choose the Direct-selection tool. ⊦
To access the Direct-selection tool when any other path tool is active, press Control.

3. Click on the path in the image window.

4. Do any of the following:

Drag an anchor point or a segment **1**.

Drag or rotate a direction line **2**.

To add an anchor point, choose the Add-anchor-point tool ♣⁺ (or hold down Control and Alt if the Direct-selection tool is currently selected), then click on a line segment (the pointer will turn into a plus sign when it's over a segment) **3**–**4**.

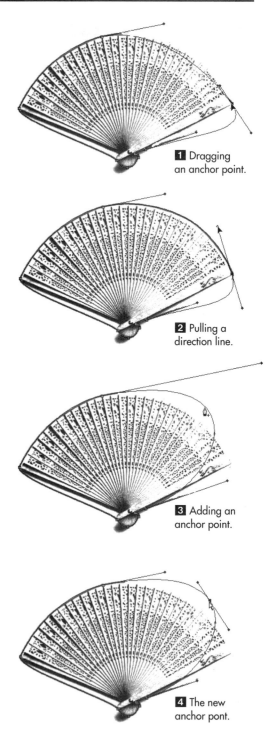

1 Dragging an anchor point.

2 Pulling a direction line.

3 Adding an anchor point.

4 The new anchor pont.

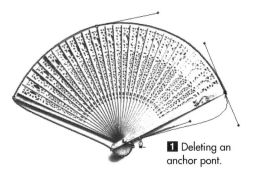

1 Deleting an anchor pont.

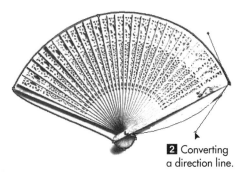

2 Converting a direction line.

To delete an anchor point from a path, choose the Delete-anchor-point tool (or hold down Control and Alt if the Direct-selection tool is currently selected), then click on the anchor point (the pointer will turn into a minus sign when it's over a point) **1**.

To convert a curved point into a corner point, choose the Convert-anchor-point tool ⌐, then click the anchor point (deselect the Convert-anchor-point tool by clicking another tool). To convert a corner point into a curved point, click the Convert-anchor-point tool, then drag away from the anchor point.

Use the Convert-anchor-point tool ⌐ to rotate half of a direction line independently **2**. Once the Convert-anchor-point tool has been used on part of a direction line, you can use the Direct-selection tool to move the other part.

To delete a segment, select it using the Direct-selection tool and make sure all the path's anchor points aren't selected, then press Backspace once. Pressing Backspace twice will delete the **entire** path!

5. Click outside the path to deselect it.

To delete a path, click the path name, then click the Trash icon.

NOTE: If the path you want to delete is a Work Path, simply drawing a new work path with the Pen tool will cause the original Work Path to be replaced.

To delete a path:

1. On the Paths palette, activate the name of the path you want to delete.

2. Alt-click the Trash icon on the Paths palette **3**.
or
Click the Trash icon, then click Yes.

To deselect a path:

1. Choose the Direct-selection tool. ✎

2. Click outside the path. The path's anchor points will be hidden.

To convert a closed path into a selection:

1. *Optional:* You can add, delete, or intersect the new selection with an existing selection.

2. Control-click the name of the path you want to convert into a selection.
or
On the Paths palette, activate the name of the closed path you want to convert into a selection, then click the Make Selection button at the bottom of the palette **1**. Alt-click the Make Selection button if you want to apply a Feather Radius to the selection (enter a low number to soften the edge slightly) **2**, choose whether or not you want edges to be Anti-aliased, or add, subtract, or intersect the path with an existing selection on the image (click an Operation option). Operation shortcuts are listed at right).

3. On the Layers palette, activate the name of the layer you want the selection to be on.

TIP To move the new selection, drag it using any selection tool.

Path-into-selection shortcuts

Make path the current selection	Control-click path name
Add path to current selection	Control-Shift-click path name
Subtract path from current selection	Control-Alt-click path name
Intersect path with current selection	Control-Alt-Shift-click path name

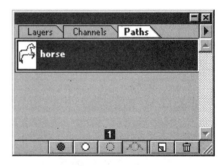

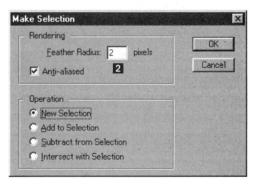

Strokes path with foreground color

2 Soft **Airbrush** stroke.

PHOTO: NADINE MARKOVA

3 The original image.

4 **Smudge** tool stroke.

When you apply color to (stroke) the edge of a path, the current tool (i.e., Paintbrush, Pencil) and its current Options palette attributes (opacity, mode) are used to produce the stroke.

To stroke a path:

1. On the Paths palette, activate the path to which you want to apply the stroke. The path can be closed or open.

2. Using the Layers palette, activate the layer on which you want the stroke pixels to appear.

3. Choose the Pencil, Paintbrush, Smudge, Airbrush, Rubber Stamp, Blur, Sharpen, Dodge, Burn, or Sponge tool.

4. On the Options palette, choose a mode.
and
Choose an Opacity (or Pressure).

5. Click the Brushes tab on the palette, then click a brush tip. The stroke thickness will match the brush tip diameter.

6. Choose a Foreground color.

7. Click the Stroke Path button at the bottom of the Paths palette **1**. (If you want to switch tools, Alt-click the Stroke Path button, choose from the Tool drop-down menu, then click OK. That tool will be used with its current Options palette settings.)
or
Choose Stroke Path (or Stroke Subpath, for an open Work Path) from the Paths palette command menu, then click OK **2**–**4**.

8. *Optional:* Click the Stroke Path button again to widen the stroke.

Stroke a Path

Use the Fill Path command to fill an open or a closed path with a color, a pattern, or imagery.

To fill a path:

1. On the Paths palette, activate the path to which you want to apply the fill.

2. Using the Layers palette, activate the layer on which you want the fill pixels to appear.

3. To fill with a solid color other than white or black, choose a Foreground color.

or

To fill with a pattern, select an area of an image using the Rectangular Marquee tool, then choose Edit menu > Define Pattern.

or

To fill with imagery, activate the layer that you want to use as a fill, then choose Edit menu > Take Snapshot.

4. Alt-click the Fill Path button at the bottom of the Paths palette ▉.

or

Choose Fill Path (or Fill Subpath for an open Work Path) from the palette command menu.

5. Choose from the Contents: Use drop-down menu ▋.

6. Enter an Opacity percentage.

7. Choose a Mode. Choose Clear mode to fill the path with layer transparency.

8. *Optional:* If a layer (not the Background) is active, check the Preserve Transparency box to recolor only existing pixels on the layer, not transparent areas.

9. *Optional:* Choose Rendering options (feathering and anti-aliasing).

10. Click OK or press Enter ▋.

TIP To fill a path using the current Fill Path dialog box settings, with the path name highlighted, click the Fill Path button at the bottom of the Paths palette.

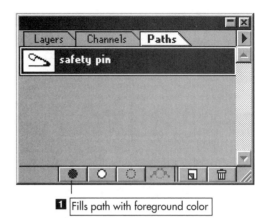

▉ Fills path with foreground color

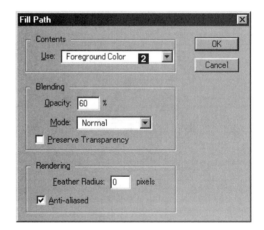

Fill a Path

Gate, ©Jeff Brice

Springhead, ©Jeff Brice

Mapping Poem, ©Jeff Brice

Trustfear, ©Alicia Buelow

Comfort, ©Alicia Buelow

Taste, ©Alicia Buelow

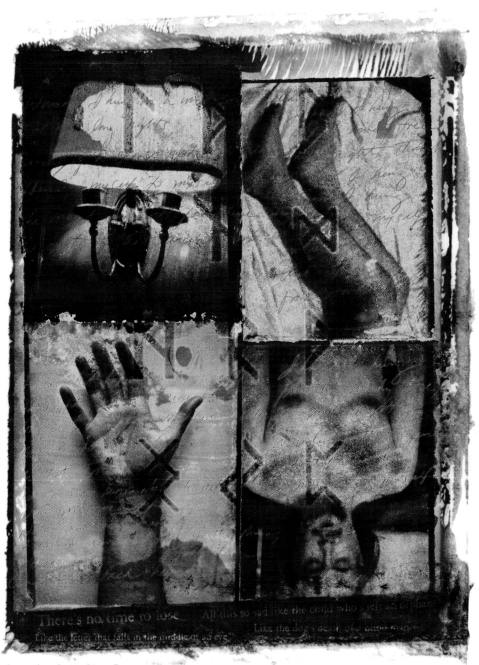

Canto nine, ©1996 Diane Fenster

Labyrinth of Lights, ©1996 Annette Weintraub

Universal Language, ©1996 Annette Weintraub

Partitions, ©1996 Annette Weintraub

Underpinnings, ©1996 Annette Weintraub

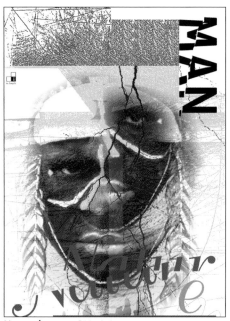

Man and nature, ©Min Wang

Transformation, ©1996 Diane Fenster

Arch, ©Jeff Brice

Sight, ©Alicia Buelow

Koolhaas, ©John Hersey

Webhouserino, ©John Hersey

Video conferencing, ©Wendy Grossman

Seasonal Specialties (tree catalog) ©1996 All Rights Reserved

Seasonal Specialties ©1996 All Rights Reserved

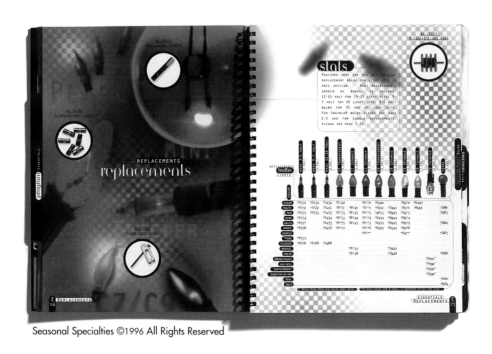

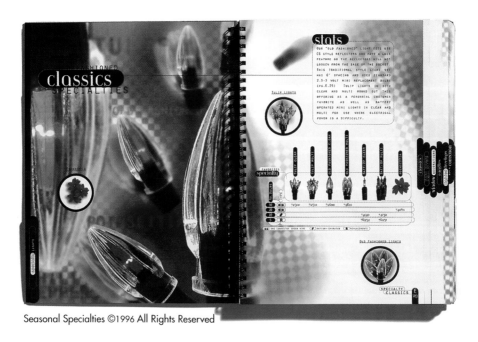

Radiowaver, ©John Hersey

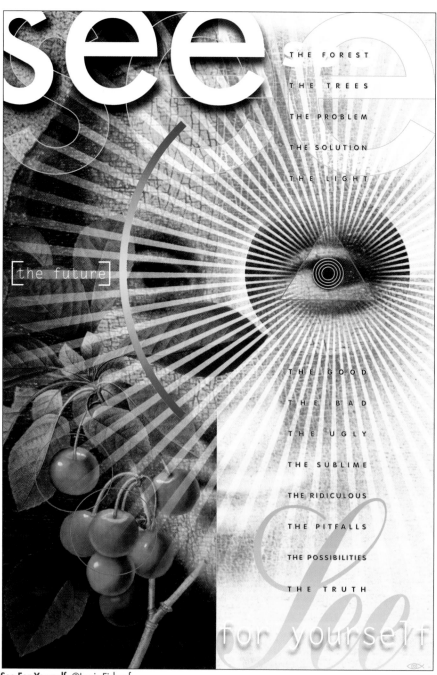

See For Yourself, ©Louis Fishauf

2 Type wrapping around a Photoshop clipping path using QuarkXPress' Runaround: Auto Image option.

3 A Photoshop clipping path layered over type in QuarkXPress.

4 If the image were imported normally, without a clipping path, it would have an opaque white background.

You can silhouette an image in Photoshop, then open or import it in another application, such as Adobe Illustrator or QuarkXPress. The area outside the image will be transparent, so it can be layered over other page elements, like text.

To clip the background from an image for use in another application:

1. Create a path around the portion of the image you want to keep.

2. Save the path, and keep it active.

3. Choose Clipping Path from the Paths palette command menu.

4. Choose the path name from the Path drop-down menu **1**.

5. Enter a number in the Flatness field. Leave this field blank to use the printer's default setting. Enter 8, 9, or 10 for high-resolution printing; enter 1, 2, or 3 for low resolution printing (300–600 dpi).

6. Click OK or press Enter.

7. Save the document in the Photoshop EPS file format (see page 244). When you open or import it into another application, only the area inside the clipping path will display and print **2**–**4**.

TIP In Adobe Illustrator, you can move, scale, rotate, reflect, or shear the silhouetted image, and the area outside it will remain transparent.

Clipping Path

175

You can create a path in Photoshop, export it to Adobe Illustrator or Macromedia FreeHand 7, and use it as a path in that program. If you like, you can then place it back into Photoshop (see page 41).

To export a path to Illustrator or FreeHand:

1. Create and save a path.

2. Choose File menu > Export > Paths to Illustrator.

3. *Optional:* Modify the name in the File Name field **1**.

4. From the Paths drop-down menu, choose an individual path name, or choose All Paths to export all the paths in the document.

5. Choose a location in which to save the path file.

6. Click OK. The path can be opened as an Adobe Illustrator document.

TIP To ensure the path fits when you reimport it into Photoshop, don't alter its crop marks in Illustrator.

TIP You may have to choose Artwork view in Illustrator to see the exported path, because it doesn't have a stroke.

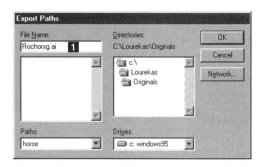

Export Path to Illustrator or FreeHand

I **N PHOTOSHOP**, type is composed of pixels. Type that is created with the Type tool appears on its own layer automatically (yay!), and can be modified like any other layer. The Type Mask tool creates a type selection, which appears above the current target layer.

This chapter covers how to create type, how to fill type with imagery using a clipping group of layers, and how to screen it back or screen back the background behind it. Special effects techniques include 3D type, fading type, and type with a drop shadow. Type can also be transformed, imported from Adobe Illustrator, filled with a gradient, filled with a pattern, or modified by applying a filter. You'll learn those techniques in other chapters.

Type resolution

Since it's composed of pixels, the resolution of type is the same as the resolution of the image. To create the smoothest possible type for high-resolution output, choose 200 dpi or higher for the image resolution. Unfortunately, increasing a image's resolution causes its file size to increase. If you want to superimpose type over an image for a particular design and you're not creating a special Photoshop type effect, import your Photoshop image into a page layout program or into an illustration program, like Adobe Illustrator, and then layer PostScript type over it.

Check the Anti-aliased box in the Type Tool dialog box for smooth rendering **1**–**2**. Photoshop uses Adobe Type Manager when rendering Adobe PostScript fonts **3**.

1 The side of a character with the **Anti-aliased** box **unchecked** in the Type Tool dialog box.

2 The **Anti-aliased** box **checked** in the Type Tool dialog box.

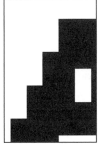

3 Adobe Type Manager turned off or not installed.

Type

Type that is created using the Type tool automatically appears on its own layer, so it can be moved, transformed, recolored, deleted, or otherwise modified without affecting pixels on any other layer.

To create type on its own layer (Type tool):

1. Choose a target layer.

2. Choose a Foreground color. (You can recolor the type later.)

3. Choose the Type tool (T). **T**

4. Click on the image where you want the type to appear. (Don't sweat it—it's a breeze to move it later.)

5. *Optional:* Check the Show: Font and Size boxes to preview the type in the dialog box **1**.

6. Enter characters in the **text** field in the Type Tool dialog box. Press Enter when you want to start a new line, otherwise all the type will appear in one line on the image.
and
Choose a typeface from the **Font** drop-down menu.
and
Choose Points or Pixels from the drop-down menu next to the Size field, then enter a number between 4 and 1000 in the **Size** field.
and
If you entered more than one line of type, enter a number between 0 and 1000 in the **Leading** field (the vertical space between lines of type).
and
Enter a number between -99.9 and 999.9 in the **Spacing** field (the horizontal space between characters).
and
Check any **Style** options. Don't double Style a font, though. For example, if you choose Garamond Italic from the Font menu, don't then apply the Italic style to it.
and

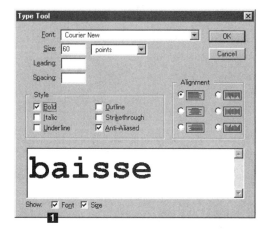

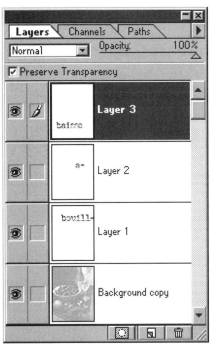

1 To produce the image below, type was placed on three separate layers so they could be moved around easily.

Click a horizontal or vertical **Alignment** icon.

and

For most purposes, you'll want to check the **Anti-aliased** box to smooth the type. This option is checked by default. Leave Anti-aliased unchecked if you're planning to output the image to a multimedia program, like Director, where anti-aliased type can appear with an ugly halo around it if it's placed against a non-white or non-uniform background color.

7. Click OK. The type will appear on a new layer and will be colored with the Foreground color **1**.

TIP To change the stacking position of the the type, drag the type layer name up or down on the Layers palette.

TIP Move the Opacity slider on the Layers palette to change the type opacity, or choose a different blending mode for the type layer. To recolor the type, see the instructions on the next page.

TIP With the type layer selected, check the Preserve Transparency box on the Layers palette to restrict painting, filling, editing, or filter effects to the letter shapes. Transparent areas on the layer won't be modified.

TIP To move the type, click the layer name on the Layers palette, choose the Move tool, then drag in the image window, or use the arrow keys to nudge it.

Type on its Own Layer

To recolor type:

1. To fill with a solid color other than white or black, choose a Foreground color.
or
To fill with a pattern, select an area of an image using the Rectangular Marquee tool, then choose Edit menu > Define Pattern.
or
To fill with imagery, activate the layer that you want to use as a fill, then choose Edit menu > Take Snapshot.

2. Click the type layer name on the Layers palette, and check the Preserve Transparency box so only the type pixels on the layer will be recolored.

3. Choose Edit menu > Fill (Shift-Backspace).

4. Choose from the Use: drop-down menu **1**.

5. *Optional:* Enter an opacity value or choose a mode. (You can also choose an opacity and mode for the type layer from the Layers palette.)

6. Click OK or press Enter.

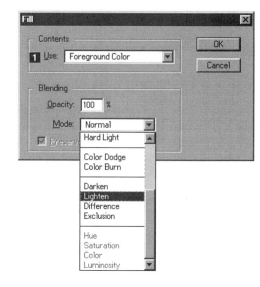

Painterly type

Choose the Paintbrush tool and a Foreground color, make sure the type layer is highlighted and the Preserve Transparency box is checked on the Layers palette, then drag across the type layer in the image window. Only existing pixels will be recolored **2**. To paint behind the type, do it on the layer directly below the type layer **3**.

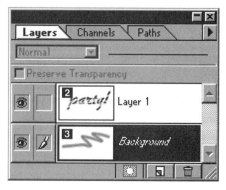

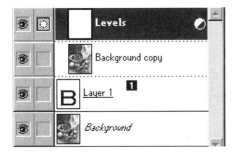

2 Screened back type.

To screen back an image with type, follow the same steps, but use an adjustment layer on the Background to lighten it, and use the topmost Levels adjustment layer to darken the type.

To screen back type:

1. Follow the steps on page 178 to create a type layer.

2. Click the name of the layer that is to be the backdrop image behind the type.

3. Choose Duplicate from the Layers palette drop-down menu, rename the duplicate layer, if you like, then click OK.

4. On the Layers palette, drag the duplicate layer name above the type layer.

5. Alt-click on the line between the two layer names to create a clipping group. A dotted line will appear and the name of the base (bottom) layer of the group will be underlined **1**. The clipping effect won't be visible until you change the duplicate layer.

6. Click on the duplicate layer name.

7. Choose New Adjustment Layer from the palette command menu.

8. Choose Levels from the Type drop-down menu, check the Group with Previous Layer box, then click OK.

9. Move the Input midtones slider to the left to lighten the midtones in the type. Pause to preview.
   and
   Move the Output shadows slider to the right to reduce the contrast in the type. Pause to preview.

10. Click OK or press Enter **2**.

11. *Optional:* Change the blending mode for the adjustment layer or the base layer to restore some background color (try Overlay, Color Dodge, or Hard Light mode). Lower the layer's opacity to soften the Levels effect.

Screen Back Type

To fill type with imagery from another document:

1. Follow the steps on page 178 to create a type layer.

2. Activate the layer in another document that contains the imagery that you want to fill the type with.

3. Choose All from the Select menu or create a selection.

4. Choose Edit menu > Copy.

5. Activate the image containing the type layer, then Control-click the type layer name.

6. Choose Edit menu > Paste Into (Control-Shift-V) **1**–**2**. A new layer with a layer mask will be created automatically, and the pasted image will be revealed through the character shapes.

7. *Optional:* With the layer thumbnail selected on the Layers palette, choose the Move tool ⊹ and drag to move the pasted image within the type shapes. Click in the space between the layer thumbnail and the layer mask thumbnail to link the mask to the layer. The position of the image inside the mask can't be changed as long as they remain linked. (Dragging with the Move tool now would move both the type shape and the image inside it, and expose the type layer underneath.)

Other ways to modify a type layer

Since type in Photoshop is composed of pixels, the ways it can be dressed up are almost limitless—just use your imagination! Here are a few suggestions:

TIP Free transform or transform it (see pages 90–91).

TIP Apply a filter to it.

TIP Fill it with a pattern (see pages 117–118) or a gradient (see pages 131–132) (remember to turn on Preserve Transparency for these fill techniques).

1 Type filled with an image using the **Paste Into** command.

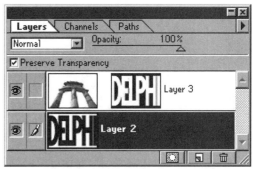

2 The bottommost layer is the original type layer; the topmost layer was created after pasting into the type selection.

Type filled with a pattern, Difference mode.

Type filled with a pattern, Fresco filter applied.

Type filled with a pattern and a gradient.

Type filled with a pattern, the Palette Knife filter applied.

1 The separate layers before being joined a clipping group.

2 The separate layers, pulled apart so you can see their stacking order.

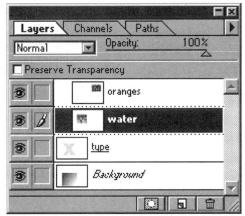

3 The Layers palette after Alt-clicking on the lines above the type layer. The type layer (the underlined name) is the base layer of the clipping group.

To fill type with imagery using a clipping group of layers:

1. Create type using the Type tool.

2. Move the type layer on the Layers palette just below the layer or layers that are to become the type fill **1**–**2**.

3. Alt-click on the line between the type layer name and the layer directly above it to create a clipping group. A dotted line will appear and the base (bottommost) layer of the group will be underlined. Only pixels that overlap the letter shapes will be visible **3**–**4**.

4. *Optional:* Activate the type layer and use the Move tool to reposition the letter shapes in the image window.

5. *Optional:* Alt-click on the lines between other layers directly above the clipping group to add them to the group.

6. *Optional:* Change the mode or opacity for any layer in the clipping group.

TIP To release a layer from a clipping group, Alt-click again on the dotted line.

TIP The opacity and mode for the clipping group are determined by those settings for the base layer (the underlined name on the Layers palette, in our example). Readjust this layer's settings to change the whole group.

4 Type filled with imagery using a **clipping group**.

Fill Type with Imagery (Clipping Group)

You can follow these instructions to create a shadow for any object on its own layer.

To create shadow type:

1. Open an image.

2. Create type using the Type tool.

3. With the type layer selected, choose Duplicate Layer from the Layers palette command menu.

4. Click OK or press Enter.

5. Click on the original type layer name (the layer below the duplicate) **1**–**2**.

6. Choose the Move tool ⊹, then drag the type slightly away from the duplicate type. You can reposition it later.

7. Choose a Foreground color for the shadow color from the Picker palette. (We chose black for our illustration.)

8. Check the Preserve Transparency box on the Layers palette so only existing layer pixels will be recolored, not the transparent areas on the layer.

9. Choose Edit menu > Fill (Shift-Backspace).

10. Choose Foreground color from the Content/Use pop-up menu, enter 100 in the Opacity field, then click OK or press Enter.

11. *Optional:* Press any of the arrow keys to nudge the type layer.

12. Uncheck the Preserve Transparency box on the Layers palette.

13. Choose Filter menu > Blur > Gaussian Blur.

14. Check the Preview box, then choose the desired degree of blurring by moving the Radius slider **3**. (Drag in the preview window to move the image inside it. Click the **+** button to zoom in or the **−** button to zoom out).

15. Click OK or press Enter (see **1** on the next page). Proceed with the next set of instructions if you want to screen the background behind the type.

1 The original type layer.

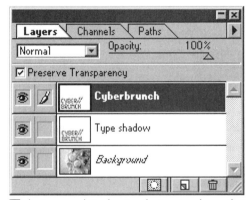

2 The Layers palette showing the two type layers that were used to create the shadow type effect.

3 Move the **Radius** slider in the Gaussian Blur dialog box to blur the type.

Shadow Type

1 After applying the **Gaussian Blur** filter to the shadow type.

2 After applying the **Levels** command with Input Levels 0, .95, and 255, and Output Levels 92 and 255 to the Background.

3 After filling the adjustment layer with a black-to-white **gradient** (upper right to lower left corner) to mask out the Levels effect in the upper right corner.

Follow these steps to heighten the contrast between the type shadow and the Background.

To screen back the background:

1. Click Background on the Layers palette.

2. Choose Layer menu > New > Adjustment Layer.

3. Choose Levels from the Type drop-down menu, then click OK.

4. Check the Preview box.

5. Move the gray Input slider a little to the left.
   and
   Move the black Output slider a little to the right.

6. Click OK or press Enter **2**–**3**.

   You can further readjust the levels using different blending modes (try Screen mode) and opacities on the Levels adjustment layer.

TIP To create more realistic shadow type on a textured background, choose Multiply mode from the Layers palette for the shadow layer, and move the Layers palette Opacity slider to lighten or darken the shadow.

To create fading type:

1. Create type on its own layer, and leave the type layer active.

2. Choose Layer menu > Add Layer Mask > Reveal All. A layer mask thumbnail will appear next to the layer name **1**.

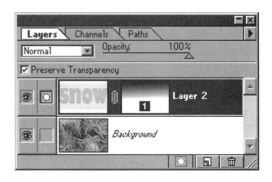

3. Choose the Gradient tool (G). ▦

4. Choose 100% Opacity, Normal mode, and Foreground to Background from the Gradient Tool Options palette.

5. Choose black as the Foreground color. (Press D to choose the default colors; press X to switch the Foreground and Background colors.)

6. Drag from the top or bottom of the selection at least halfway across the type. The type layer mask will fill with a black-to-white gradient. Type will be hidden where there is black in the layer mask **2**.

TIP Click on the layer thumbnail on the Layers palette to modify the layer; click on the layer mask thumbnail to modify the layer mask. (Read more about layer masks in Chapter 12.)

2 Fading type.

Fading Type

To keep in mind if you work with a type selection

- To **move** a type selection: Use the Type Mask tool (not the Move tool) to drag it or use the arrow keys to nudge it. Hold down Shift and press an arrow key to move the type selection 10 screen pixels at a time.

- If you drag a type selection using the Move tool, you'll cut away and move pixels from the active layer. You'll be knocking out letter shapes from the image and moving the underlying pixels in the shape of characters. This method creates a floating selection layer. To drop the floating selection onto the active layer and leave the selection marquee active, choose Layer menu > Defloat; to drop and deselect the floating selection, choose Select > None (Control-D).

- You can choose from two methods to **copy** pixels from only within a type selection: Choose Edit menu > Copy to copy pixels only from the active layer or choose Edit menu > Copy Merge to copy pixels from all visible layers below the selection. Position the type selection over the desired pixels before using either copy command.

- To paste imagery into the type selection, activate another layer or another image, copy an area from that image, click back on the image that contains the type selection, then choose Edit menu > Paste Into. The type selection will be deselected.

- If you save the type selection to a new **channel** (click the Save Selection as Channel button on the Channels palette), it can then be viewed on the Channels palette and loaded onto any layer or layer mask, and at any time.

3D type. (For this image, we blurred the Background.)

The Type Mask tool creates a selection in the shape of type characters. You might want to create a type selection for a variety of reasons: to copy layer imagery in the shape of letters; to mask (limit) an adjustment layer effect to a type selection; or to add a layer mask (Reveal All or Hide All).

To create a type selection (Type Mask tool):

1. Activate the layer on which you want the type selection to appear.

2. Choose the Type Mask tool.

3. Click in the image window where you want the selection to appear.

4. Follow steps 4–7 on pages 178–179.

To create 3D type:

1. Create or open an image in RGB mode with a gradient or a texture on the Background.

2. Choose the Type Mask tool and create a type selection.

3. Click the Save Selection as Channel button on the Channels palette.

4. Choose Select menu > None (Control-D).

5. On the Layers palette, activate the texture layer.

6. Choose Filter menu > Render > Lighting Effects.

7. From the Texture Channel drop down menu, choose the number of the channel that contains the type.

8. Choose Spotlight for the Light Type; position the lighting ellipse so it falls nicely across the type; adjust the Height slider for the desired degree of three-dimensionality; and make any other adjustments to the lighting. Uncheck the "White is high" box to make the shadows appear on the lower right.

9. Click OK.

(Continued on the following page)

More stuff to do to the 3D type:

1. After following steps 1–9 on the previous page, activate the channel that contains the type, choose Duplicate Channel from the Channels palette command menu, enter a name ("soft shadow"), then click OK.

2. Activate the duplicate channel.

3. To enlarge the type area, choose Filter menu > Other > Maximum, move the Radius slider to 2, then click OK.

4. To soften the edge of channel, choose Filter menu > Blur > Gaussian Blur. Move the Radius slider to the desired degree of softening.

5. Activate the 3D type effect layer on the Layers palette.

6. Choose Duplicate Layer from the Layers palette command menu.

7. Repeat steps 6–9 on the previous page to create the 3D look, but this time choose the larger type channel as the Texture Channel. For our image, we inverted the layer after applying the Lighting Effects filter. You can also fiddle with the Mountainous slider and other settings in the Lighting Effects dialog box.

8. *Optional:* Lower the duplicate layer's opacity until you reach a pleasing balance between the larger 3D type and the original 3D type.

3D type

To deselect a type mask selection:

Choose Select menu > None (Control-D). (If you press Backspace or choose Edit menu > Clear, you will remove pixels that were within the boundaries of the type selection.)

TIP Double-click the type selection with the Type Mask tool to reopen the Type Tool box (this only works for a Type Mask tool selection).

3D Type; Deselect Type Mask Selection

FILTERS 16

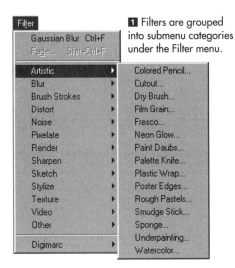

1 Filters are grouped into submenu categories under the Filter menu.

PHOTOSHOP'S FILTERS can be used to produce an myriad of special effects, from slight sharpening to wild distortion. Use filters like Blur or Sharpen for subtle retouching; use filters like Color Halftone, Find Edges, Emboss, or Wind to stylize an image; use the Artistic, Brush Strokes, Sketch, or Texture filters to make a layer look hand-rendered; or create a wide variety of beautiful lighting illusions using the Lighting Effects filter.

This chapter has three components: techniques for applying filters; an illustrated compendium of all the Photoshop filters; and lastly, a handful of step-by-step exercises using filters.

Filter basics

Filters are grouped into thirteen submenu categories under the Filter menu **1**. Any third-party filter added to the program can have its own submenu. (See the Photoshop User Guide for information about installing third-party filters.)

How to apply filters

Filters can be applied to a whole target layer or to a selected area of a target layer. For a soft transition between the filtered and non-filtered areas, feather the selection before you apply a filter.

Some filters are applied in one step by selecting them from a submenu. Other filters are applied via dialog boxes in which one or more variables are specified. Choose Filter menu > Last Filter (Control-F) to reapply the last used filter using the same settings. Choose a filter from its submenu to choose different settings. To open the dialog box for the last used filter with its last used settings, use the Control-Alt-F shortcut.

The **Groucho** filter

Filters cannot be applied to an image in Bitmap or Indexed Color mode, or to a 48-bit RGB or 16-bit grayscale image.

Using a filter dialog box

Some filter dialog boxes have a Preview box, which you should check if you want to display the filter's effects in both the image window and in the preview window in the filter dialog box **1**. Drag in the preview window to move the image inside it.

With some filter dialog boxes open, the pointer becomes a square when it's passed over the image window, in which case you can click to preview that area of the image.

Click the "+" button to zoom in on the image in the preview box, or click the "–" button to zoom out **2**. Or press the up or down arrow on the keyboard to magnify or reduce a selected field by one unit (or .1 unit, if available).

A flashing line below the preview size value indicates the filter effect is taking its sweet time to render in the preview window. On a slow machine, you might have enough time to go make a sandwich.

A flashing line below the Preview check box means the filter effect is taking its sweet time to preview in the image window.

How to lessen a filter's effect

The Fade command lessens filter effects and Image menu > Adjust effects (not other commands). After applying a filter, choose Filter menu > Fade (Control-Shift-F). Choose an opacity amount, and a mode, if desired **3**, then click OK. If you Undo the Fade command, the complete filter effect will be undone.

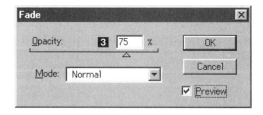

To lessen a filter's effect with an option to test different blending modes, and without limiting yourself to one Undo, do the following:

1. Duplicate the image layer to which the filter will be applied.

To maximize a filter's effect

- To heighten the effect of some filters, like Emboss (illustrated below), make sure the target layer has good brightness/contrast values. To heighten contrast in a layer before applying a filter to it, choose Image menu > Adjust > Levels, move the black Input slider to the right and the white Input slider to the left, then click OK.

- To recolor a layer after applying a filter that strips color (i.e., Charcoal filter), use the Image menu > Adjust > Hue/Saturation dialog box (check the Colorize box).

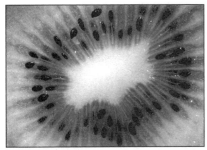

The original image.

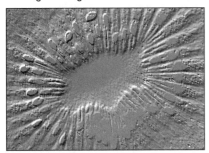

Emboss filter.

1   **2**

2. Apply the filter to the duplicate layer.

3. Use the Layers palette Opacity slider to lessen (fade) the effect of the filter.

4. Choose a different mode from the mode drop-down menu. The instructions on page 156 use this technique.

Because the filter was applied to a copy of the original layer, you can come back later and readjust the mode or opacity of the filter effect layer to blend it differently with the original layer, create a layer mask for the duplicate layer to hide or change the filter effect, or discard the filter layer entirely. When the image is finalized, merge the duplicate layer with the original.

Use a layer mask to control filter effects

A layer mask can be used to limit the effect of a filter. The edge between the white and black areas of the of a layer mask, can be soft, hard, painterly, etc., depending on the type of brush strokes you use to paint the black areas of the mask. By choosing Add Layer Mask > Reveal Selection when a selection is active and then applying a filter (try Brush Strokes > Spatter, Pixilate > Pointillize, Stylize > Wind, Distort > ZigZag or Ripple), the filter effect will be visible on the edge between black and white areas of the layer mask.

Or, create a black-to-white gradient in the layer mask and then apply a filter to the layer image (not the layer mask). The filter effect will apply fully in the image where areas of white are on the mask and fade to nil in areas of the image that correspond to black areas in the mask.

To limit the effect of a filter

Create a selection first on a layer to have a filter affect only pixels within the selection **1**. To achieve a soft-edged transition around the filtered area, feather the selection before applying the filter **2**.

Texture mapping via a filter

For some filters, like Conté Crayon, Displace, Glass, Lighting Effects, Rough Pastels, Texture Fill, and Texturizer, in lieu of using a preset pattern to create a texture effect, you can load in another image to use as the pattern for the texture effect. Lights and darks in the loaded image are used to create the peaks and valleys in the texture. The image you're using for the mapping must be saved in the Photoshop file format.

If the filter dialog box contains a Texture drop-down menu with a load option, select that option, locate a color or grayscale image in the Photoshop format, then click OK.

Apply a filter to an individual channel

To create a subtle effect, modify pixels of a single color component in an image by applying a filter to only one of a target layer's channels (Add Noise is a nice one to experiment with) **1**. Click a channel color name on the Channels palette, apply the filter, then click the top channel on the palette (Control-~) to redisplay the composite image **2**.

To make filter effect look less artificial

If the imagery you're creating lends itself to experimentation, try creating your own formulas by testing different variables in a filter dialog box or by applying more than one filter to the same image. If you come up with a sequence that you'd like to use more than once, save it in an action.

The original image.

1

2

The Wind filter applied to type. Check the Preserve Transparency box on the Layers palette for the type layer if you want the filter effect to spread outside the letter shapes. Uncheck Preserve Transparency to limit a filter effect to the letter shapes.

PHOTO: PAUL PETROFF

All the filters illustrated

Artistic filters

Original image

Colored Pencil

Cutout

Dry Brush

Film Grain

Fresco

Neon Glow

Paint Daubs

Palette Knife

Artistic filters

Original image

Plastic Wrap

Poster Edges

Rough Pastels

Smudge Stick

Sponge

Watercolor

Underpainting

Blur filters

Original image

Blur More

Gaussian Blur

Motion Blur

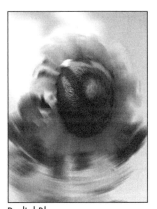

Radial Blur

Smart Blur (Normal)

Smart Blur (Edges Only)

Smart Blur (Overlay Edge)

Blur Filters

Brush Strokes filters

Original image

Accented Edges

Angled Strokes

Crosshatch

Dark Strokes

Ink Outlines

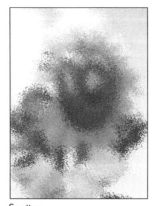

Spatter

Sprayed Strokes

Sumi-e

Brush Strokes Filters

Distort filters

Original image

Diffuse Glow

Displace

Glass

Ocean Ripple

Pinch

Polar Coordinates

Ripple

Shear

Distort Filters

Distort filters

Spherize

Twirl

Wave (Type: Square)

Wave (Type: Sine)

Zigzag

Noise filters

Original image

Add Noise

Median

Pixelate filters

Original image

Color Halftone

Crystallize

Facet

Fragment

Mezzotint (Short Strokes)

Mezzotint (Medium Dots)

Mosaic

Pointillize

Render filters

Original image

Clouds

Difference Clouds

Lens Flare

Sharpen filters

Sharpen Edges

Sharpen More

Unsharp Mask

Render Filters; Sharpen Filters

Sketch filters

Original image

Bas Relief

Chalk & Charcoal

Charcoal

Chrome

Conté Crayon

Graphic Pen

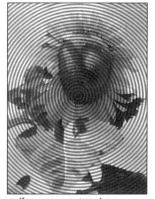

Halftone Pattern (Circle)

Halftone Pattern (Dot)

Sketch Filters

Sketch filters

Original image

Note Paper

Photocopy

Reticulation

Stamp

Torn Edges

Water Paper

Stylize filters

Original image

Diffuse

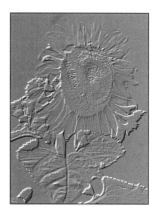

Emboss

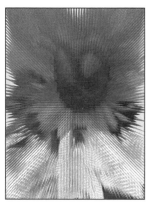

Extrude

Find Edges

Glowing Edges

Solarize

Tiles

Tiles, then Fade (Overlay mode)

Stylize filters

Original image

Trace Contour

Wind

Texture filters

Craquelure

Grain Enlarged

Grain Horizontal

Patchwork

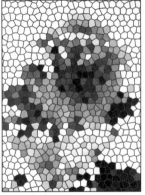

Stained Glass

Texturizer

Image

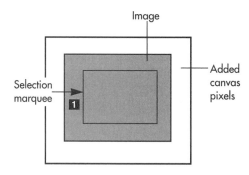

Selection
marquee

Added
canvas
pixels

1

A few filter exercises

Apply the Ripple, Twirl, or Zigzag filter to a target layer with a white border to produce a warped paper texture.

To create a wrinkled edge:

1. Use Image menu > Canvas Size to add a white border around a one-layer image.

2. Choose the Rectangular Marquee tool.

3. Enter 8 in the Feather field on the Marquee Options palette.

4. Drag a selection marquee across about three quarters of the image (not the border) **1**.

5. Choose Select menu > Inverse (Control-Shift-I). The added canvas area will become the active selection.

6. Apply the Filter menu > Distort > Ripple **2**, Twirl **3**, or Zigzag **4**, or a combination thereof. Click the zoom out button (–) in the filter dialog box to preview the whole image.

PHOTO: PAUL PETROFF

2 A wrinkled edge produced using the **Ripple** filter (Amount 100, Medium).

3 A wrinkled edge produced using the **Twirl** filter (Angle -300).

4 A wrinkled edge produced using the **Zigzag** filter (Amount 40, Ridges 8, Around center).

Create a Wrinkled Edge

A variety of textures can be created using the Add Noise filter as the starting point.

To create a texture from nothing:

1. Create a new document, Contents: White.

2. Choose Filter menu > Noise > Add Noise.

3. Move the Amount slider to a number between 400 and 700 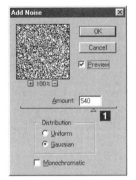, click Gaussian, then click OK or press Enter .

4. Choose Filter menu > Blur > Gaussian Blur.

5. Enter 3 in the Radius field, then click OK or press Enter.

6. Choose Filter menu > Stylize > Find Edges.

7. Choose Image menu > Adjust > Levels.

8. Move the black Input slider a ways to the right and move the white Input slider to left, pause to preview, then click OK or press Enter ❸.

9. Choose Filter menu > Sharpen > Sharpen Edges a few times.

2 A new, blank document, after applying the Add Noise filter.

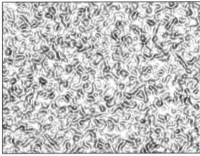
3 Spaghetti.

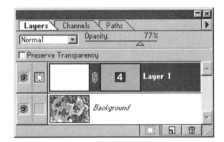

By adding an interesting black or gray texture to a layer mask, you can control the blending of what is seen in a layer and the layers below it. Areas of black in a layer mask will hide pixels in the layer and reveal imagery from the layer below.

To use a layer mask to apply a texture:

1. Open an image.

2. Create a new layer, and fill it with a color or shade.

3. Create layer mask for the new layer by clicking the Add Layer Mask button on the Layers palette ▣, and leave the layer mask thumbnail active.

4. Apply a filter or series of filters to the mask ❹–❺:

5

Create Texture; Apply Texture

1 The original image.

2 Theirs.

3 Ours.

The Texture filters (Craquelure, Grain, Mosaic Tiles, Patchwork, and Texturizer) will produce a texture effect on a white layer mask. For other filters, first apply the Add Noise filter to the layer mask to create light and dark pixels for the next filter or filters you apply to work with.

Try applying any of the following filters after applying a Texture filter or the Add Noise filter: Artistic > Dry Brush (small stroke size), Palette Knife (small stroke size), Plastic Wrap (use Levels to increase contrast), Sponge, or Watercolor.

5. *Optional:* To intensify a filter's effect, apply the Distort > Twirl or Ripple, or Stylize > Wind filter afterward.

To fade a filter's effect, use the Filter menu > Fade command.

6. *Optional:* Use the Levels command to heighten contrast in the layer mask to achieve a more dramatic light-to-dark contrast.

We've come up with a way to turn a photograph into a watercolor using the Median Noise and Minimum filters. Compare it to Photoshop's Watercolor filter.

Our watercolor filter:

1. Duplicate the layer that you want to turn into a watercolor.

2. With the duplicate layer active, choose Filter menu > Noise > Median.

3. Move the Radius slider to a number between 2 and 8.

4. Click OK or press Enter.

5. Choose Filter menu > Other > Minimum.

6. Move the Radius the slider to 1, 2, or 3.

7. Click OK or press Enter **1**–**3**.

8. *Optional:* Apply the Sharpen More filter.

Our Watercolor

In the following instructions, the Mosaic filter is applied using progressive values to a series of rectangular selections, so the mosaic tiles gradually enlarge as the effect travels across the image. Using a gradient in a layer mask, on the other hand, would gradually fade of the Mosaic effect without changing the size of the mosaic tiles .

To apply the Mosaic filter using graduated values:

1. Choose a target layer.

2. Choose the Rectangular Marquee tool.

3. Marquee about a quarter or fifth of the layer, where you want the mosaic tiles to begin.

4. Choose Filter menu > Pixelate > Mosaic.

5. Enter 6 in the Cell Size field **2**.

6. Click OK or press Enter.

7. With the selection still active and the Rectangular Marquee tool still chosen, drag the marquee to the next adjacent quadrant **3**. Hold down Shift while dragging to constrain the movement.

8. Repeat steps 4–7 until you've finished the whole image, entering 12, then 24, then 30 in the Cell Size field. To create larger pixel blocks, enter higher numbers—like 8, 16, 28, and 34—in the Cell Size field.

9. Deselect (Control-D) **4**.

1 The Mosaic filter applied using a gradient in the layer mask.

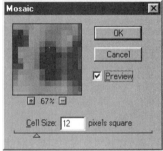

2 Enter a number in the Cell Size field in the Mosaic dialog box. Enter progressively higher numbers each time you repeat step 5.

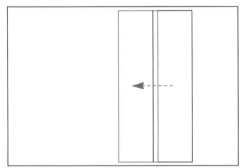

3 Apply the Mosaic filter to a rectangular selection, move the marquee, then reapply the filter, etc.

4 A graduated mosaic.

Mosaic Filter

1 The original image.

2 The final image.

Turn a photograph into a painting or a drawing:

1. Choose Duplicate Layer from the Layers palette command menu, then click OK.

2. Choose Filter menu > Stylize > Find Edges.

3. With the duplicate layer active, click the Add Layer Mask icon.⊡

4. Paint with black at below 100% opacity on the layer mask to reveal parts of the layer below **1**–**2**.

5. *Optional:* Lower the opacity of the duplicate layer.

6. *Optional:* For a dramatic effect of colors on a dark background, activate the layer icon, then choose Image menu > Adjust > Invert.

TIP To produce magic marker drawing, apply the Trace Contour filter, and apply Filter menu > Other > Minimum (Radius of 1 or 2) in place of step 2, above.

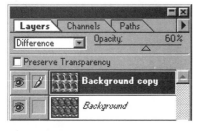

3 The original pattern.

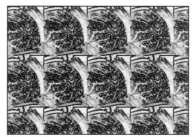

A pattern variation

Fill a layer with a pattern **3**, duplicate the pattern layer, then apply the Find Edges filter to the duplicate layer, fill it with a Foreground color, 60% Opacity, Color Mode. Finally, choose Overlay or Difference mode for the duplicate layer **4**.

4 A texturized pattern.

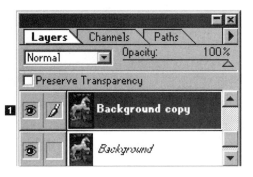

To create an illusion of motion, select an object on one layer to be the stationary object, and then apply the Motion Blur filter to the same image on another layer.

To Motion Blur part of an image:

1. Activate the layer that contains the imagery you want to motion blur.

2. Choose Duplicate Layer from the Layers palette command menu, rename the duplicate layer, if you like, then click OK.

3. Activate the Background **1**.

4. Alt-click the Eye icon for that layer to hide all the other layers.

5. Choose Filter menu > Blur > Motion Blur.

6. Enter a number between -360 and 360 in the Angle field or drag the axis line **2**. (We entered -17 for our image.)
and
Enter a number between 1 and 999 in the Distance field (the amount of blur). (We entered 50 for our image.)
and
Click OK or press Enter.

7. Alt-click the Eye icon for the Background on the Layers palette to redisplay all the other layers.

8. Activate the duplicate layer.

9. Select an object on the duplicate layer that you want to remain stationary **3**.

10. Choose Select menu > Feather (Control-Shift-D).

11. Enter 5 in the Feather Radius field, then click OK or press Enter.

12. Choose Select menu > Inverse (Control-Shift-I).

13. Press Delete, then deselect (Control-D) **4**.

14. *Optional:* Move the stationary image on the duplicate layer using the Move tool or change that layer's opacity.

3 Select an object.

PHOTO: CARA WOOD

4 The completed **Motion Blur**.

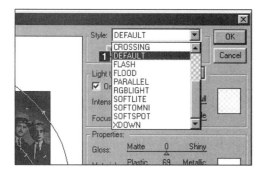

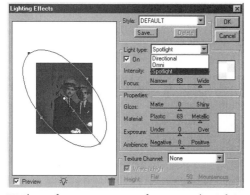

2 Choose from a cornucopia of options in the **Lighting Effects** dialog box to create your own lighting effects.

The Lighting Effects filter produces a tremendous variety of lighting effects. You can choose from up to 17 different light sources and you can assign to each light source a different color, intensity, and angle.

NOTE: For the Lighting Effects filter to work, at least 20 MB of RAM must be allocated to Photoshop.

To cast a light on an image:

1. Make sure your image is in RGB Color mode.

2. Choose a target layer.

3. *Optional:* Select an area on the layer to limit the filter effect to that area.

4. Choose Filter menu > Render > Lighting Effects.

5. Choose Default or choose a preset lighting effect from the Style drop-down menu **1**.

Do any of the following optional steps to adjust the light **2**:

6. Choose from the Light Type drop-down menu. Choose Spotlight to create a narrow, elliptical light.

7. Move the Intensity slider to adjust the brightness of the light. Full creates the brightest light **3**. Negative creates a black light effect.

8. Move the Focus slider to adjust the size of the beam of light that fills the ellipse shape **4**–**5**. The light source starts from where the radius touches the edge of the ellipse.

3 The default spotlight ellipse with Full Intensity.

4 The default spotlight ellipse with Wide Focus. The light is strongest at the sides of the ellipse.

5 The default spotlight ellipse with Narrow Focus.

(Continued on the following page)

Lighting Effects Filter

9. If you want to change the color of the light, click on the color swatch, then choose a color from the Color palette.

10. In the preview window:

Drag the center point of the ellipse to move the whole light.

Drag either endpoint toward the center of the ellipse to increase the intensity of the light **1**.

Drag either side point of the ellipse to change the angle of the light and to widen or narrow it **2**–**3**.

11. Move the Properties sliders to adjust the surrounding light conditions on the target layer.

The **Gloss** property controls the amount of surface reflectance on the lighted surfaces.

The **Material** property controls which parts of the image reflect the light source color—Plastic (the light source color is like a glare) or Metallic (the object surface glows).

The **Exposure** property lightens or darkens the whole ellipse **4**–**5**.

The **Ambience** property controls the balance between the light source and the overall light in the image **6**–**7**. Move this slider in small increments.

Click the **Properties** color swatch to choose a different color from the Color Picker dialog box for the ambient light around the spotlight.

12. Click OK or press Enter.

TIP The Texture Channel option is discussed on page 187.

TIP Shift-drag (the ellipse) to keep the angle constant and change the size of the ellipse. Control-drag to keep the size constant and change the angle or direction of the ellipse.

TIP To create a pin spot, choose Spotlight from the Light Type drop-down menu, move the Intensity slider to about 80,

1 The default spotlight ellipse after dragging the end points inward to narrow the light beam.

2 The spotlight ellipse ro`.ated to the left by dragging a side point.

3 The spotlight ellipse after dragging the radius inward to make the light beam more round.

4 The spotlight ellipse with the Exposure Property set to Over.

5 The spotlight ellipse with the Exposure Property set to Under.

6 The spotlight ellipse with a Positive Ambience Property.

7 The spotlight ellipse with a Negative Ambience Property.

The default Omni light is round. The effect is like shining a flashlight perpendicular to the image.

1 Drag a new light source onto the preview box. A new ellipse will appear where the mouse is released.

move the Focus slider to about 30, and drag the side points of the ellipse inward. Move the whole ellipse by dragging its center point to cast light on a particular area of the image.

TIP If the background of an image was darkened too much from a previous application of the Lighting Effects filter, apply the filter again to add another light to shine into the dark area and recover some detail. Move the Exposure Properties and Ambience Properties sliders a little to the right.

TIP To see the image in the Preview box without the ellipses, drag the light bulb icon just inside the bottom edge of the Preview box **1**. Delete the extra light when you're finished.

TIP To delete a light source ellipse, drag its center point over the Trash icon.

TIP Check the Light Type/On box to preview the lighting effects in the preview box.

TIP To duplicate a light source ellipse, Alt-drag its center point.

TIP The last used settings of the Lighting Effects filter will remain in the dialog box until you change them or exit Photoshop. To restore the default settings, choose a different style from the Style drop-down menu, then choose Default from the same menu.

TIP To add your own Lighting Effects settings to the Style drop-down menu, click Save before clicking OK.

TIP Click Delete to remove the currently selected style from the drop-down menu.

Lighting Effects Filter

A custom lighting effect

To produce , we chose RGB Color mode, chose a target layer (the figures), and chose Filter menu > Render > Lighting Effects.

In the Lighting Effects dialog box, we:

■ Chose Spotlight from the Light Type drop-down menu.

■ Set the Intensity halfway toward Full.

■ Set the Focus toward Wide.

■ Dragged the side points of the ellipse inward to make it narrower.

■ Dragged the centerpoint of the ellipse to cast the light over the face on the left in the image.

■ Set the Exposure Property slightly toward Over to brighten the light source.

■ Moved the Ambience Property slider to 2 to darken the background of the image.

■ Dragged the endpoint of the Radius slightly inward to focus the beam of light more intensely on the face.

■ When we were satisfied with the light source on one face, we Alt-dragged the centerpoint of the ellipse to duplicate the light, and move the duplicate light over the face on the right **2**.

■ To create a subtle backlight, we dragged the light bulb icon into the Preview area to create another light source, rotated the ellipse sideways, and set the Intensity to be less Full than the other lights. We left the Focus setting between Narrow and Wide and left the Properties setting alone **3**.

TIP Apply Lighting Effects to the Background of an image first, then to successive layers above it.

1 The original RGB image.

2 The three ellipses used to produce the image below.

3 The image after applying the Lighting Effects filter with our own settings.

ACTIONS 17

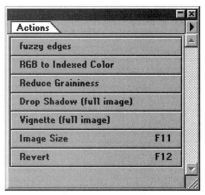

1 **Actions** palette in **Button** mode. To turn Button mode on or off, choose **Button Mode** from the Actions palette command menu.

An included command has a black check mark; an excluded command has none.

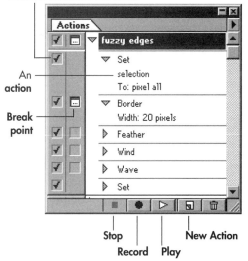

2 With the **Actions** palette in **List** mode, you can exclude a command, insert a pause, rearrange the order of commands, record an additional command, rerecord a command, delete a command, or save an action to an action set file.

A **SEQUENCE OF** menu operations can be recorded as an action. The action can then be played back on a single file or on a group of files within the same folder (called a "batch" of files) using the same commands, with the same dialog box settings, and in the same order in which they were recorded. Or, a pause can be inserted in an action, at which point you can choose different dialog box settings during the playback or perform an operation that could not be recorded. You can also add commands to an action after it's recorded.

Actions are particularly useful when you want to produce consistent image editing results on multiple images. You can use an action to apply a series of Adjust commands or a sequence of filter applications. Or, you can save concise steps into an action for preparing a file for print or converting it to a different file format. The Actions palette is used to record, play back, edit, delete, save, and load actions **1**–**2**. Each action can be assigned its own keyboard shortcut for quick access.

By the way, the Commands palette is history. Adobe decided the Actions palette could be used in its place. Some people aren't too happy about that.

As you create an action, the commands you use are recorded. When you're finished recording, the commands will be appear as a list on the Actions palette.

NOTE: Some operations, like painting brush strokes or using an editing or selection tool, can't be recorded. Sad, but true.

To record an action:

1. Open an image or create a new image.

2. Click the New Action button at the bottom of the Actions palette **1**.

3. Enter a name for the action **2**.

4. *Optional:* Assign a keyboard shortcut Function key and/or display color to the action.

5. Click Record **3**.

6. Execute the commands you want to record as you would normally apply them to any image. When you enter values into a dialog box and then click OK, those settings will record (but not if you click Cancel).

7. Click the Stop button to stop recording **4**. The action will now be listed on the Actions palette.

TIP To reorder the sequence of commands in an action, see page 220. To give yourself some leeway for experimentation, record an action on a copy of a file and then replay the action on yet another copy or on the original.

TIP Double-click an action name on the palette to open the Action Options dialog box, where you can rename the action or reset its shortcut or color.

TIP Include the Save command in an action with caution. It's useful if the action will be used for batch processing, but less useful if you're doing creative work. To delete a Save or any other command from an action, see page 220.

Stop Record   New Action

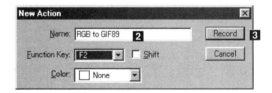

You can insert a stop into an action that will interrupt the playback, at which point you can manually perform a non-recordable (and *only* a non-recordable) operation, like creating a selection or drawing brush strokes. When the manual operation is finished, you can resume the playback.

To insert a stop in an action:

1. As you're creating an action, pause at the point at which you want the stop to appear.
or
Click the command name in an existing action after which you want the stop to appear.

2. Choose Insert Stop from the Actions palette command menu.

3. Type an instruction for the person replaying the action so they'll know which command to perform **1**. It's a good idea to specify in your stop message that after performing a manual step, the user should click the Play button on the Actions palette to resume the playback.

4. *Optional:* Check the Allow Continue box **2** to include a Continue button in the stop alert box **3**. **NOTE:** With Allow Continue unchecked, you will still be able to click Stop at that point in the action playback and then click the play icon on the palette to resume the action playback.

5. Click OK or press Enter.

6. The stop will be inserted below the previously highlighted command in the action **4**. To move it to a different position, drag it upward or downward on the Actions palette.

TIP If an action is replayed while the Actions palette is in Button mode, the Play icon won't be accessible for resuming the playback after a stop. Click the action name again to resume play instead. Choose List mode for the palette when you're using stops.

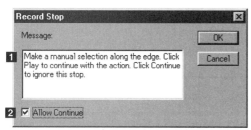

Enter a **message** in the Record Stop dialog box to guide the user during playback. Check the **Allow Continue** box to create a Continue button which the person replaying the action can press to bypass the stop command and resume playback.

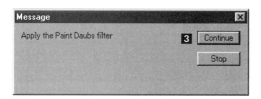

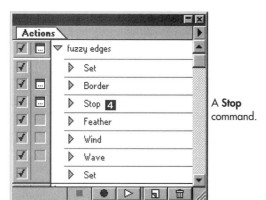

A **Stop** command.

To exclude or include a command from playback:

1. Make sure the Actions palette is in List—not Button—mode.

2. On the Actions palette, click the right-pointing triangle next to an action name to expand the list, if necessary.

3. Click in the leftmost column to remove the check mark and exclude that command from playback **1**. (Click in the same spot again to restore the check mark and include the command.)

The "fuzzy edges" action **expanded** on the Actions palette. The Feather step is unchecked to **exclude** it from playback.

A command can be inserted into an existing action. Dialog box settings, however, will not be recorded when you do so. See our the sidebar on this page for a workaround to this limitation.

To insert a menu command into an action:

1. Click the command name in the action after which you want the new menu command to appear.

2. Choose Insert Menu Item from the Actions palette command menu.

3. Choose the desired command from the menu bar.

or

Start typing a command name into the Find field, then click Find **2**.

4. Click OK or press Enter. The menu command will be inserted into the action. When it's played back, the action will automatically pause at this juncture, at which point you can choose dialog box settings, then click OK (or click Cancel). The action playback will resume.

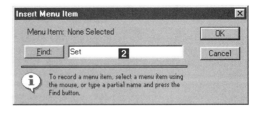

To include dialog box settings in an inserted command

To include dialog box settings with an inserted command, choose Record "[command name]" again, change the dialog box settings, if desired, click OK, then click next to the command name to make the dialog icon ▣ appear. This will insert a pause for the dialog box to open when this step is reached, at which point new settings can be entered.

Or double-click the command name and enter settings in the dialog box. The action will still halt at this point to allow you to accept, change, or cancel the dialog box settings.

Exclude a Control; Insert a Control

More playback options

- To play an action starting from a specific command on the list, click that command name, then click the Play button or choose Play from "[command name]" from the Actions palette command menu.

- To play a single command in a multi-command action, click the command name, then Control-click the Play button or choose Play Only "[command name]" from the Actions palette command menu.

To replay an action on an image:

1. Open the image on which you want to play back the action.

2. Choose List mode for the Actions palette (uncheck Button mode). (In Button mode, you can only execute the whole action, and any previously excluded commands won't play back.)

3. Click an action name on the palette ▉.

4. Click the Play button on the palette ▉.

NOTE: Batch processing will end at a stop command in an action. Remove inserted stops from the action for batch playback.

To replay an action on a batch of images:

1. Choose List mode for the Actions palette.

2. Make sure all the files for batch processing are contained in one folder.

3. Choose Batch from the Actions palette command menu.

4. Choose Source: Folder ▉.
   and
   Click Choose.
   and
   Locate the desired batch folder, then click OK.

5. Choose an action from the Action drop-down menu.

6. Choose Destination: None to leave the files open; or choose Save and Close to save the files over the originals; or choose Folder to save files to a new folder (click Choose to designate the destination folder).

7. *Optional:* If you chose Folder for the previous step and checked the Override Action "Save In" Commands box, the image will save to the folder designated in step 5 during playback when a Save command occurs in the action.

8. Click OK or press Enter. The batch processing will begin.

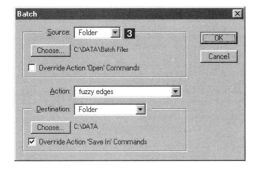

Using the batch option, you can import non-Photoshop images and process them using an action. This procedure can be used to process images from a digital camera plugged into your computer. The import option is like using File > Import to open an image, except in this case it's automatic.

To replay an action on a batch of non-Photoshop images:

1. Choose Batch from the Actions palette command menu.

2. Choose Source: Import ▋.

3. Choose an import option from the From drop-down menu ▋. (These options are the same as in the File > Import dialog box.)

4. Follow steps 5–8 on the previous page.

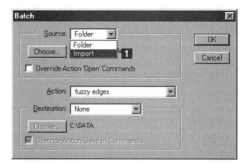

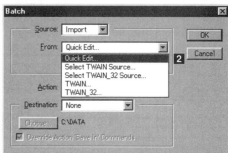

NOTE: To save the current list of actions as a set for later use, follow the instructions on page 224 **before** you clear the palette.

To delete a command from an action:

1. Highlight the command you want to delete.

2. Click the trash icon at the bottom of the Actions palette, then click OK.

NOTE: If commands are reordered, the action may produce a different overall effect on the image on which it is played.

To change the order of commands:

1. On the Actions palette, click the right-pointing triangle next to an action name to expand the list, if it's not already expanded ▋.

2. Drag a command upward or downward on the list ▋–▋.

The Invert command moved upward on the list.

When a pause (also called a "break point") is inserted into an action, the dialog box for that command will open during playback. When the pause occurs, you can choose different settings or click OK to proceed with the settings used when the action was originally recorded. A pause can only be set for a command that uses a dialog box.

To insert a pause (break point) into an action:

1. Make sure the Actions palette is in List mode (not Button mode).

2. On the Actions palette, click the right-pointing triangle next to the action name to expand the list, if it's not already expanded.

3. Click in the second column from the left (next to the command name) to display the dialog box icon **1**. (Click again in the same spot if you want to remove the icon and remove the pause.)

The action will pause when this command is encountered, at which point you can enter new values, accept the existing values, or cancel out of the dialog box. The playback will resume after you close dialog box.

Actions palette with an action expanded. Click next to the individual command name to insert a pause and show the dialog icon.

Insert a Pause (Break Point)

To add a command (or commands) to an action:

1. On the Actions palette, click the right-pointing triangle next to an action's name to expand the list, if it's not already expanded, then click the command name after which you want the new command to appear.

2. Choose Start Recording from the Actions palette command menu.

3. Perform the steps to record the commands you want to add.

4. Click the Stop button to stop recording **1**. You can drag any command upward or downward to a different position in the action.

TIP To copy a command from one action to another, expand both action lists, then Alt-drag the command you want to copy from one action to the other. If you don't hold down Alt while dragging, you'll cut the command from the original action. Be careful if you copy any Save commands—they may contain particular info for the original action.

To rerecord a whole action using different dialog box settings:

1. Click on the name of the action you want to revise.

2. Choose Record "[action name]" Again from the Actions palette command menu. The action will play back, stopping at commands that use dialog boxes.

3. When each dialog box opens, enter new settings, if desired, then click OK. When the dialog box closes, the Record Again rerecording will continue.

To stop the rerecording, click Cancel in a dialog box or click the Stop button on the Actions palette.

To rerecord one command in an action:

1. Double-click the command on the action list.

2. Enter new settings.

3. Click OK. Click Cancel to have any revisions be disregarded.

Duplicate an action if you want to experiment with it or add to it and don't want to mess around with the original.

To duplicate an action:

Click on the name of the action you want to duplicate, then choose Duplicate "[action name]" from the Actions palette command menu.

or

Drag the name of the action you want to duplicate over the New Action button at the bottom of the Actions palette **1**.

TIP To duplicate a command in an action, click on the command name, then choose Duplicate "[command name]" from the palette command menu. Or drag the command over the New Action button at the bottom of the Actions palette.

To duplicate an action, drag its name over the New Action button at the bottom of the Actions palette.

To delete an entire action:

1. Highlight the action you want to delete.

2. Click the trash icon at the bottom of the Actions palette, then click OK.

or

Alt-click the trash icon.

Rerecord Command; Duplicate Action

It's a good idea to save actions to a file to guard against loss due to an application or system crash or inadvertent use of the Delete or Clear Actions command.

To save all the actions on the Actions palette to a file:

1. Choose Save Actions from the Actions palette command menu **1**.

2. Type a name for the action.

3. Choose a location in which to save the action file.

4. Click Save. The new file will be regarded as one set, regardless of the number of actions it contains. Actions are automatically stored in the Adobe Photoshop 4.0 Preferences file. If this file is deleted to cure a problem in Photoshop, any actions not saved to a separate file will be deleted in the process.

To load an additional actions set onto the Actions palette:

1. Click the action name below which you want the loaded actions to appear.

2. Choose Load Actions from the Actions palette command menu.

3. Locate and highlight the actions set you want to append.

4. Click Open.

To replace the current actions set with a different actions set:

1. Click the action name below which you want the loaded actions to appear.

2. Choose Replace Actions from the Actions palette command menu.

3. Locate and highlight the actions set you want to load.

4. Click Open.

PREFERENCES 18

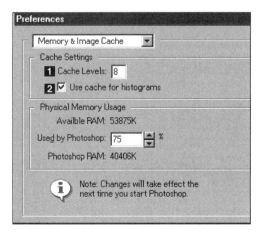

To access the preferences dialog boxes quickly, use the **Control-K** shortcut to open the General Preferences dialog box, then use any of the shortcuts illustrated above to access other dialog boxes, or click **Next** on the right side of the dialog box to cycle through them.

PREFERENCES **ARE** default settings that apply to the application as a whole, such as which ruler units are used, or if channels display in color. Most preferences changes take effect immediately; a few take effect on re-launching. To access the preferences dialog boxes the fast-and-easy way, see the illustration at left. (Or use the File menu > Preferences submenu.)

NOTE: To reset all the default preferences, open the Prefs subdirectory inside the Photoshop directory, then delete the PHOTOSHO.PSP file.

Image Cache Preferences

1 A Cache Levels value between 1 and 8 helps speed up screen redraw when you're editing or color adjusting high resolution images. A low-resolution version of the image is saved in a cache buffer and is used to update the on-screen image. The higher the Cache Levels number, the more buffers are used, and the speedier the redraw.

2 Check the "Use cache for histograms" box for faster, but slightly less accurate, histogram display in the Levels and Histogram dialog boxes.

Image Cache Preferences

General Preferences

1 Choose the Photoshop **Color Picker** to access the application's own Color Picker. If you're trying to mix a color in Photoshop to match a color in Macromedia Director or Netscape Navigator, use the Windows Color Picker.

2 Choose an **Interpolation** option for reinterpretation of an image as a result of resampling or transforming. Bicubic is slowest, but the highest quality. Nearest Neighbor is the fastest, but the poorest quality.

3 Check **Anti-alias PostScript** to optimize the rendering of EPS images in Photoshop.

4 Check **Export Clipboard** to have the current Clipboard contents stay on the Clipboard when you quit Photoshop.

5 Check **Short PANTONE Names** if your image contains Pantone colors and you are exporting it to another application.

A tool tip.

6 Check **Show Tool Tips** to see an onscreen display of the name of the tool or icon currently under the cursor.

7 Check **Beep When Done** for a beep to sound after any command, for which a progress bar displays, is completed.

8 With **Dynamic Color Sliders** checked, the Color palette sliders update as you move them. Turn this option off to speed performance.

9 With **Save Palette Locations** checked, palettes that are open when you exit Photoshop will appear in their same location when you re-launch.

10 To restore the palettes' default groupings when you launch Photoshop, click **Reset Palette Locations to Default.**

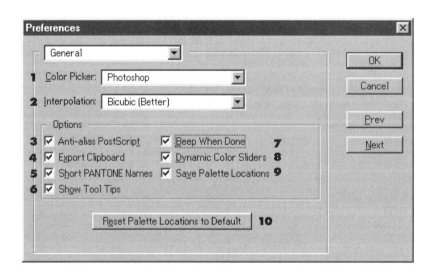

Saving Files Preferences

1 For each **Image Preview** type, choose Never Save to save files without previews, choose Always Save to always save files with the specified previews, or choose Ask When Saving to assign previews for each individual file when you save it for the first time **1**.

2 Check **2.5 Compatibility** to automatically save a flattened, Photoshop version 2.5 copy in every 3.0 document. This option increases the file's storage size. Turn this option off if you don't need it.

3 Check **Save Metric Color Tags** if you are exporting your file to QuarkXPress and are using EFIColor in that program.

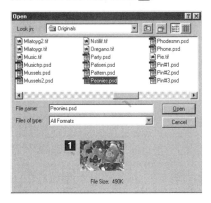

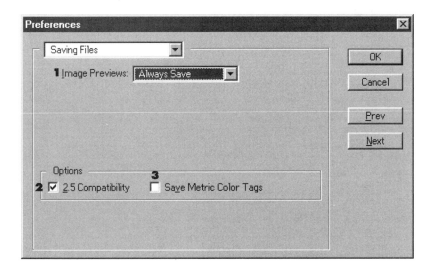

Saving Files Preferences

Display & Cursors Preferences

1 Choose whether **CMYK Composites** for the RGB screen version of a CMYK file will be rendered Faster, but simpler, or Smoother and more refined.

2 Check **Color Channels in Color** to display individual RGB or CMYK channels in their particular color. Otherwise, they will display grayscale.

3 Check **Use System Palette** to have the Apple System Palette be used rather than the document's own color palette. Turn this option on to correct the display of erratic colors on an 8–bit monitor.

4 Check **Use Diffusion Dither** to have Photoshop use a grainy dot pattern to simulate transitions between colors that are absent from the limited palette of an 8-bit, 256 color monitor.

5 Uncheck **Video LUT Animation** to disable the interactive screen preview if you are using a video card that is causing conflicts between Photoshop and your monitor. With Video LUT Animation turned on, changes made in a Photoshop dialog box are reflected immediately on the entire screen, not just in the image window or in a selection. With this option unchecked, you must check the Preview box in a dialog box to preview changes in the image window.

6 For the **Painting Cursors** (Gradient, Line, Eraser, Pencil, Airbrush, Paintbrush, Rubber Stamp, Smudge, Blur, Sharpen, Dodge, Burn, and Sponge tools) choose **Standard** to see the icon of the tool being used, or choose **Precise** to see a crosshair icon, or choose **Brush Size** to see a round icon the exact size and shape of the brush tip (up to 300 pixels). For the non-painting tools (Marquee, Lasso, Polygon Lasso, Magic Wand, Crop, Eyedropper, Pen, Gradient, Line, and Paint Bucket), choose **Other Cursors**: Standard or Precise.

Standard cursor **Precise** cursor **Brush Size** cursor

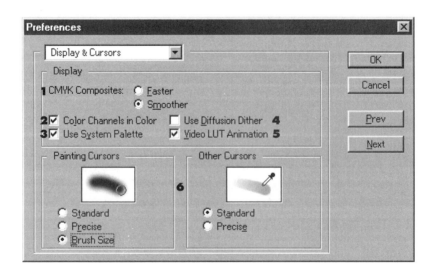

Transparency & Gamut Preferences

1 A checkerboard grid is used to represent transparent areas on a layer (areas that don't contain pixels). You can choose a different **Grid Size**.

2 Change the **Grid Colors** for the transparency checkerboard by choosing Red, Orange, Green, Blue, or Purple from the drop-down menu, or choose Light, Medium, or Dark.

3 To change the color used to indicate out-of-gamut colors on an image if you're using the **Gamut Warning** command, click the Color square, then choose a color from the Color Picker. You can lower the Gamut Warning color Opacity to make it easier to see the actual image color underneath.

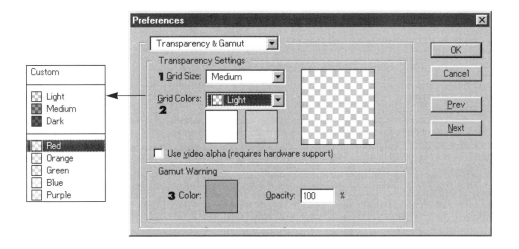

Grid Size: Large; Grid Colors: Medium

Units & Rulers Preferences

1 Choose a unit of measure from the Rulers Units: drop-down menu for the horizontal and vertical rulers that display in the image window. (Choose View > Show Rulers to display the rulers.)

2 To create multiple column guides, enter a Column Size: Width and Gutter width.

TIP If you change the measurement units for the Info palette **1**, the ruler units will change in this dialog box also, and vice versa.

TIP You can also open this dialog box by double-clicking either ruler in the image window.

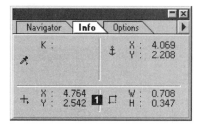

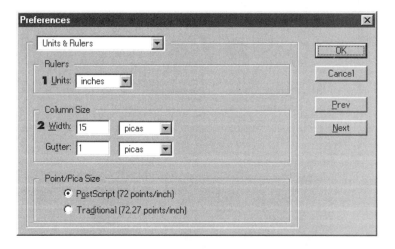

Guides & Grid Preferences

1 Choose a preset color for the removable ruler **Guides** from the **Color** drop-down menu. Click the color square to choose a color from the Color Picker.

2 Choose Lines or Dashed Lines for the **Guides Style**.

3 Choose a preset color for the non-printing **Grid** from the **Color** drop-down menu. Click the color square to choose a color from the Color Picker.

4 Choose Lines or Dashed Lines for the **Grid Style**.

5 To have grid lines appear at specific unit-of-measure intervals, choose a unit of measurement, then enter a new value in the **Gridline every** field.

6 To add grid lines between the thicker grid line increments chosen in the Gridline every field, enter a number in the **Subdivisions** field.

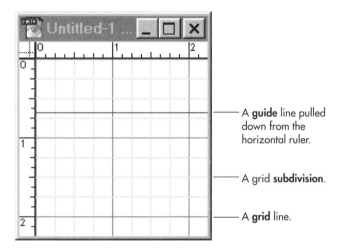

— A **guide** line pulled down from the horizontal ruler.

— A grid **subdivision**.

— A **grid** line.

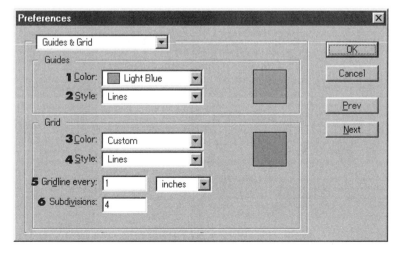

Plug-ins & Scratch Disk Preferences

NOTE: For changes made in this dialog box to take effect, you must exit and re-launch Photoshop.

1 Click **Plug-Ins Folder: Choose** if you need to relocate the plug-ins folder. Photoshop needs to know where to find this folder in order to access the plug-in contents. Photoshop's internal Plug-Ins module shouldn't be moved out of the Photoshop folder unless you have a specific reason for doing so (we're not talking about third-party plug-ins here). Moving it could inhibit access to the Acquire, Export, and File Format commands.

2 The **Primary** (and optional Secondary) **Scratch Disk** is used when available RAM is insufficient for processing or storage. Choose an available hard drive from the Primary drop-down menu. Startup is the default.

3 As an optional step, choose an alternate **Secondary** hard drive to be used as extra work space when necessary. If you have only one hard drive, of course you'll only have one scratch disk.

TIP If your scratch disk is a removable cartridge, removing the cartridge while Photoshop is running may cause the program to crash.

TIP To see how much RAM is currently being used while Photoshop is running, choose Scratch Sizes from the drop-down menu at the bottom of the image window ❶. The number on the left is the amount of memory needed for all currently open images and the Clipboard. The number on the right is the total amount of RAM available to Photoshop.

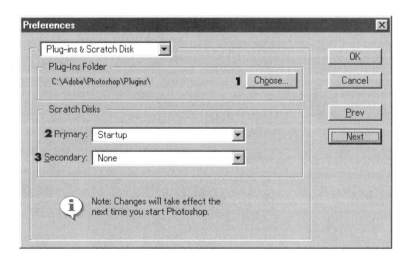

Resolution of output devices

Hewlett Packard LaserJet	300 or 600 dpi
Apple LaserWriter	300 or 600 dpi
IRIS SmartJet	300 dpi (looks like 1600 dpi)
3M Rainbow	300 dpi
QMS Colorscript	300 dpi
Canon Color Laser/Fiery	400 dpi
Linotronic imagesetter	1,200–4,000 dpi

AN IMAGE CAN be printed from Photoshop to a laser printer, to a color printer (thermal wax, dye sublimation, etc.), or to an imagesetter. A Photoshop image can also be imported into and printed from a drawing application, like FreeHand or Illustrator, a layout application, like QuarkXPress or PageMaker, a multimedia application, like Director, or prepared for viewing online.

Printer settings are chosen in the Print dialog box and the Page Setup dialog box (File menu). The following pages contain output tips, information about file compression, instructions for outputting to various types of printers, and instructions for creating duotones or a percentage tint of a Pantone color. Also included is a color separation walk-through, which explains the basic steps for calibrating your system and color correcting an image.

Press and hold on the Sizes bar in the lower left corner of the image window to display a thumbnail preview of the image in relationship to the paper size and other Page Setup specifications.

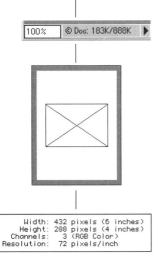

```
Width:      432 pixels (6 inches)
Height:     288 pixels (4 inches)
Channels:     3 (RGB Color)
Resolution:  72 pixels/inch
```

Hold down Alt and press and hold on the Sizes bar to display file information.

NOTE: Only currently visible layers and channels will print.

To print to a black-and-white laser printer:

1. Choose File menu > Print (Control-P).

2. For a picture in Grayscale or RGB Color mode, click Print as: Gray **1**.

For a CMYK Color image, make sure the Print Separations box is unchecked so the composite image will print.

3. Click OK or press Enter.

TIP To print only a portion of an image, select the area with the Rectangular Marquee tool, then click Print Range: Selection in the Print dialog box.

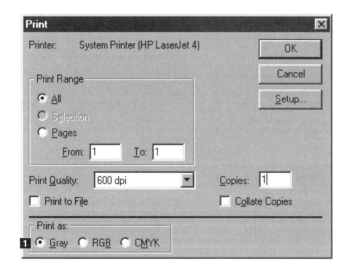

Laser Printer

To print to a Hewlett Packard LaserJet with halftone enhancement features:

1. Choose File menu > Page Setup (Control-Shift-P).

2. Click Screens ■.

3. Check the Use Printer's Default Screens box. (Don't change the default Paper, Layout, Reduce, or Orientation settings. Read about the other Page Setup options on pages 238–239.) Click OK, then click OK again.

4. Choose File menu > Print (Control-P).

5. If the picture is in CMYK Color mode, make sure the Print Separations box is unchecked.

6. Click OK or press Enter.

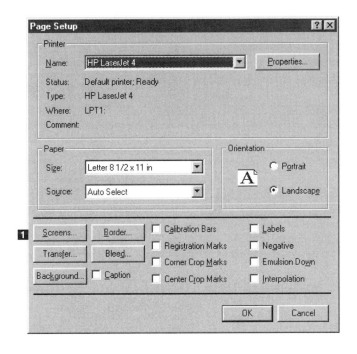

Unless your service bureau tells you otherwise, you should never send an RGB file to
a color or high-end printer. To see how an
image looks in CMYK mode in Photoshop
before you print it, choose Image menu >
Mode > CMYK Color before you open the
Print dialog box. Clicking Print as: CMYK
in the Print dialog box performs the same
function without a screen preview.

To print to a PostScript color printer:

1. To print to a PostScript Level 1 printer,
choose Image menu > Mode > CMYK
Color. CMYK color will be simulated
on screen.

or

To print to a PostScript Level 2 printer,
choose Image menu > Mode > Lab
Color.

2. Choose File menu > Page Setup
(Control-Shift-P).

3. Choose the correct color printer driver
option from the Name drop-down
menu **1**. (A printer driver must be
installed in your system to appear on
this menu.)

4. Click OK or press Enter.

5. Choose File menu > Print (Control-P).

6. Click Encoding: Binary **2**.

7. Click OK or press Enter.

TIP For a PostScript Level 1 printer, click
Screens in the Page Setup dialog box,
then check the Use Same Shape for All
Inks box. For a PostScript Level 2
printer, check the Use Accurate Screens
box, but don't change the ink angles.

TIP If the printout from a CMYK Color file
is too dark, lighten the image using the
Levels dialog box (Control-L). Move
the gray Input slider a little to the left
and the black Output slider a little to
the right. Save a copy of the file.

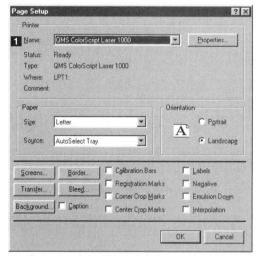

This illustration shows the Print dialog box for a **CMYK
Color** image.

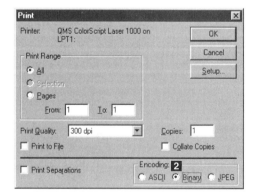

To prepare a file for an IRIS or dye sublimation printer or an imagesetter:

1. To print on a PostScript Level 1 printer, choose Image menu > Mode > CMYK Color.

or

To print on a PostScript Level 2 printer, choose File menu > Page Setup, click Screen, check the Use Accurate Screens box, then click OK twice. Ask your service bureau whether the file should be in CMYK Color or Lab Color mode.

2. Choose File menu > Save a Copy (Control-Alt-S).

3. Choose a location in which to save the file.

4. Choose Photoshop EPS from the Save As drop-down menu, then click Save.

5. Choose Preview: TIFF (8 bits/pixel) **1**.

6. Choose Encoding: Binary. (Leave the DCS option off.)

7. If you've changed the screen settings in the Halftone Screens dialog box, then check the Include Halftone Screen box.

8. Click OK or press Enter.

TIP Ask your service bureau to recommend an image resolution for the color printer or imagesetter you plan to use before saving and printing the file.

TIP If your image is wider than it is tall, ask your service bureau if it will print more quickly if you rotate it first using Photoshop's Rotate Canvas command.

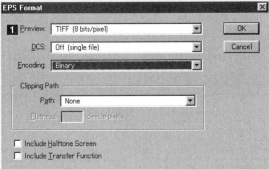

High-End Printer

Photoshop's Trap command slightly over-laps solid color areas in an image to help prevent gaps that may occur due to press misregistration or movement. Trapping is only necessary when two distinct, adjacent color areas share less than two of the four process colors. You don't need to trap con-tinuous-tone or photographic images.

NOTE: Photoshop's Trap command spreads colors, unlike some other applications, which also may use the choke method. Consult with your press shop before using this command, and apply it to a copy of your image; store your original image without traps.

To apply trapping:

1. Open the image to which you want to apply trapping, and make sure the image is in CMYK Color mode.

2. Choose Image menu > Trap.

3. Enter the Width value your press shop recommends **1**.

4. Click OK or press Enter.

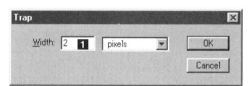

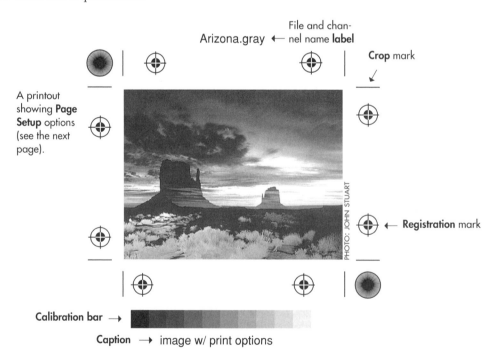

Arizona.gray ← File and chan-nel name **label**

Crop mark

A printout showing **Page Setup** options (see the next page).

PHOTO: JOHN STUART

← **Registration** mark

Calibration bar →

Caption → image w/ print options

The Page Setup dialog box

1 An image will print faster with Portrait Orientation than with Landscape Orientation. If your image is wider than it is tall, choose Image menu > Rotate Canvas > 90°CW. Then you can print it in Portrait Orientation.

2 To print a colored background around the image, click Background, then choose a color.

3 To print a black border around an image, click Border, then specify a measurement unit and a width.

4 Choose Bleed to print crop marks inside the image at a specified distance from the edge of the image.

5 Calibration Bars creates a Grayscale and/or color calibration strip outside the image area.

6 Registration Marks creates marks a print shop uses to align color separations.

7 Crop Marks creates short little lines that a print shop uses to trim the final printed page.

8 Labels prints the document's title and channel names.

9 Ask your print shop whether to choose the Negative or Emulsion Down film option.

10 Interpolation reduces jaggies when outputting to some PostScript Level 2 printers.

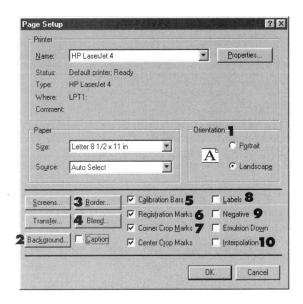

Page Setup Options

Preparing files for other applications

The people at the last stage of your project, ironically, are the people you should chat with first. In order to create printing plates from your file, you'll need to furnish your print shop with paper or film output. Nowadays, many print shops perform this service in house, which makes sense. Before outputting your file, ask your print shop or publisher if they have any specifications for the paper or film output you give them, and make sure the image is saved at the appropriate resolution for the target output device. Also ask what halftone screen frequency (lpi) the print shop will use and output your file at that frequency. You might also ask your prepress shop if you should save your file with special settings for a particular printer, such as in a particular image mode. Let the prepress shop calculate the halftone screen angle settings for you—that's their department.

Photoshop to QuarkXPress

To color separate a Photoshop image from QuarkXPress, first convert it to CMYK Color mode. Different imagesetters require different formats, so ask your prepress house whether to save your image in the TIFF or EPS file format, and whether to turn on the DCS option **1**. The DCS (Desktop Color Separation) option pre-separates the image in Photoshop, and it produces five related files, one for each CMYK channel and one for the combined, composite, CMYK channel. If you need to preview a DCS image in QuarkXPress, choose On (72 pixel/inch grayscale) or On (72 pixel/inch color). A color preview can balloon the storage size of an image.

Leave the Include Halftone Screens and Include Transfer Functions boxes unchecked. Your prepress shop will choose the proper settings for these options.

Photoshop to PageMaker

Save your image in the EPS or TIFF format.

To keep a background transparent

To import a Photoshop image into a drawing or page layout application and maintain its transparent background, save it as a clipping path (see page 175).

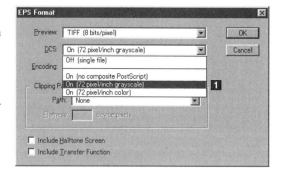

Photoshop and CorelDRAW

To Copy and Paste from Photoshop to CorelDRAW, select an area of a Photoshop layer and copy it, then in a CorelDRAW image window, choose Paste. CorelDRAW will list the pasted object as an image object. You can apply some editing commands to the pasted image object.

To Copy and Paste a CorelDRAW object into Photoshop, select and copy an object in CorelDRAW, then in an Photoshop image window, choose Paste. The object will appear as an area of pixels on a separate layer.

To drag and drop from Photoshop to CorelDRAW, drag a selection from a Photoshop window into a CorelDRAW window. The object will be listed in CorelDRAW as a color bitmap. Most editing commands will be available for the color bitmap object. You cannot drag and drop from CorelDRAW to Photoshop.

Photoshop to a film recorder

Color transparencies, also called chromes, are widely used as a source for high quality images in the publishing industry. A Photoshop file can be output to a film recorder to produce a chrome. Though the output settings for each film recorder may vary, to output to any film recorder, the pixel count for the height and width of the image file must conform to the pixel count the film recorder requires for each line it images. If the image originates as a scan, the pixel count should be taken into consideration when setting the scan's resolution, dimensions, and file storage size.

For example, let's say you need to produce a 4 x 5-inch chrome on a Solitaire film recorder. Your service bureau advises you that to output on the Solitaire, the 5-inch side of your image should measure 2000 pixels and the file storage size should be at least 10 megabytes. (Other film recorders may require higher resolutions.) Choose File menu > New, enter 2000 for the Width (in pixels) and 4 inches for the Height, enter a Resolution value to produce an Image Size of at least 10MB, and choose RGB Color Mode. Click OK to produce the image entirely within Photoshop, or note the resolution and dimensions, and ask your service bureau to match those values when they scan your image.

If the image is smaller than 4 x 5 inches and you would like a colored background around it, click Background in the Page Setup dialog box, then choose the color your service bureau recommends.

Photoshop to Illustrator

To export a **layer**, choose the Move tool, then drag a layer from the Photoshop image window into an Illustrator 7 image window. The layer will arrive as a 72 ppi pixel image in an outlined box.

To export a Photoshop **path**, use the Export > Path to Illustrator command (see page 176). The path does not have to be selected, though it should be a saved path, not a work path. In Illustrator, use File > Open to open the saved Photoshop path file, and use it like any other Illustrator path object. The path will arrive with its own crop marks. If you don't change them, you can save the file in the Illustrator 7 format, then Place the file in Photoshop (but don't rescale or reposition its bounding box, or you'll mess up the registration in Photoshop).

To place a Photoshop image as a **bitmap object** in Illustrator, save it in the Photoshop EPS file format in Photoshop, and use the Open command in Illustrator. Or, use Illustrator's File menu > Place command, and choose the Placed EPS option. Either way, the image will appear in an outlined box, and it can be transformed, but not edited.

You can apply some filters to a Photoshop image if it was opened as an object using the Illustrator's Open command, including the Adjust Color, Invert Color, Object Mosaic, and Photoshop plug-in filters that have been made available as plug-ins to Illustrator.

Photoshop to Painter

When you open a Photoshop image in Painter:

Photoshop **layers** will be converted into floaters in Painter and Photoshop paths will be converted into paths in Painter.

A Photoshop **layer mask** will be converted into a floater with a floater mask in Painter. If you reopen the image in Photoshop, however, the layer mask effect will become permanent and the mask itself will be deleted.

The fourth **channel** in a Photoshop file will become a mask in Painter if there were no paths in the original Photoshop file. To display the mask in Painter and force its name to appear on the Objects: P. List palette, choose the Path Adjuster tool and click in the image window or click the

If your clipping path won't print:

If your high-end printer generates a Limitcheck error when printing a document that contains a clipping path, it may be because the path contains too many points. Follow these steps to reduce the number of points on a path:

1. Activate the clipping path on the Paths palette.

2. Convert the path into a selection.

3. Delete the original clipping path, but leave the selection active.

4. Choose Make Work path from the Paths palette command menu to turn the selection into a path, entering a Tolerance value of 4–6 pixels.

5. Follow steps 2–7 on page 175 to reconvert the path into a clipping path.

third Visibility button on the P. List palette. The channel will be blank if you reopen the file in Photoshop.

If you import a Photoshop file with a transparent **background** into Painter, Painter will create a white background for it. If you reopen the image in Photoshop, it will have a new, white background layer, which will contain any brush strokes that were applied to the background in Painter.

If you apply a **blending mode** to a layer in Photoshop and then open the image in Painter, the mode effect may look different, but the original effect will reappear if you reopen the file in Photoshop.

Painter to Photoshop

You can make a round trip without losing layers or floaters. Choose File menu > Save As, then choose Photoshop 3.0 from the Type drop-down menu. If you save a Painter 4.0 file with floaters in the Photoshop 3.0 file format and then open it in Photoshop, each floater (or floater group) will be assigned its own layer. Painter shapes will also be placed on their own separate layers in Photoshop, and keep its original opacity.

If you save a Painter file with a selection path or mask group in Photoshop 3.0 format (check the Save Mask Layer box in the Save As dialog box) and then open the file in Photoshop, the mask, complete with any feathering, will appear as a mask in channel #4, and any Painter paths will appear on Photoshop's Paths palette. If the Painter image contains more than one selection path, activate the path you're planning to use as a mask in Photoshop before you save it in Painter.

Photoshop produces superior color separations than Painter because Painter doesn't read CMYK files, and because Photoshop offers greater control over print specifications.

Painter to Photoshop

The EPS format is a good choice for importing a Photoshop image into an illustration program, like Adobe Illustrator, or a page layout program, like QuarkXPress or PageMaker.

To save an image as an EPS:

1. If the image is going to be color separated from QuarkXPress or Illustrator, choose Image menu > Mode > CMYK.

2. Choose File > Save a Copy (Control-Alt-S). This command saves a flattened version of the image, and discards and any alpha channels in the file.

3. Enter a name in the File name field.

4. Choose a location in which to save the file.

5. Choose Save As: Photoshop EPS.

6. Click Save.

7. Choose Preview: TIFF (1 bit/pixel) for a grayscale preview, or choose TIFF (8 bits/pixel) for a color preview **1**.
and
For most purposes, you should choose Encoding: Binary. Binary Encoded files are smaller and process more quickly than ASCII files. However, for some applications, PostScript "clone" printers, or printing utilities that cannot handle Binary files, you'll have to choose ASCII.
and
Click OK or press Enter. The original, non-flattened version of the file will remain open.

TIP If you've changed the frequency, angle, or dot shape settings in the Halftone Screens dialog box, then check the Include Halftone Screen box.

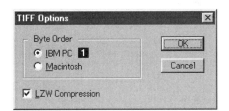

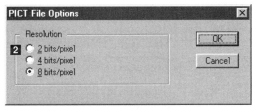

A TIFF file can be imported by QuarkXPress or PageMaker. A CMYK TIFF can be color separated from QuarkXPress.

To save an image as a TIFF:

1. Follow the first four steps on the previous page.

2. Choose Save As: TIFF.

3. *Optional:* Not all programs can import a TIFF with an alpha channel. If your target application does not, check the "Don't Include Alpha Channels" box to discard any alpha channels.

4. Click Save.

5. Click Byte Order: IBM PC **1**.

6. *Optional:* Check the LZW Compression box to reduce the file size. No image data will be lost.

7. Click OK or press Enter.

A PICT or BMP file can be opened in most drawing and multimedia applications. Choose whichever format is appropriate for your target application.

To save an image as a PICT or BMP:

1. Follow the first four steps on the previous page.

2. Choose Save As: PICT File.
or
Choose Save As: BMP File.

3. Click Save.

4. Choose a Resolution/Depth option **2**–**3**. (For an image in Grayscale mode, check 2, 4, or 8 bits/pixel.)

5. Click OK or press Enter.

TIP When saving a color image as a PICT for a multimedia application, choose a resolution of 16 bits/pixel or less.

Save as TIFF; Save as PICT

Only about 50 shades of an ink color can be printed from one plate, so print shops are sometimes asked to print a grayscale image using two or more plates instead of one to extend its tonal range. The additional plates can be gray or a color tint, and are usually used to print midtones and highlights. You can convert an image to Duotone mode in Photoshop to create a duotone (two plates), tritone (three plates), or quadtone (four plates).

The Duotones folder in the Photoshop application folder contains duotone, tritone, and quadtone curves that you can use as is or adapt for your own needs (click Load in the Duotone Options box).

NOTE: Duotone printing is very tricky, so you should ask your print shop for advice. **A duotone effect can't be proofed on a PostScript color printer.** In fact, only a press proof will give you accurate feedback.

To produce a duotone:

1. Choose Image menu > Mode > Grayscale. An image with good contrast will work best.

2. Choose Image menu > Mode > Duotone.

3. Choose Type: Duotone **1**.

4. Click the Ink 2 color square **2**. Ink 1 should be the darkest ink, and the lightest ink should be the highest ink number.

5. To choose a matching system color, like a Pantone color, click Custom. Choose from the Book pop-up menu, then type a color number or click a swatch. Subtle colors tend to look better in a duotone than bright colors.
or
To choose a process color, click Picker, then enter C, M, Y, and K percentages.

6. Click OK or press Enter.

7. For a process color, enter a name next to the color square.

8. Click the Ink 2 curve **3**.

Threes and fours

Printing a **tritone** (three inks) or a **quadtone** (four inks) requires specifying the order in which the inks will print on press. You can use the **Overprint Colors** dialog box to adjust the on-screen representation of various ink printing orders, but these settings won't affect how the image actually prints. Ask your print shop for advice about printing.

Click a color square to choose a color.

Click a curve to modify it.

Enter a name for a process color.

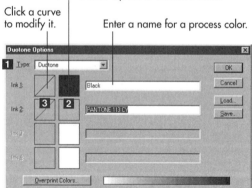

In the Duotone Options dialog box, choose Duotone from the Type drop-down menu, then click the Ink 2 color square.

The image's **highlights**

The image's **midtones**

The image's **shadows**

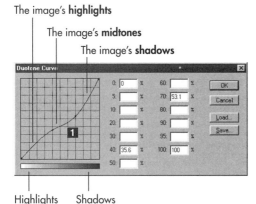

Highlights   Shadows

Reshaping the duotone curve for an ink color affects how that color is distributed among an image's highlights, midtones, and shadows. With the curve shape in screenshot above, Ink 2 will tint the image's midtones. To produce a pleasing duotone, try to distribute Ink 1 and Ink 2 in different tonal ranges (for example, black as Ink 1 in the shadow areas, somewhat in the midtones and a little bit in the highlights; and an Ink 2 color in the remaining tonal ranges—more in the midtones and light areas and less in the darks).

9. Drag the curve upward or downward in the Duotone Curve dialog box ▇. To achieve a duotone effect, the Ink 1 curve must be different from the Ink 2 curve.

10. Click OK or press Enter.

11. Click the Ink 1 curve, then repeat steps 9 and 10.

12. *Optional:* Click Save to save the current settings to use with other images.

TIP To reduce black ink in the highlights, lower the black ink (Ink 1) curve 5 percent setting to zero. To reduce color in the shadows, lower the color ink (Ink 2) curve 100 percent setting to around 85 percent.

TIP If you're using a Pantone color and you're going to output the image from an illustration or page layout program, turn on Short Pantone Names in the File > Preferences > General dialog box.

This is a great low-budget way to expand the tonal range of a grayscale image: it's still printed as a monotone (using one plate).

To print a grayscale image using a Pantone tint:

1. Open a grayscale image.

2. Choose Image menu > Mode > Duotone.

3. Choose Monotone from the Type dropdown menu.

4. Click the Ink 1 color square, then open the Custom Colors dialog box.

5. Choose the desired Pantone color, then click OK.

6. In the Duotone Options dialog box, click on the Ink 1 curve.

7. In the 100% field, enter the desired tint percentage value ▇. Leave the 0% field at 0 and all other fields blank. Click OK.

8. Click OK to close the dialog box.

9. Save the file in EPS format (see page 244).

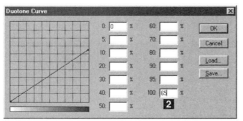

The Duotone Curve dialog box for a monotone print. The 100% field value has been lowered to the desired Pantone tint percentage.

Color Reproduction

Color reproduction basics

One of the key—and potentially problematic—issues in output is obtaining good CMYK color reproduction on an offset press. Read this section to familiarize yourself with the various stages in the output process.

The output image will resemble the image you see on screen only if the monitor is carefully calibrated for that output. Each offset press, for example, has its own settings. In order to produce consistent and predictable output, you must enter monitor and press characteristics information into Photoshop.

RGB-to-CMYK conversion

Photoshop determines how to convert an RGB image to CMYK mode and how to display a CMYK mode preview based on the current settings in the File menu > Color Settings dialog boxes, which are discussed on the following pages.

The major steps in color separation are:

■ Calibrate the monitor.

■ Enter Printing Inks and Separation settings.

■ Obtain a color proof using those settings.

■ Match the on-screen preview to the proof.

Monitor settings

Calibrating your monitor involves using either a third-party utility installed in your computer to balance the Red, Green, and Blue components on screen, or using the Gamma control panel to adjust, by eye, the color balance, the white and black areas of color, and neutral gray. See page 253 to learn more about the Gamma control panel.

Once a monitor is calibrated, you need to enter the following info in Photoshop's Monitor Setup dialog box **1**: The Gamma value used to calibrate the monitor, the White Point for that particular monitor,

Questions to ask your print shop about color separations

Color separating is an art. As a starting point, ask your print shop the following questions so you'll be able to choose the correct scan resolution and settings in the Printer Inks Setup and Separation Setup dialog boxes:

What lines per inch setting is going to be used on the press for my job? This will help you choose the appropriate scanning resolution.

What is the dot gain for my paper stock choice on that press? Allowances for dot gain can be made using the Printer Inks Setup dialog box.

Which printing method will be used on press—UCR or GCR? GCR produces better color printing and is the default choice in the Separations Setup box. (GCR stands for Gray Component Replacement, UCR stands for Undercolor Removal.)

What is the total ink limit and the black ink limit for the press? These values can also be adjusted in the Separations Setup box.

Note: Change the dot gain, GCR or UCR method, and ink limits **before** you convert your image from RGB Color mode to CMYK Color mode. If you modify any of these values after conversion, you must convert the image back to RGB Color mode, adjust the values, then reconvert to CMYK Color mode.

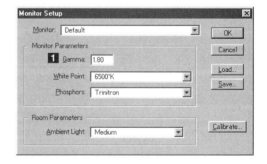

and the room (ambient) lighting around the monitor give Photoshop a clearer idea of the on-screen viewing characteristics. Check with your monitor manufacturer to choose settings for your monitor.

Print and separation settings

Another key factor in color reproduction is the type of output device to be used. In the following section, we discuss offset press output. (Online imaging issues are discussed in Chapter 20.) A monitor is an RGB device that uses light to additively blend colors. An offset press is a CMYK device that uses opaque inks to subtractively blend colors.

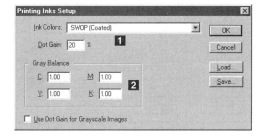

In the Printing Inks Setup dialog box, you need to enter the characteristics of the offset press 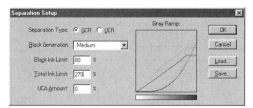, such as the ink type associated with a particular print press and the dot gain for that press. Consult with your print shop for these settings.

You can even match (calibrate) a screen image to a color proof by adjusting the values in the Gray Balance settings in this dialog box **2**. More about this later. Stay tuned.

Other characteristics of the offset press are entered into the Separation Setup dialog box **3**, but since these settings are particular for each press shop, you must consult with your press shop for this information. In short, the Separation Type tells Photoshop about the type of press used: Does the press use the GCR (gray component replacement) or UCR (undercolor removal) method, and how does the print shop handle black ink. The Black Generation amount controls how much black ink is used when translating RGB components of light into CMY inks. Adjustments must be made to prevent inks from becoming muddy when they're mixed together. Black is substituted for areas of CMY ink mixing, and how much black is substituted is determined by the Black Generation amount. Finally, each press shop uses different

3 In this Separation Setup screen shot, the Black Ink Limit and the Total Ink Limit values have been changed to values suggested by the printshop, and the graph reflects the new values.

amounts of ink coverage on each separation plate. Some shops use less than 100% maximum ink coverage for each plate. Ask your press shop for these percentage settings.

Separation tables

Once you're satisfied with a set of color proofs from a particular print shop, rather than reenter this information every time you need to do RGB-to-CMYK conversion for that shop, you can use the Separation Tables dialog box to build a table containing the Printing Inks Setup and Separation Setup settings. Click Save **2** in the Separation Tables dialog box to build a table file. Next time you output in that particular press situation, load in the custom Separation Table you created and saved for that press.

But remember, these settings affect RGB-to-CMYK image mode conversions. If you readjust any settings in the Printing Inks or Separations dialog box, you will have to reconvert your image from RGB to CMYK mode again using the new settings. Keep a copy of your image in RGB Color mode so you'll have the option to readjust and reconvert it.

Match the on-screen image to a color proof

After converting your image to CMYK Color mode, ask your output service or press shop to produce a color proof of the image using the Color Settings you just entered.

As we mentioned above, use the Gray Balance settings (Printing Inks Setup dialog box) to match the CMYK preview of an on-screen image to a proof. By matching the two images—on-screen and printed proof—you can then rely more confidently on the accuracy of Photoshop's CMYK Color preview.

Load in any custom Separation Table or reenter all the individual Setup dialog

Total Ink coverage readout

To display total ink coverage percentages on the Info palette for image pixels currently under the pointer, choose **Total Ink** from the pop-up menu next to the leftmost eyedropper on the Info palette **1**. This readout is based on the current Separation Setup settings.

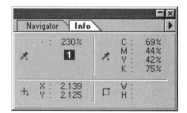

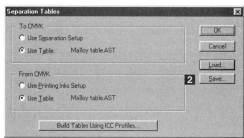

Click **Load** in the Separation Tables dialog box to load in a custom table with specific Printing Inks and Separation Setup settings.

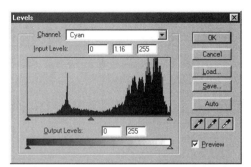

Gray balance adjustments are made to individual channels (Cyan, in this case) using the Levels dialog box. The gray midtones slider is moved to achieve a better color match between the on-screen image and a proof. Jot down the Input Levels value, since you won't be saving these dialog box settings.

File compression

To reduce the storage size of an image, use a compression program like DriveSpace or WinZip. Compression using this kind of software is non-lossy, which means the compression doesn't cause data loss.

If you don't have compression software, choose File menu > Save a Copy, choose TIFF from the Save As drop-down menu, and check the **LZW Compression** box in the TIFF Options dialog box. If you want to save the file without alpha channels, also check the Don't Include Alpha Channels box. LZW compression is non-lossy, which is good, but, and here's the rub, some applications won't import an LZW TIFF, and still other applications will import an LZW TIFF only if it doesn't contain an alpha channel.

If you're saving an image for print output, we don't recommend using the **JPEG** file format or the Compress EPS/JPEG command because JPEG compression is lossy, and additional image data is lost with each compression. The data loss may not be noticeable on screen, but it may be very noticeable on high resolution output. JPEG is more suitable for Web output.

box settings that were used to produce the proof.

Open the CMYK mode image, and adjust the overall light and dark values of the on-screen CMYK mode preview to match the proof by increasing or decreasing the Dot Gain setting in the File menu > Color Settings > Printing Inks Setup dialog box. Increasing the Dot Gain will darken the on-screen preview. Click OK to view the effect.

Next, to match the color of the monitor to the proof, with the CMYK Color mode image open and the proof in hand, open the Image menu > Adjust > Levels dialog box. Choose an individual ink color from the Channel menu and move only the Input Levels gamma slider (the gray triangle) to achieve a better color match between the two images. Repeat, if necessary, for the remaining individual ink colors. Jot down the gamma settings from the top middle field for each ink color on a piece of paper, then click Cancel. **Do not click OK** at this point—you'll **ruin** your CMYK image if you do so.

Open the File menu > Color Settings > Printing Inks Setup dialog box, enter the settings for each ink color that you jotted down from the Levels dialog box in the C, M, Y, and K Gray Balance fields, then click OK. If the original Gray Balance values are not 1.0, then multiply the new values by the old values to arrive at the correct value.

The preview of all CMYK mode images will now reflect the new Printing Inks settings, but the actual image information will only be changed if the image is converted to RGB Color mode and then back to CMYK Color mode.

Follow the instructions on this page and the next page to adjust your monitor for Photoshop. These are the first steps in monitor-to-output calibration. See the Photoshop User Guide for information about calibrating your system. You should do the Monitor Setup and Gamma adjustment before performing the color correction walk-through, which begins on page 255.

NOTE: After choosing monitor specs and making your desktop gray (instructions on the next page), adjust the brightness and contrast knobs on your monitor and do not change them (put tape on them, if necessary). Then follow instructions on the next page to adjust the Gamma.

To choose Monitor Setup options:

1. Choose File menu > Color Settings > Monitor Setup.

2. Choose your monitor name from the Monitor drop-down menu. If it's not listed, consult the documentation that was provided with your monitor to find the closest equivalent **1**.

3. Choose the manufacturer of your CRT from the Phosphors drop-down menu. This information should also be provided with your monitor.

4. Choose Low, Medium, or High from the Ambient Light drop-down menu, whichever is most applicable.

5. Click OK or press Enter.

TIP Leave the Gamma at 1.80 and the White Point at 6500°K, unless you have a specific reason to change it (if you're outputting to videotape, for example, which requires a higher gamma).

TIP The Monitor Setup affects color substitution when an image is converted from RGB Color mode to CMYK Color mode.

TIP Try to keep the light in your computer room consistent while you're working. Not so easy.

Monitor Setup Options

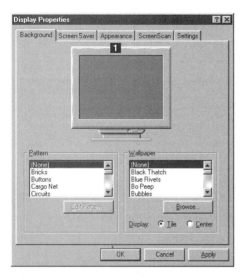

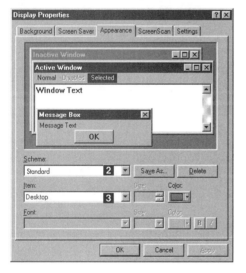

A colored Desktop can influence your perception of colors in a Photoshop image. Make the Desktop gray to alleviate this problem.

To make the Desktop gray:

1. Click the Start button on the Taskbar > Settings > Control Panels.

2. Double-click the Display icon.

3. Choose the Appearance tab **1**.

4. Choose the Windows Standard scheme **2**.

5. Choose Desktop from the Item drop-down list **3**.

6. Choose a gray color from the Color drop-down list.

7. Click OK.

8. Choose File menu > Exit.

Careful adjustment of the Gamma sliders will produce a neutral on-screen gray and will hopefully remove any color cast, if there is one, from your screen.

To adjust the Gamma:

1. Choose File menu > Color Settings > Monitor Setup.

2. Click the Calibrate button.

3. Compare the black, midtone, and white of the Gamma calibration bar grays to a photographic progressive grayscale bar.

4. Click the White Pt button, then move the White Point sliders until the right-most square on the calibration bar matches the photographic bar.

5. Click the Black Pt button, then move the Black Pt sliders until the dark calibration squares look neutral.

6. Click the Balance button, then move the Balance sliders until the gray calibration squares look neutral.

7. Move the Gamma Adjustment slider to blend the light and dark bars.

8. *Optional:* Click Save Settings, then rename and save the Gamma settings.

If you convert an image to CMYK Color mode, its colors are automatically forced into printable gamut. In certain cases, however, you may want to see which areas are out-of-gamut (non-printable) in RGB, and change some of them manually. In the following instructions, you'll choose the Gamut Warning command to display out-of-gamut colors in gray, and use the Sponge tool to desaturate those areas to bring them into printable gamut.

NOTE: The Gamut Warning command uses the current separation table settings, so enter your Setup info first (see page 249).

To correct out-of-gamut colors:

1. Convert your image to RGB Color or Lab Color mode.

2. Choose View menu > Gamut Warning.

3. *Optional:* To select and restrict color changes to the out-of-gamut areas, choose Select menu > Color Range, choose Out of Gamut from the Select drop-down menu **1**, then click OK.

4. Choose the Sponge tool. ⊛

5. Choose Desaturate from the drop-down menu on the Toning Tools Options palette, and choose a Pressure percentage.

6. Click the Brushes tab, then click a tip.

7. Choose a target layer.

8. Drag across the gray, out-of-gamut areas **2**. As they become desaturated, they will redisplay in color. Don't desaturate colors too much, though, or they'll get muddy. (To turn off the Gamut Warning, choose View menu > Gamut Warning again.)

TIP To preview the image in CMYK in a second window, choose View menu > New View. With the new window active, choose View menu > CMYK Preview. Resize and move the new window so both windows are visible.

Desaturate another way

You can use the Image menu > Adjust > Hue/Saturation command instead of the Sponge tool to correct out-of-gamut colors in the selected areas. Move the Saturation slider to the left to desaturate.

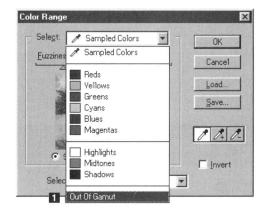

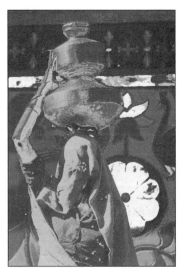

2 For illustration purposes, out-of-gamut colors in this image are shown in white instead of the usual gray.

A color correction walk-through

The following is a walk-through session to color correct an image using the Levels, Curves, Color Balance, and Unsharp Mask commands. Adjustment layers are used whenever possible so you'll be able to easily readjust the image tone and color later, if your heart desires.

If your image is intended for on-screen output, do all your correction in RGB color mode. If you're working with a CMYK scan, do all your correction in CMYK Color mode. Adobe recommends using RGB color mode for color correction on output intended for separation, converting the image to CMYK Color mode using the proper separation setup settings, and then fine-tuning in CMYK Color mode after you get your color proofs back.

NOTE: Make sure your monitor is calibrated before performing the following steps.

The basic steps

■ Scan or acquire a Photo CD image into Photoshop

■ Set the Black and White points

■ Limit tonal values

■ Adjust the neutral gray

■ Color balance

■ Perform Selective Color adjustments (optional)

■ Unsharp Mask

✏ The first step

Open a single layer, flattened version of an image in RGB or CMYK Color mode in Photoshop. Use Save a Copy to create a flattened version of the image, if necessary.

On the Info palette, press the leftmost dropper icon and choose RGB Color **1**, and press the rightmost dropper icon and choose CMYK Color. Leave the palette visible and accessible for the following instructions.

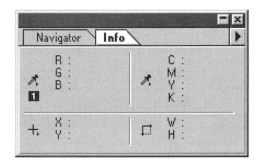

The first step in color correction is to set the black and white points (the darkest shadow and lightest highlight values) to preserve image detail in those areas.

✋ Set the black and white points by eye using Threshold mode (method 1)

1. On the Layers palette, activate the Background of an RGB Color image.

2. Choose Image menu > Adjust > Levels.

3. Uncheck the Preview box, then Alt-drag the black Input slider until small sections of the shadows of the image appear on the white area of the image window ▊.

4. Alt-drag the white Input slider until small sections of the highlights of the image appear on the black area of the image window ▊.

5. Move the gray midtone Input slider (don't hold down Alt) to darken or lighten the midtones.

6. Jot down on paper all the Input readouts that are displayed at the top of the dialog box, check the Preview box, then click Cancel.

7. Activate the Background, Control-click the Create New Layer button, choose Type: Levels, then click OK.

8. Enter all the values noted in step 7, above, into the appropriate Input Levels fields, then click OK.

9. Activate the Background, then set the Info palette readouts to Grayscale. Pass the cursor over the darkest and lightest areas of the image. If the darkest K value falls between 95 and 100%, double-click the adjustment layer to open the Levels dialog box, then move the black Input slider outward. If the lightest K value falls between 5 and 0% white, move the white Input slider outward to lower the contrast. This will lower the percentage values for the Black and White points. Click OK.

▊ Alt-dragging the **black** Input Levels slider reveals the **darkest** areas of the image first.

▊ Alt-dragging the **white** Input Levels slider reveals the **lightest** areas of the image first.

Threshold mode not working?

To use the Threshold mode, first of all, your monitor must be set to 256 colors. Choose this color depth setting in Control Panels > Display > Settings. Second, in order to preview these changes in the Levels dialog box, your video card must be of the type that allows for color table animation. If it isn't, you can acquire a color table animation extension for your video card that will enable you to use the Threshold mode feature.

Set the Black and White Points

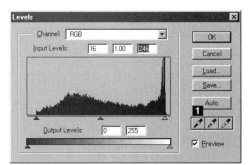

Double-click the black or white point eyedropper icon to open the Color Picker dialog box, then set target values for the black and white points in the image.

A detail of the **Color Picker** dialog box. The HSB fields have been set to values specified by the press shop for the black point value in an image. Clicking now with the black point eyedropper in the Levels dialog box will lighten the darkest areas of the image to 95% black.

✒ Set the black and white points via the Levels eyedroppers using target values (method 2)

1. Ask your press shop which target values should be entered for the black and white points.

2. To create an adjustment layer above the Background, Control-click the Create New Layer button, choose Type: Levels, then click OK.

3. Double-click the black point eyedropper icon **1**.

4. Click in the area of the image that you want to be the darkest—but not too dark, so some detail is retained. Display the rulers, then drag guides from the vertical and horizontal rulers to that spot so you can quickly relocate it.

5. In the Color Picker, enter the C, M, Y, and K values your press shop recommends or enter 0, 0, and 5, respectively, for HSB values **2**, then click OK.

6. Click the black point eyedropper icon.

7. Click on the same pixel area you clicked on in step 4, above. Use the Info palette and the guides to locate the same pixel values.

8. Double-click the white point (third) eyedropper icon.

9. Click in an area of the image that you want to be the lightest, without sacrificing too much detail. (Set up guides to easily relocate the same spot.) In the CMYK area of the Color Picker, enter C, M, Y, and K values your press shop recommends, or in the HSB area of the picker, enter 0 for H and S and 95 for B, then click OK.

10. Click the White point eyedropper icon. Click on the same pixel area you clicked on in step 9, and find the same

(Continued on the next page)

pixel values using the Info palette and the guides.

11. Move the gray midtone Input slider to darken or lighten the midtones.

12. Click OK.

TIP You can also set target black and white values using the eyedroppers in the Curves dialog box.

TIP Be careful if you're viewing pixel values in the Info palette with the Levels dialog box closed, because the adjustment layer will show the current RGB values on the Info palette, but only the current K value will display in the CMYK part of the Info palette. If the Background is active and the adjustment layer is visible, the Info palette will display all the current pixel readouts.

If you bypassed the steps for setting the Black and White points or were not satisfied with the resulting high and low pixel values, you can further limit the tonal values in the image via the Levels dialog box.

🖎 Limit tonal values

1. Open the Info palette.

2. You can use the existing Levels adjustment layer, or Control-click the New Layer icon to create an adjustment layer above the Background, choose Type: Levels, then click OK. You can perform adjustments on separate adjustment layers, and then show/hide them individually, or show them all together.

3. Move both Output sliders inward slightly to soften the darkest black and lightest white in the image ▣. Or enter 12 and 244, respectively. Use the Info palette to confirm that the adjustments fall within the percentage range your press shop specified (but remember that the Levels dialog box fields don't work in percentage values), then click OK.

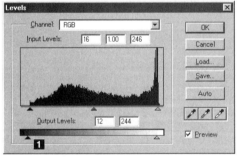

Move the black and white Output Levels sliders inward slightly to tone down the darkest black and lightest white in the image.

Limit tonal values using Curves

To limit tonal values using the Curves dialog box, click on the grayscale bar, if necessary, to make it display percentage values, then drag the low point of the curve upward five percentage points, to 5%, and drag the high point of the curve downward five percentage points, to 95%.

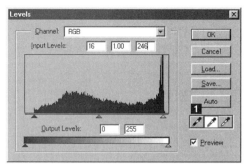

After clicking the gray point eyedropper icon in the Levels dialog box, pass the pointer over the image to find an area with similar RGB readouts.

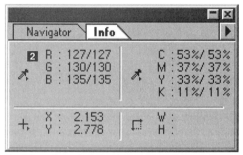

The **Info** palette showing the RGB breakdown of pixels under the pointer. While the Levels dialog box is open, two RGB readouts are displayed: before Levels adjustment and after Levels adjustment. (To reset the Info palette readouts, click on the palette's eyedropper icon and choose RGB color from the drop-down menu.)

✏ Adjust the neutral gray

1. Open the Info palette.

2. Use the existing Levels adjustment layer, or Control-click the Create New Layer button to create an adjustment layer above the Background, choose Type: Levels, then click OK.

3. Click the gray eyedropper **1**.

4. Note the RGB values on the Info palette as you pass the cursor over the image. Reset the palette readouts, if necessary.

5. When you find an area with close to equal R, G, and B readouts **2**, in the range from 100 to 160 (like R=120, G=115, B=110), click on that area with the gray eyedropper.

The overall image color balance will readjust based on the area you clicked on, but the brightness level in that area won't change. Click elsewhere if you want to readjust the neutral gray balance. The Info palette readout should now display similar R, G, and B values.

6. Click OK.

If the image still has an undesirable color cast, you can use the Color Balance or Curves command to correct it. The Color Balance dialog box is easier to use, since it displays the relationship of color opposites, and works on the Shadows, Midtones, and Highlights areas of an image via separate groups of sliders, but you can't use it to adjust individual color channels. Using the Curves command, you can perform adjustments on an individual color channel or on all the channels together, so it provides a greater degree of control over an individual color's adjustment, but the curves are a little tricky to manipulate. Take your pick.

✏ Color balance the image

Control-click the Create New Layer icon to create an adjustment layer above the Background, then follow the steps on page 124 (Color Balance) or page 126 (Curves).

If, after obtaining color proofs, there's still a lingering color imbalance in part of the image, you can correct that color component via the Selective Color command, which adjusts the amount of ink used on press for individual process colors. You can even change the amount of a process color used in specified color combinations (the amount of cyan used in green, for example) without affecting the percentage of that color used in other color combinations.

☜ Perform selective color adjustments

1. Make sure the image is in CMYK mode.

2. Flatten the image to adjust the whole image, then choose Image menu > Adjust > Selective Color.
or
Create an adjustment layer using Type: Selective Color.

3. Choose the color you want to adjust from the Colors drop-down menu **1**.

4. Click Relative to add or subtract a percentage of a process color from the selected color. Using this method, other colors will adjust in tandem with the color you're currently adjusting, but you can't tell which ones.

Click Absolute to add or subtract an exact process color amount from the selected color. Use this method to adjust individual color components precisely according to your print shop's specifications.

5. Enter the percentages in the Cyan, Magenta, Yellow, and/or Black fields that your print shop specifies, or adjust those sliders.

☜ Unsharp Mask

Apply the Unsharp Mask filter to the Background (see pages 44–45). Don't merge the adjustment layer into the Background yet.

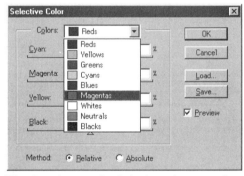

1 In the Selective Color dialog box, choose an ink color from the **Colors** drop-down menu, then move the sliders to adjust the printing percentage for that color.

WEB & MULTIMEDIA 20

Visit Peachpit Press' web site: http://www.peachpit.com.

ARTWORK BY JOHN GRIMES

THIS CHAPTER covers the preparation of Photoshop images for use in multimedia (on-screen) and on the World Wide Web (online). Conversion to Indexed Color mode is covered first, then, using Photoshop images in Director, and finally, saving images for viewing on the Web.

Some multimedia and video programs and some computer systems will not import a Photoshop image containing more than 256 colors (8-bit color). You can reduce the number of colors in an image's color table by converting it to Indexed Color mode, or to optimize its display on the Web.

NOTE: Converting a multi-layer image to Indexed Color mode will cause its layers to be flattened. Use the Save As command to work on a copy of the image.

To convert an image to Indexed Color mode:

1. Make sure the image is in RGB Color mode.

2. Choose Image menu > Mode > Indexed Color.

3. Choose a Palette **1**:

You can choose Exact if the image contains 256 or fewer colors. No colors will be eliminated.

Choose Adaptive for the best color substitution.

Choose System (Macintosh) if you're going to export the file to an application that only accepts the Macintosh default palette.

Choose System (Windows) if you're planning to export the image to the Windows platform.

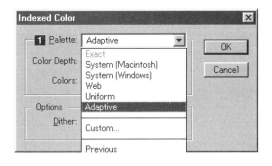

(Continued on the followimg page)

Choose Web if the image is intended for Web viewing. This option limits the Color Table to only colors available in the most commonly used Web browsers.

To create your own palette, choose Custom, click OK, then edit the Color Table, if you want. (Click Save if you want to save the table for later use. Click Load to load in a previously saved table.) Click OK and skip the remaining steps.

Choose Previous to reuse the custom palette from the last used Custom or Adaptive palette option.

4. If you chose the Adaptive palette, you can choose a Color Depth to specify the number of colors in the table **1**. If you choose 4 bits/pixel, the table will contain 16 colors; if you choose 8 bits/pixel, the table will contain 256 colors. The fewer bits/pixel in the image, the more dithered it will be. You can also enter your own value in the Colors field.

5. Choose Dither: None, Diffusion, or Pattern. None will cause areas that contain sharp color transitions to appear posterized, so it's an option that's best suited for flat-color images. Diffusion may produce the closest color substitution, but it can also produce a dotty effect in those areas. The Pattern option, which adds pixels in a more structured arrangement, is available only when the System (Macintosh) palette is used (see step 3).

6. Click OK or press Enter.

TIP If you want to control which colors will be chosen for the palette, create a selection or selections that contain the colors you want to be in the palette before converting your image to Indexed Color mode, then choose the Adaptive palette for step 3 on the previous page.

Painting in Indexed Color mode
In Indexed Color mode, the Pencil, Airbrush, and Paintbrush tools produce only fully opaque strokes. For those tools, leave the Opacity slider on the Options palette at 100%. Dissolve is the only tool mode that will produce a different stroke at a lower opacity.

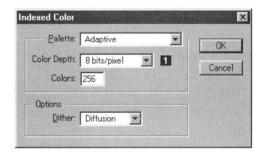

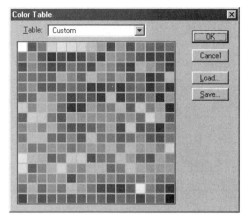

1 Click a color in the Color Table dialog box, or drag across a series of colors.

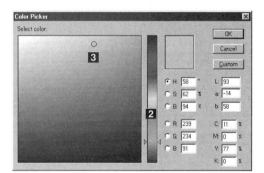

To edit an Indexed Color table:

1. Choose Image menu > Mode > Color Table. The Color Table will display all the picture's colors.

2. Click on a color to be replaced **1**.
or
Drag Select a bunch of colors by dragging across them.

3. Move the slider up or down on the vertical bar to choose a hue **2**, then click a variation of that hue in the large rectangle **3**.

4. Click OK to exit the Color Picker.

5. Click OK or press Enter.

TIP You can convert a Grayscale picture directly to Indexed Color mode and then modify its color table to add arbitrary color to the image. Try the Black Body or Spectrum table.

For the best results, choose a warm first color and a cool last color, or vice versa, for steps 3 and 5 below.

To reduce an Indexed Color table to two colors and the shades between them:

1. Choose Image menu > Mode > Color Table.

2. Drag across the Color Table from the first swatch in the upper left corner to the last swatch in the lower right corner.

3. Choose a first color from the Color Picker: move the slider up or down on the vertical bar to choose a hue **2**, then click a variation of that hue in the large rectangle **3**.

4. Click OK.

5. Choose a last color from the Color Picker.

6. Click OK to exit the Color Picker.

7. Click OK or press Enter.

Edit an Indexed Color Table

You can create a painterly effect by generating an Indexed Color image from an RGB Color image, and then pasting the Index Color image back into the RGB Color picture.

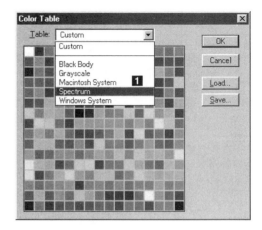

To recolor an RGB image:

1. If the image is not in RGB mode, choose Image menu > Mode > RGB Color.

2. Follow the steps on pages 261–262 to convert the image to Indexed Color mode.

3. Choose Image menu > Mode > Color Table.

4. Choose Table: Spectrum **1**.

5. Click OK or press Enter.

6. Choose Select menu > All.

7. Choose Edit menu > Copy.

8. Choose File menu > Revert.

9. Click Revert to restore the image to RGB Color mode.

10. Choose Edit menu > Paste to paste the Indexed Color image onto a new layer.

11. Double-click the new layer name **2**.

12. Choose from the Mode drop-down menu **3**. Try Dissolve (at below 80% opacity), Multiply, Soft Light, Difference, or Color.

13. *Optional:* Change the Opacity percentage to reveal more of the original image.

14. *Optional:* Move the black Underlying slider to the right to restore shadows from the underlying layer.
and/or
Move the white Underlying slider to the left to restore highlights from the underlying layer.
and/or
To restore midtones, Alt-drag to split either slider.

15. Click OK or press Enter.

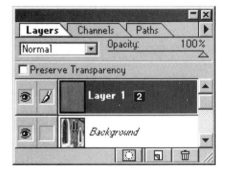

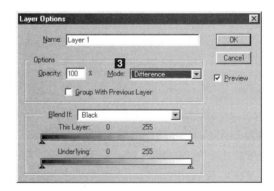

Recolor an RGB Image

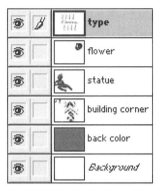

The initial composition of the Director frame in the illustration below was developed using Photoshop's layers (left). Each Photoshop **layer** became a separate **cast member** in Director.

A frame from a Director movie of an interactive map. Each street name is a button link to another point in the movie.

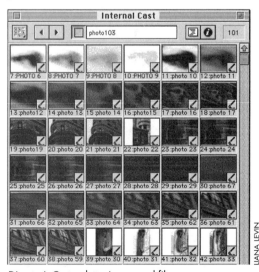

Director's Cast palette. Image and filter sequences were composed using Photoshop layers and then copy-and-pasted onto Director's Cast palette.

From Photoshop to Director

Bitmap imagery, button shapes, bitmap type, and even some transitions can be developed in Photoshop to use in Director, Macromedia's multimedia application. You can use Photoshop's Layers palette like a storyboard to develop an image sequence. Stack, hide, and show picture elements on individual layers, then use each layer as an individual cast member in Director. Assembling an image via layers in Photoshop is like using the Score in Director to assemble cast members on the Stage.

Ways to use the Layers palette as a storyboard

■ Show and hide layers in a sequence to preview how you want those objects to appear or disappear in Director.

■ Move layers in the image window via the Move tool to test animated motion.

■ Lower or increase a layer's opacity to preview a fade-out/fade-in effect.

■ To maximize your animation flexibility, select the various elements of a one-layer image, then copy-and-paste them onto individual layers. Each element could become a separate cast member in Director.

■ Use a layer's pixels as a separate cast member in Director. Control-click on a layer name (not the Background) to select all the pixels on that layer, and use Edit menu > Copy to copy the pixels to the Clipboard. In Director, choose a cast member window on the Cast palette, then choose Edit menu > Paste Bitmap. The Photoshop pixel imagery will become bitmap imagery in Director, but it may be slightly less smooth in color areas.

You could also save the Photoshop file in the .PCT (PICT) or .BMP format (choose 16 Bits/pixel) and use Director's Import command to load it onto the Cast palette. A major disadvantage of this method: it flattens all the layers. In Director's Import dialog box, use the appropriate format to import the image.

NOTE: Importing imagery into Director in a non-bitmap format can produce a small file size, but you can't edit the cast member, you can't apply Xtras filters to it, and you may not be able to drop white out using the ink effect of Background Transparent for non-type objects.

RGB vs. Indexed Color images

Either method you use to import imagery from Photoshop into Director—using the copy and paste method or saving a file as a .PCT or .BMP in Photoshop and importing it in Director—will produce an RGB bitmap file with a 16-bit color depth, which is overly large. To find out the file size of a selected cast member, click the info icon on the Cast palette in Director. Use Transform Bitmap to reduce the size of the cast member to 8-bit to speed up the movie's playback.

To reduce the size of the Director bitmap, in Photoshop, you can convert the RGB file to Indexed Color mode using the System palette (Windows) and an 8-bit or lower color depth resolution.

If you use the Adaptive palette, each Photoshop Indexed Color file that you import into Director will arrive with its own color palette. Loading multiple cast members with assorted palettes can slow the movie playback. Use the Copy and Paste option when you have a small number of Indexed Color files to import, and use the File > Import option if you have a large number of Indexed Color files to import that don't have to be edited in Director. Remember to use the appropriate format in the Import dialog box.

While you can use Director to transform a bitmap RGB image from Photoshop and lower its color depth, you'll achieve better

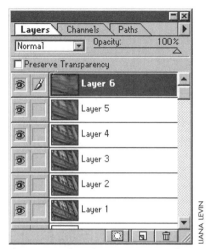

The Layers palette showing a Motion Blur filter sequence. Each layer was copy/pasted into Director as a separate cast member.

This 50K image was saved as an RGB PICT in Photoshop, pasted as Bitmap into Director, and then reduced to 8-bit depth in Director. Note the graininess in the sky.

This 150K image was imported as .PCT and kept at 16-bit depth. It has smooth tone transitions, but it has a larger file size than the image above.

1 This image was converted to Indexed Color mode (8-bit depth) in Photoshop and then pasted into Director as Bitmap, and it's a 50K file. The sky is smooth in this smaller size image, like the 150K image on the previous page.

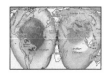
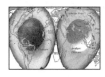
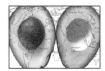
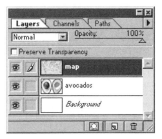

2 This illustration shows a few of the twenty steps that are used to gradually lower the opacity of the map layer. For each opacity level, the Save a Copy command was used to save a flattened copy of the original.

results if you do this in Photoshop via Indexed Color mode **1**.

Creating transitions using transparency

In some multimedia applications, Director 5, for one, you have the option to lower a sprite's opacity. Fade-outs and fade-ins can be created in Photoshop for any object on its own layer above the Background. Follow these steps to create exportable, transparent objects using Photoshop for an application in which you can't change opacities. Create a new document with a white Background, and drag-and-drop or copy-and-paste the chosen object onto its own layer above the Background. With the layer containing the object active, save a flattened version of the image in the .PCT or .BMP format using the File menu > Save a Copy command. You can create a new folder for the series of files you'll be saving **2**.

In the original two-layer document that will remain open, lower the topmost layer's opacity to 95%, and save the image again in the new folder in the .PCT or .BMP format using the Save a Copy command. Repeat these steps to create each separate cast member for the transition, lowering the opacity of the topmost layer each time by 5 or 10 percent. In the multimedia application, use the Import command to load the whole series of files.

How to copy a pixel object with an anti-aliased edge into Director

Director displays an object's anti-aliased edges with a white or colored halo, which will be noticeable if the background behind the object is any color other than white. The halo will also be noticeable if the object moves across a background that isn't uniform or that changes gradually.

This halo problem won't arise if you Import as .PCT to Director for type created in Photoshop. To avoid this problem when using Copy/Paste, select an object in Photoshop without its anti-aliased edge, Control-click on a layer name to select the object, then zoom in to at least 200% view so you can really see the object's edge. Choose Select menu > Modify > Contract and contract the selection by 1 or 2 pixels to remove the anti-aliased edge 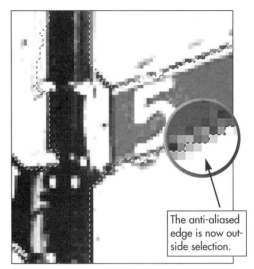. Finally, copy the object selection and paste it into Director. A soft-edged shape, like a shadow, will have a dotty dissolve along its edge when it's pasted as Bitmap in Director.

Director and Photoshop filters

Photoshop compatible plug-in filters are now accessable from within Director 5. To use them, make a copy of the Filters folder (Photoshop folder > Plug-ins > Filters), then place it in the Xtras folder within the Director folder. Make sure the Photoshop Filters file was also installed in the Program folder > Macromedia > Dir 5.0 > Dir532 > Xtras folder.

The filters are accessed via the Xtras menu > Filter Bitmap and/or Xtras menu > Auto Filter, and only work on Bitmap cast members.

As of this writing the Gallery Effects filters were working within Director 5, but the new Effects filters were not.

The anti-aliased edge is now outside selection.

1 After using the Magic Wand tool to select the white background around the signpost and then inversing the selection, some of the original anti-aliased edge remained. Select menu > Modify > Contract (by one pixel) was used shrink the selection inward.

Two pasted bitmap cast members in Director 5. The member on the left was copied without contracting the selection in Photoshop. The member on the right was copied after contracting the selection in Photoshop to remove its halo.

Four golden rules for Web image creation

- Let the image **content**—whether it's flat color or continuous-tone—determine which **file format** you use.

- Use as **low** a **pixel size** of the image as is practical, balancing the file size with aesthetics (number of colors). And remember the fail-safe option for flat-color images for viewing on both Mac and Windows browsers: Load the Indexed Color Web palette onto the Swatches palette.

- Try reducing the image's **color depth**.

- View your Web image through a **Web browser** on computers other than your own so you can see how quickly it actually downloads and how good (or bad) it looks.

Photoshop to the World Wide Web

The basic formula for outputting a Photoshop image for on-line viewing may seem straightforward: Design the image in RGB mode, and save it in the file format used by Web browsers (the applications that combine text, images, and HTML code into a viewable page on the World Wide Web). However, when you load and view an image via a Web browser, you may be disappointed to find that not all colors or blends display well on the Web, and your image may take an unacceptably long time to download and render, which is a function of its storage size. If an image looks overly dithered (grainy and dotty), or was subject to unexpected color substitutions, or takes too long to view on a Web page, it means your design is not outputting well.

Four important issues that you'll need to address for on-line output are discussed on the following pages: the pixel size of the image, the color palette, the color depth, and the file format (GIF or JPEG).

Image size

In order to calculate the appropriate image size for your image, you must know beforehand your intended viewers' monitor size and modem speed. In most cases, you should be designing your image for a 13-inch monitor, the most common monitor size, and a 14.4 kbps modem, the most common modem speed. By mid-1997, 28.8 kbps will be the most common modem speed.

The maximum size of an image that can be viewed on a 13-inch monitor is 480 pixels high by 640 pixels wide. The Web browser window will display within these parameters, so your maximum image size will occupy only a portion of the browser window—about 8 inches high (570 pixels) by 7 inches wide (500 pixels).

The image resolution only needs to be 96 ppi, which is the per-square-inch resolution of an IBM PC monitor.

Assuming dimensions of, say, 500 by 400 pixels (7 by 6 inches), a flattened image in the PICT format will be about 600K, according to its Document Sizes reading on the Info bar in the lower left corner of the image window in Photoshop. This size value, however, reflects how much RAM is occupied when the image is opened in Photoshop. The same file saved in the GIF or JPEG file format will be much smaller due to the compression schemes built into these formats.

To determine a file's actual storage size, highlight the file name in the Explorer, then right-click on the file name and choose Properties. This, by the way, is a more accurate measure of a file's storage size than the View > Details readout in the Explorer.

The degree to which a GIF or JPEG file format compresses depends on how compressable the image is. Both formats cause a small reduction in image quality, but it's worth the size reduction tradeoff, because your image will download faster on the Web. A file size of about 50K traveling on a 14.4 kbps modem with a one second per kilobyte download rate will take about a minute to download, about 30 seconds on a 28.8 kbps modem. (Is this a test question?)

A document with a flat background color and a few flat color shapes will compress a great deal (expect a file size in the range of 20 to 50K). A large document (over 100K) with many color areas, textures, or patterns (an Add Noise texture covering most of the image, for example) won't compress nearly as much. Continuous-tone, photographic images may compress less than flat color images when you use the GIF format. If you posterize a continuous-tone image down to somewhere between four and eight levels, the resulting file size will be similar to that of a flat color image, but you will have lost the continuous color transitions in the bargain. JPEG is the better format choice for a photographic-type image.

Create a browser window layer

Take a screen shot of your browser window, open the file in Photoshop, and paste it into a Web design document as your bottommost layer. Now you can design for that specific browser window's dimensions. (Thanks to Darren Roberts for this hot tip.)

Size comparisons of GIFs

20K GIF, from a 5-level posterized image.

120K GIF, from a continuous-tone image.

To summarize, if an image must be large (500 x 400 pixels or larger), ideally, it should contain large areas of only a few flat colors. If you want the image to be more intricate in color and shape, restrict its size to only a section of the Web browser window.

By the way, patterned imagery that completely fills the background of the browser window is usually created using a tiling method in a Web page creation program or using HTML code.

GIF: the great compromise

GIF is an 8-bit file format, which means a GIF image can contain a maximum of 256 colors. Since a majority of Web users have 8-bit monitors, which can display a maximum of 256 colors, not the thousands or millions of colors that make images look pleasing to the eye, GIF is the standard format to use, and a good choice for images that contain flat color areas and shapes with well-defined edges, like type.

To prepare an image for the GIF format and to see how the image will truly look when viewed via the browser, set your monitor's resolution to 256 colors (not Thousands or Millions), choose File menu > Preferences > Display and Cursors, check the Use Diffusion Dither box, then click OK.

Your color choices for a GIF image should be based on what a Web browser palette can display. Most browser palettes are 8-bit, which means they can display only 256 colors. Colors that aren't on the palette are simulated by dithering, a display technique that intermixes color pixels to simulate other colors. To prevent unexpected color substitutions or dithering, make sure you use the browser palette for your image. Color substitutions are particularly noticeable in flat color areas, and can make you want to disown an image.

Using the GIF89a Export command, you can create an adaptive palette using the

GIF

most common colors in the image—instead of just the colors in the system palette. This concentrates the range of 256 colors to those that are most needed in the image, which helps preserve image quality. Unfortunately, this adaptive palette probably won't match the browser's palette exactly. What to do?! Read on.

Photoshop's Web palette

A more fail-safe approach is to use Photoshop's Web palette, which you can choose if you convert an image to Indexed Color mode. Here's the Web palette's built-in guarantee: colors in the image will display properly on the current browsers on both the Macintosh and Windows platforms. Here's the rub: In order to create a palette that works on both platforms, since the Mac and Windows browser palettes share only 216 out of 256 possible colors, your image will be reduced to 216 colors, even less than in the GIF format. Don't distress. This is a small loss in a continuous-tone image, and it will actually lower its file size. Ready to sign up?

To create a Web palette:

1. Open an image, and if it's not already in RGB Color mode, convert it now.

2. Choose Image menu > Mode > Indexed Color.

3. Choose Palette: Web **1**.

4. Click OK.

5. Choose Image menu > Mode > Color Table.

6. Click Save.

7. Choose a location for and enter a name for the Web color table, click Save, then Click OK.

8. Choose Replace Swatches from the Swatches palette command menu.

9. Locate and highlight the Web table you just saved, then click Open. The swatches will now be the 216 colors common to both Macintosh and

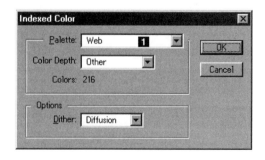

Windows Web browsers. Use only those swatches when you choose flat colors for your Web image.

TIP If you want to apply a gradient fill to a large area of your image and you plan to use the GIF format, create a top-to-bottom gradient. Top-to-bottom gradients produce smaller file sizes than left-to-right or diagonal gradients.

Color depth

If you lower an image's color depth, you will reduce the actual number of colors it contains, which will in turn reduce its file size and speed up its download time on the Web. You can reduce the number of colors in an 8-bit image to fewer than the 256 colors it contained originally in the Indexed Color dialog box or the GIF89a Export dialog box. By choosing the Adaptive palette option, you'll have the ability to reduce the number of colors in the palette and, thus, in the image.

Photoshop provides previews for both Indexed Color and GIF89a exports, so you can test how an image will look with fewer colors. Color reduction may produce dithered edges and duller colors, but you'll get the reduction in file size that you need. Always preview the image at 100% view to evaluate color quality, by the way.

Color depth (and thus, file size) can also be greatly reduced by first using the Hue/Saturation command to colorize the image and make it monotone and then reducing the number of colors substantially (to as low as 4-bit), which won't diminish the quality of the already monotone image.

GIF89a Export

Use the GIF89a format if you require transparency (you want to mask out the image's background or a portion of the image itself) and interlacing (the image displays in progressively greater detail as it downloads onto the Web page). Transparent GIF is a good choice for an image that will display

Color depth

Number of colors	Bit depth
256	8
128	7
64	6
32	5
16	4
8	3
4	2
2	1

Color Depth; GIF89a Export

on a Web page that has a non-uniform background pattern.

To prepare an RGB image for the Web using GIF89a Export:

1. Choose File menu > Export > GIF89a Export.

2. Choose Palette: Adaptive **1**.
and
Choose the number of colors (color depth) from the Colors drop-down menu, or enter a specific number.

3. Click Preview to preview the image using the present palette and color depth settings. You can drag the image in the preview window, if you like, and you can also zoom in or out using the zoom tool in the dialog box. Click to zoom in, Alt-click to zoom out.

4. Click OK to close the preview window.

5. Try to further lower the color depth level, previewing the results, to see if a lower color depth is tolerable.

6. Leave the Interlaced box checked if you want to display the image in progressively greater detail on the Web page. Uncheck this option if the image contains small type, because interlacing can cause a longer wait for the type to become sharp enough to read.

7. If you're dissatisfied with the image quality, hold down Alt and click Reset to restore the original export settings, then readjust the settings.

8. Click OK when you're satisfied (or as satisfied as you're gonna get) with the GIF export preview.

9. Choose a location in which to save the file, enter a name for the file, then click Save.

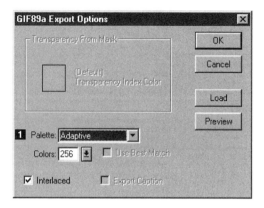

GIF9a Export

The original image.

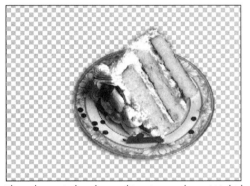

The cake copied and pasted into its own layer. We hid all the other layers before saving in the GIF format.

To create a transparent GIF:

NOTE: For a one-layer image, do all the following steps. For an image on its own transparent layer, start with step 4.

1. Select the part of the image you want to keep and be non-transparent. If you want to produce a soft-edged transition to transparency, feather the selection using a low value (1 to 3 pixels). Feathering will prevent the fringe of pixels on the edges of areas next to the selection from appearing on the background of your Web page. Don't use feathering if you're selecting a hard-edged, flat color image. A high feathering value will produce noticeable halos along the edge of the image when it's viewed through a browser.

2. Choose Edit menu > Copy.

3. Choose Edit menu > Paste. The imagery will appear on its own layer.

4. Hide any layers that you don't want to be visible in the final GIF image, and also hide the Background, even if it's all white.

5. Choose File menu > Export > GIF89a Export.

6. Choose Palette: Adaptive, and click Preview to preview the GIF file.

7. Try lowering the number of colors via the Colors drop-down menu or by entering a value.

8. Preview again to evaluate the image quality with a lower color depth.

9. The Transparency Index Color—which is the color for transparent areas—is set to the Netscape background color by default. To choose your own color for the transparent areas, click on the Transparency Index Color box, choose a new color, then click OK. This color will only be visible on a large feathered edge when the image is viewed in the browser.

GIF89a Export

If you want your image to fade or to appear as an irregular shape on a flat color area, create two layers in your Photoshop document, one that contains a flat color chosen with the Web palette loaded into the Swatches palette and one that contains the image with a soft, feathered edge or that has an irregular shape. Hide all the other layers except these two. Use the GIF89a Export command, but don't change the default Transparency color, since transparency isn't created with this type of GIF.

If you're planning to change the background on your Web page using a large flat color background image or via HTML code, though, you must make the Transparency Index Color box match the background the GIF will appear on top of. Otherwise, default gray will display in the soft edge areas of a large feathered edge (yech).

JPEG: the sometimes solution

The JPEG format may be a better choice for preserving color fidelity if your image is continuous tone (contains gradations of color or is photographic) and it's aimed toward viewers who have 24-bit monitors, which have the capacity to display millions of colors.

A JPEG plus: it can compress a 24-bit image to as small a file as the GIF format can compress an 8-bit image.

JPEG's shortcomings: First, a JPEG file has to be decompressed when it's downloaded for viewing on a Web page, which takes time. Secondly, JPEG is not a good choice for flat-color images or type, because its compression methods tend to produce artifacts along the well-defined edges of these kinds of images. And third, not all Web viewers use 24-bit monitors, and a JPEG image will be dithered on an 8-bit monitor, though dithering in a continuous-tone image is less noticeable than in an image that contains flat colors.

You can lower your monitor's setting to 8-bit to preview what the image will look

To match colors between Photoshop and other applications

If you try to mix a color in Photoshop using the same RGB values as a particular color used in Director or Netscape Navigator, you probably won't be able to achieve an exact match, because Director and Navigator use the Windows Color Picker to determine RGB color values (the number attached to each R, G, and B component), whereas Photoshop, by default, uses its own Color Picker.

To be able to mix colors using the RGB sliders on the Color palette in Photoshop to match colors used in Director, you should use the Windows Color Picker rather than Photoshop's own Color Picker: Choose Preferences > General, choose Windows from the Color Picker drop-down menu, then click OK. Remember to reset this preference back to the Photoshop Color Picker when you're finished.

like in an 8-bit setting. If it doesn't contain type or objects with sharp edges, then the JPEG image will probably survive the 8-bit setting conversion.

JPEG format files can now be saved as progressive JPEG, which is supported by the Netscape Navigator browser, and which displays the image in increasing detail as it downloads onto the Web page.

If you choose JPEG as your output format, you can experiment by creating and saving several versions of the image using varying degrees of compression. Open the JPEG versions of the image in Photoshop and view them at 100% or a more magnified view. Decide which degree of compression is acceptable by weighing the file size versus diminished image quality. Be sure to leave the original image intact to allow for potential future revisions.

Each time an image is resaved as a JPEG, some original image data is destroyed, and the more the image is degraded. The greater the degree of compression, the greater the data loss. To prevent this data loss, edit your image in Photoshop format and then save a JPEG copy when the image is finalized.

To save a copy of an image in JPEG format:

1. Choose File menu > Save a Copy (Control-Alt-S).

2. Choose Save As: JPEG.

3. Choose a location and enter a name for the file.

4. Click Save.

5. Enter a number between 0 and 10 for Image Options: Quality or choose from the four drop-down menu options.
   or
   Move the slider left or right to choose from the quality options.

   A Maximum setting will compress the image the least (between 5:1 and 15:1),

(Continued on the following page)

Save a Copy of an Image in JPEG Format

and preserve image quality the most, but the resulting file size from this setting will be larger than with any other setting.

Try all four settings on different versions of the original, and then reopen the JPEGs in Photoshop to weigh the image quality versus file size question.

6. Choose Format Options ◼: Baseline ("Standard") to minimize the amount of data loss during compression.
or
Choose Format Options: Baseline Optimized to optimize image quality during compression.
or
Choose Progressive to produce a progressive JPEG file. This type of file will display in the Web browser in several passes, with more detail revealed with each pass. Choose the desired number of passes (scans) from the Scans drop-down menu.

7. Click OK or press Enter.

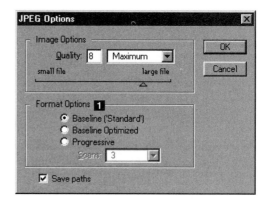

PNG: the future solution?

PNG is a new file format, and it isn't widely supported by Web browsers yet, but it may become more popular in the near future. PNG supports 24-bit color images, it has an interlacing option, and it offers even more impressive compression than the present JPEG format. PNG also supports alpha channels of 256 levels of gray that can be used to define areas of transparency. With 256 levels of masking gray, you can create a very soft fade to transparency, so you'll be able to display soft shadows and glowing shapes on the Web.

To save an image in PNG format:

1. In Photoshop, choose File menu > Save a Copy (Control-Alt-S).

2. Choose a location in which to save the file, enter a name for the file, then choose PNG in the Save As box.

PNG

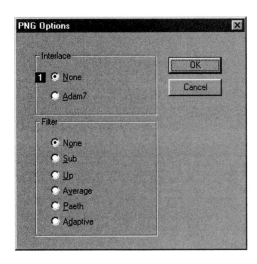

3. Click Save.

4. Choose Interlace: None or Adam7 1.

5. Choose a filter option for the method by which the file will be compressed. (See the Adobe Photoshop User Guide for information on filter options.)

6. Click OK.

Dithering about

Dithering is a technique in which pixels from two palette colors are intermixed to give the impression of a third color, and it's used to make images that contain a limited number of colors (256 or fewer) appear to have a greater range of colors and shades. Dithering is usually applied to continuous-tone images to increase their tonal range, but—argh, life is full of compromises—it can make them look a little dotty.

Dithering usually doesn't produce aesthetically pleasing results in flat color graphics, so these kinds of images usually aren't dithered. The browser palette will dither pixels to create the required color, however, if the palette doesn't contain a color used in the flat graphic. It's best to work with colors from the Web palette loaded into the Swatches palette for those types of images.

Continuous-tone imagery is, in a way, already dithered. Some continuous-tone imagery looks fine on a Web page with no dithering and 256 colors. The fewer the colors the palette of a non-dithered continuous-tone image contains, the more banding will occur in its color transitions; if dithering is turned on, the more dithering you'll see. You can decide which lesser of these two evils your own eye prefers.

One more consideration: Dithering adds noise to the file, so compression with dithering on is not as effective as when dithering is off. So, with dithering on, you may not be able to achieve your desired degree of file compression. As is the case with most Web output, you'll have to strike a balance between aesthetics and file size.

Dithering

In Photoshop, you can access a dithering option when you convert an image to Indexed Color mode. You can't control dithering with the GIF89a Export option; this command dithers an image automatically.

On the fringe: to alias or anti-alias

To make an object anti-aliased, pixels are added along its edge with progressively less opacity to smooth the transition between the object and its background. An object with an aliased edge is sharp, and has no extra pixels along its edge.

When images are composited in Photoshop, anti-aliasing produces smooth transitions between existing shapes and added shapes. Along the edge of a selection created using a tool with an anti-aliased edge, though, there may be a leftover fringe from the color of the former surrounding pixels. If you copy and paste this type of shape onto a flat color background, the fringe may become evident, and it can look mighty peculiar. To eliminate the fringe, before you create your selection, uncheck the Anti-aliased box on the Options palette for the Marquee or Lasso tool. You'll create a hard-edged selection, with no extra pixels along its edge.

To select imagery on its own layer with out selecting semi-transparent pixels on its anti-aliased edge, Control-click the layer name. You'll get a tighter selection this way than you would get using the Magic Wand tool.

When you're initially selecting a shape on a flat color background (all on one layer), use the Magic Wand tool with a low Tolerance setting (1-5). Click on the flat background with Anti-aliased unchecked, zoom in (400-500%) to see the edge of the shape, then choose Select menu > Inverse to select the shape (not its background). At this point, if the edge of the selection created using the Control-click or Magic Wand method still includes too many soft-edged pixels, choose, Select menu > Modify > Contract, and enter a 1 or 2 pixel value for the amount by which the selection edge will shrink inward. Reapply the command until the soft edge is eliminated.

With the GIF89a Export's ability to export a shape on its own layer with a transparent background, the fringe problem is diminished, provided a careful selection was made on the shape initially. If you still detect a fringe edge using the GIF preview, click Cancel, activate the shape's layer, then apply the Layer menu > Matting > Defringe command using a value of 1 or 2 pixels.

In Photoshop, you can produce a tile that can then be used to produce a seamless, repetitive, background pattern on a Web page using HTML code. These instructions get the longest-set-of-instructions-in-the-book award.

To create an almost seamless tile for a repetitive pattern:

1. Create a new 3x3 inch document, 72ppi, RGB Color mode, Contents: White.

2. Alt-click the Create New Layer button at the bottom of the Layers palette to create a New layer, and name it "Frame."

3. Choose a Foreground Color.

4. Using the Rectangular Marquee tool, Shift-drag a square selection near the center of the layer.

5. Choose Edit menu > Stroke.

6. Enter Width: 1 pixel, choose Location: Center, then click OK.

7. Choose Select menu > None.

8. Create another new layer, and name it "Design."

9. Draw the pattern. Hard-edge lines will be easiest to work with. Try not to cross more than two edges at a time as you draw.

To copy the edges of the design:

1. Make sure the Design layer is active 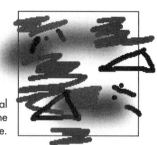.

2. Choose the Rectangular Marquee tool, Style: Normal.

3. Drag a vertical selection adjacent to and just touching the left edge of the frame, if there are any strokes that extend beyond that edge **2**.

4. Choose Edit menu > Copy.

5. Choose Edit menu > Paste.

6. If necessary, choose the Move tool, then press the up or down arrow to align the new pasted layer strokes with the strokes on the Design layer. Zoom in, if you need to.

7. Repeat steps 1–6 for all edges with strokes that cross them **3**.

To move the new edge layers over the opposite edge of the design:

1. Choose the Move tool.

2. Activate an edge layer that resulted from pasting.

3. Shift-drag the layer to position the strokes from one edge across to the opposite edge of the design, stopping so the strokes extend slightly beyond the edge of the frame **4**. Repeat this step for each pasted edge layer.

4. Choose the Magic Wand tool, and choose a Tolerance of 2 on the Magic Wand Options palette.

5. Activate the Frame layer.

6. Click within the Frame shape. The inner part should now be selected.

7. Choose Edit menu > Copy Merged to copy pixels from the visible layers.

8. Choose Edit menu > Paste. The new layer will be positioned above the Frame layer.

9. Activate the Frame layer.

10. Choose the Magic Wand tool.

11. Click again within the Frame shape.

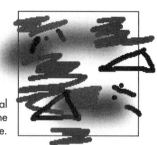

1 The original design pattern with the Frame layer visible.

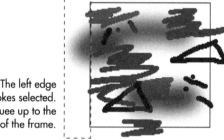

2 The left edge strokes selected. Marquee up to the edge of the frame.

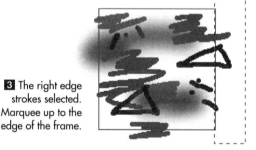

3 The right edge strokes selected. Marquee up to the edge of the frame.

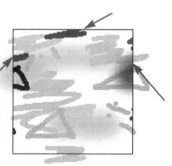

4 The stroke layers after they have been moved to the opposite side of the design (shown here grayed out).

Tile Pattern

1 The Frame layer selected with the Copy Merged/Paste layer visible.

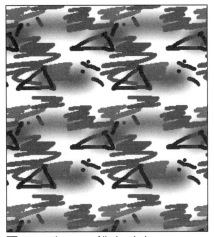

2 A new document filled with the pattern.

12. Hide the Design layer and all the edge layers to prevent soft, semi-transparent strokes from combining with their duplicates on the Copy Merged/Paste layer **1**.

13. Choose Edit menu > Define Pattern.

14. Choose Select menu > None.

15. Create a new file whose Width and Height are much larger than the tile document, 72 ppi, RGB mode, Contents: White.

16. Choose Edit menu > Fill.

17. Choose Use: Pattern, 100% opacity, Normal mode.

18. Click OK. The new image will be filled with your pattern tile **2**. If there are any noticeable seams, reopen the tile design file, delete the layer that contains the Copy Merged/Paste view of the design (above the Frame layer), and then reposition the edge layer. Repeat steps 5–18 starting on the previous page.

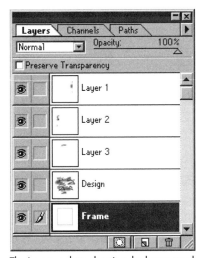

The Layers palette showing the layers used to produce the pattern fill.

Tile Pattern

Using layers for Web design

Since you can use Photoshop to create both imagery and special display text effects, it's a good application for designing Web pages. You can use Photoshop's Layers palette to preview and compose the elements of your Web page design. Create separate layers for such items as a particular background color, a tiled pattern, or imagery. And create aliased or anti-aliased headline text in Photoshop, and enhance it in various ways: Add a shadow, distortion, a glow, texture, or fill it with imagery. Photoshop text is rasterized, so, unlike PostScript text, you don't need to worry about whether the desired fonts are installed in the viewer's system. With elements on separate layers, you can restack, reposition, scale down, color adjust (for a screened back effect, for example), or show/hide different elements of the Web page. You can even save different versions of the page and decide later which design to use.

In a layered document, the Copy Merged command will allow you to copy a selection that includes pixels from all visible layers that fall within the selection area. This is a great way to create a "flattened" area of an image. Create a new document, then paste. That flattened area will be on its own new layer. You can duplicate layers to try out different design ideas on the same image, then show/hide individual layers to judge the duplicates.

You can duplicate a layer several times and move the layer imagery to try out an animation sequence (show/hide consecutive layers). Or apply a filter at progressively higher values to preview a filter transition.

When the design is finalized, save the layered version for any future revisions. You can copy-and-paste or drag-and-drop imagery on different layers into a final output document, or duplicate a layer into its own document using the Duplicate Layer command (choose New as the Destination document).

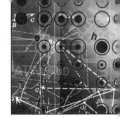

APPENDIX A: KEYBOARD SHORTCUTS

File menu

New...	Control N
Open...	Control O
Close...	Control W
Save	Control S
Save as...	Control Shift S
Save a Copy...	Control Alt S
Page Setup...	Control Shift P
Print...	Control P
Preferences > General...	Control K
Load in last Preferences settings	Alt choose File menu > Preferences > General
Quit	Control Q

Edit menu

Undo	Control Z

The Clipboard

Cut	Control X *or* F2
Copy	Control C *or* F3
Copy Merged	Control Shift C
Paste	Control V *or* F4
Paste Into	Control Shift V
Fill...	Shift-Backspace

Image menu

Adjust commands

Levels...	Control L
Auto Levels	Control Shift L
Curves...	Control M
Color Balance...	Control B
Hue/Saturation...	Control U
Desaturate	Control Shift U
Invert	Control I
Display last dialog box settings	Alt choose command
Make Curves grid larger/smaller	Alt click on grid

Layer menu

New > Layer via Copy	Control J
New > Layer via Cut	Control Shift J
Group with Previous	Control G
Ungroup	Control Shift G
Free Transform	Control T
Transform > Numeric...	Control Shift T
Arrange > Bring to Front	Control Shift]
Bring Forward	Control]
Send Backward	Control [
Send to Back	Control Shift [
Merge Down	Control E
Merge Visible	Control Shift E

Select menu

All	Control A
None	Control D
Inverse	Control Shift I
Feather	Control Shift D

Filter menu

Reapply last filter chosen	Control F
Open last Filter dialog box	Control Alt F
Fade... (last Filter or Image menu > Adjust command)	Control Shift F
Cancel a filter while a Progress dialog box is displayed	Control . (period) *or* Esc

View menu

CMYK Preview	Control Y
Gamut Warning	Control Shift Y
Zoom In	Control +
Zoom Out	Control -
Fit on Screen	Control 0 *or* double-click Hand tool
Actual Pixels	Control Alt 0 *or* double-click Zoom tool
Show/Hide Edges	Control H
Show/Hide Path	Control Shift H
Show/Hide Rulers	Control R
Show/Hide Guides	Control ;

Snap to Guides	Control Shift ;
Lock Guides	Control Alt ;
Show/Hide Grid	Control "
Snap to Grid	Control Shift "

Display sizes

Enlarge display size	Control Space bar click (works with some dialog boxes open)
Reduce display size	Alt Space bar click (works with some dialog boxes open)
Magnify selected area	Drag with Zoom tool
Zoom in (window size unchanged)	Control Alt +
Zoom out (window size unchanged)	Control Alt -

Toolbox

Show/Hide Toolbox and palettes	Tab
Show/Hide palettes but not Toolbox	Shift Tab
Open tool Options palette	Double-click any tool other than Type, Hand, or Zoom

Hand tool

Temporary Hand tool with any other tool selected	Space bar

Eyedropper tool

Select color for the non-highlighted color square (Color palette)	Alt click color
Temporary Eyedropper tool with Paint Bucket, Gradient, Line, Pencil, Airbrush, or Paintbrush tool selected	Alt

Eraser tool

Magic eraser, restores last saved version	Alt drag
Constrain eraser to 90° angle	Shift drag

Gradient Editor

Create New gradient	Control N
Select first or next gradient color marker to the right	Tab
Select last or next gradient color marker to the left	Shift Tab
Save only selected gradient as a file	Control Shift click Save button

Save selected gradient as a Curves map file	Control Alt click Save button

Line tool
Constrain to 45° or 90° angle	Shift drag

Paintbrush, Pencil, Airbrush, Rubber Stamp, Smudge tool
Constrain to 90° angle	Shift drag
Precise crosshair cursor for brushes	Caps Lock

Pen tool
Add anchor point with Direct Selection tool highlighted	Control Alt click line segment
Delete anchor point with Direct Selection tool highlighted	Control Alt click anchor point
Constrain straight line segment or anchor point to 45° angle	Shift drag
Delete last created anchor point	Backspace
Erase path being drawn	Backspace Backspace
Temporary Direct Selection tool with any Pen tool selected	Control
Temporary Convert Anchor Point tool with the Path Select tool	Control
Select whole path (Direct Selection tool)	Alt click path
Switch between Add Anchor Point and Delete Anchor Point tools	Alt (over a point)
Temporary Add or Delete Anchor tool (Pen tool selected) or (Direct Selection tool selected)	Control Alt (over point or segment)
Fill selection with Background color	Control Backspace
Fill selection with Background color and Preserve transparency	Control Alt Backspace

Sharpen/Blur tool
Switch between Sharpen and Blur	Alt drag picture *or* Alt click Sharpen/Blur tool on Toolbox

Smudge tool
Temporary Finger Painting tool	Alt drag

Selection tools
Add to a selection	Shift drag
Subtract from a selection	Alt drag

Intersect a selection	Alt Shift drag
Constrain marquee to square or circle	Drag and press Shift
Draw marquee from center	Drag and press Alt
Move marquee (Marquee tool selected)	Drag marquee
Move marquee in 1-pixel increments	Arrow keys
Move marquee in 10-pixel increments	Shift and Arrow keys
Float selection pixels (Move tool selected)	Control drag selection
Copy (float) selection pixels	Alt drag selection
Drop a floating selection	Control E
Float selection in same position	Control Alt up arrow, then down arrow
Fill selection with Foreground color	Alt Backspace
Fill selection with Foreground color and Preserve transparency	Control Alt Backspace
Switch Masked Areas/Selected Areas (Quick Mask mode)	Alt click Quick Mask icon on Toolbox

Rectangular Marquee and Elliptical Marquee tools

Draw selection from center	Drag and press Alt
Square or circlular selection	Drag and press Shift

Magic Wand tool

Add to a selection	Shift click
Subtract from a selection	Alt click

Lasso tool

Create straight side in a selection	Alt click

Polygon Lasso tool

Create curved side in a straight-sided selection	Alt drag
Constrain to 45°	Shift click

Dialog boxes

Restore original settings	Hold down Alt, click Reset
Delete to the right of the cursor	del
Highlight next field	Tab
Highlight previous field	Shift Tab
Increase/decrease number in highlighted field by 1 unit	Up or down arrow

| Increase/decrease number in highlighted field by 10 units | Shift and Up or down arrow |
| Cancel out of dialog box | Esc |

Palettes

Hide/Show Brushes	F5
Show/Hide Picker	F6
Show/Hide Layers	F7
Show/Hide Info	F8
Show/Hide Actions	F9
Shrink palette to a bar	Double-click palette tab *or* Alt click palette zoom box

With any painting or editing tool selected

| Move tool | Control |
| Opacity percentage (Options palette) | Keypad key 0=100%, 1=10%, 2=20%, etc. *or* type two numbers quickly, 41=41%, etc. |

Layers, Channels, and Paths

Load a layer, channel, or path as a selection	Control click layer, channel, or path name
Add to current selection	Control Shift click layer channel, or path name
Subtract from current selection	Control Alt click layer, channel, or path name
Intersect current selection	Control Alt Shift click layer, channel, or path name
Delect selected layer, channel, or path	Alt click palette Trash icon
Create new layer, channel, or path and set options	Alt click New [ ] button

Channels palette

RGB Channels

RGB	Control ~
Red	Control 1
Green	Control 2
Blue	Control 3

CMYK Channels

CMYK	Control ~
Cyan	Control 1
Magenta	Control 2

Yellow	Control 3
Black	Control 4

Layers palette

Select/deselect Preserve Transparency option on Layers palette	press /
Select a layer via a pop-up menu in image window (Move tool selected) *or* (any other tool selected)	Control press, choose layer from pop-up menu
Select a layer from the image window (Move tool selected)	Control press object in image
Hide/show all other layers	Alt click layer eye icon
Add new adjustment layer	Control click Create New Layer button
Add new layer mask, but invert mask effect	Alt click Create Layer Mask button
Switch between layer mask view and composite view	Alt click Layer mask thumbnail
Temporarily turn off layer mask effect	Shift click Layer mask thumbnail
Create a clipping group	Alt click line between layers
Merge down a copy of the selected layer	Alt choose Merge Down command
Merge copies of all visible layers into bottommost visible layer	Alt choose Merge Visible command
Merge copies of all linked layers into selected layer	Alt choose Merge Linked command

Channels palette

Open Load Selection dialog box	Alt click Load Channel as Selection button
Open Channel Options dialog box	Alt click Save Selection as Channel button
Switch display between alpha channel and composite (topmost) channel	Shift click alpha channel
Deselect a particular color channel	Shift click a color channel

Swatches palette

Delete a swatch	Control click swatch
Replace swatch with new color swatch	Shift click swatch to be replaced

| Insert new swatch between two swatches | Alt Shift click swatch |
| Select for Background color (Toolbox) | Alt click a swatch |

Navigator palette

| Zoom in to specific location | Control drag in preview box |
| Enter a view %, keep text field highlighted | Shift Enter |

Actions palette

Turn on current command and turn off all other commands	Alt click check mark
Turn on current command's break point & turn off all other breakpoints	Alt click break point
Start recording an action without opening the New Action dialog box	Alt click Create New Action button
Play an action from a selected command forward to end	Control click Play button
Play an entire action	Control double-click action name

Paths palette

Open Fill Path dialog box	Alt click Fill Path button
Open Stroke Path dialog box	Alt click Stroke Path button
Open Make Selection dialog box	Alt click Load Path as Selection button
Open Make Work Path dialog box	Alt click Make Work Path from Selection button

Brushes palette

Delete selected tip	Control click tip
Select previous tip (Painting tool selected)	press [
Select next tip (Painting tool selected)	press]
Select first tip/last tip (Painting tool selected)	press Shift [or press Shift]

Color palette

Color bar

Choose color for non-highlighted square	Alt click Color bar
Display Color Bar dialog box	Control click Color bar
Cycle through Color bar styles	Shift click Color bar

Free Transform

Move bounding border	Drag inside border
Rotate bounding border	Drag outside border
Scale bounding border	Drag handle
Scale proportionally	Hold Shift and drag handle
Skew bounding border	Control Shift drag handle
Distort bounding border	Control drag handle
Create Perspective effect	Control Alt Shift drag handle
Perform symmetrical transformation	Hold Alt with other shortcuts above
Apply transformation to selected pixels	Press Enter *or* double-click inside border
Cancel transformation in progress	Esc
Undo the last step in transformation	Control Z

Context-sensitive menus

Display context-sensitive menus	Right click on image (any tool selected) *or* Right click on some palette icons for options

Tools

Airbrush	A
Blur/Sharpen	R
Crop	C
Default colors	D
Dodge/Burn/Sponge	O
Elliptical/Rectangular Marquee	M
Eraser	E
Eyedropper	I
Gradient	G
Hand	H
Lasso/Polygon Lasso	L
Line	N
Magic Wand	W
Move	V
Paintbrush	B
Paint Bucket	K
Pen/Direct selection/Add-anchor-point/ Delete-anchor-point/ Convert-anchor-point	P

Pencil	Y
Rubber Stamp	S
Smudge	U
Standard mode/Quick Mask mode	Q
Standard windows/Full screen with menu bar/Full screen with no menu bar	F
Switch foreground/ background colors	X
Type/Type Mask	T
Zoom	Z

Default F key assignments

Cut	F2
Copy	F3
Paste	F4
Hide/show Brushes palette	F5
Hide/show Picker palette	F6
Hide/show Layers palette	F7
Hide/show Info palette	F8
Hide/show Actions palette	F9
Revert	F12
Fill	Shift F5
Feather	Shift F6
Select menu > Inverse	Shift F7

Miscellaneous

Update font list after opening suitcase	Shift click on image with Type tool

Print preview box

Picture information	Alt press on Sizes bar

Alpha channel
A special 8-bit grayscale channel that is used for saving a selection.

Anti-alias
The blending of pixel colors on the perimeter of hard-edged shapes, like type, to smoooth undesirable stair-stepping (jaggies).

ASCII
(American Standard Code for Information Interchange) A standard editable format for encoding data.

Background color
The color applied when the Eraser tool is used, the canvas size is enlarged, or a selection is moved on the Background of an image.

Bézier curve
A curved line segment drawn using the Pen tool. It consists of anchor points with direction lines with which the curve can be reshaped.

Binary
In Photoshop, a method for encoding data. Binary encoding is more compact than ASCII encoding.

Bit
(Binary digit) The smallest unit of information on a computer. Eight bits equal one byte. (see Byte)

Bit depth
The number of bits used to store a pixel's color information on a computer monitor.

Bitmap
The display of an image on a computer screen via the geometric mapping of a single layer of pixels on a rectangular grid. In Photoshop, Bitmap is also a one-channel mode consisting of black and white pixels.

Blend (see Gradient)

Brightness (see Lightness)

Burn
To darken an area of an image.

Byte
The basic unit of storage memory. One byte equals eight bits. One kilobyte (K, Kb) equals 1,024 bytes. One megabyte (M, MB) equals 1,024 kilobytes. One gigabyte (G, Gb) equals 1,024 megabytes.

Canvas size
The size of an image, including a border, if any, around it.

Channel
An image component that contains the pixel information for an individual color. A grayscale image contains one channel, an RGB image contains three channels, and a CMYK image contains four channels.

Clipboard
An area of memory used to temporarily store selection pixels. The Clipboard is accessed via the Cut, Copy, and Paste commands.

Clipping
In Photoshop, the automatic adjustment of colors to bring them into printable gamut.

Clone

To copy image areas using the Rubber Stamp tool.

CMYK

(Cyan, Magenta, Yellow, and Black) The four ink colors used in process printing. Cyan, magenta, and yellow are the three subtractive primaries. When combined in their purest form, they theoretically produce black, but in actuality, they produce a dark muddy color. CMYK colors are simulated on a computer monitor using additive, red, green, and blue light. To color separate an image from Photoshop, convert it to CMYK Color mode.

Color correction

The adjustment of color in an image to match original artwork or a photograph. Color correction is usually done in CMYK Color mode in preparation for process printing.

Color separation

The production of a separate sheet of film for each ink color that will be used to print an image. Four plates are used in process color separation, one each for Cyan, Magenta, Yellow, and Black.

Color table

The color palette of up to 256 colors of an image in Indexed Color mode.

Continuous-tone image

An image, like a photograph, in which there are smooth gradations between shades or colors.

Contrast

The degree of difference between lights and darks in an image. A high contrast image is comprised of only very light and very dark pixels.

Crop

To trim away part of an image.

Crop marks

Short, fine lines placed around the edges of a page to designate where the paper is to be trimmed at a print shop.

DCS

(Desktop Color Separation) A file format in which a color image is broken down into five PostScript files: Cyan, Magenta, Yellow and Black for high resolution printing, and an optional low resolution file for previewing and laser printing.

Digitize

To translate flat art or a transparency into computer-readable numbers using a scanning device and scanning software.

Dimensions

The width and height of an image.

Dither

The mixing of adjacent pixels to simulate additional colors when available colors are limited, such as on an 8-bit monitor.

Dodge

To bleach (lighten) an area of an image. Also, a so-so car model.

Dot gain

The undesirable spreading and enlarging of ink dots on paper.

Dpi

(Dots Per Inch) A unit used to measure the resolution of a printer. Dpi is sometimes used to describe the input resolution of a scanner, but "ppi" is the more accurate term.

Duotone

A grayscale image printed using two plates for added tonal depth. A tritone is printed using three plates. A quadtone is printed using four plates.

Dye sublimation

A continuous-tone printing process in which a solid printing medium is converted into a gas before it hits the paper.

8-bit monitor

A monitor in which each pixel stores eight bits of information and represents one of only 256 available colors. Dithering is used to simulate additional colors.

EPS

(Encapsulated PostScript) An image file format containing PostScript code and, in the case of Photoshop, an optional PICT or TIFF image for screen display. EPS is a commonly used format for moving files from one application to another and for imagesetting and color separating.

Equalize

To balance an image's lights and darks.

Feather

To fade the edge of a selection or mask a specified number of pixels (the feather radius).

Fill

To fill a selection with a shade, color, pattern, or blend.

Film negative

A film rendition of an image in which dark and light areas are reversed.

Floating selection

An area of an image that is surrounded by a marquee and can be moved or modified without affecting underlying pixels.

Font

A typeface in a distinctive style, such as Futura Bold Italic.

Foreground color

The color applied when a painting tool is used or type is created.

Gradient fill

In Photoshop, a graduated blend between colors that is produced by the Gradient tool.

Grayscale

An image containing black, white, and up to 256 shades of gray, but no color. In Photoshop, Grayscale is a one-channel image mode.

Halftone screen

A pattern of tiny dots that is used for printing an image to simulate smooth tones.

Highlights

The lightest areas of an image.

Histogram

A graph showing the distribution of an image's color and/or luminosity values.

HSB

See Hue, Saturation, and Brightness.

Hue

The wavelength of light of a pure color that gives a color its name—such as red or blue—independent of its saturation or brightness.

Imagesetter

A high-resolution printer (usually 1,270 or 2,540 dpi) that generates paper or film output from a computer file.

Indexed color

In Photoshop, an image mode in which there is only one channel and a color table containing up to 256 colors. All the colors of an Indexed Color image are displayed on its Colors palette.

Interpolation

The recoloring of pixels as a result of changing an image's dimensions or resolution. Interpolation may cause an image to look blurry when printed. You can choose an interpolation method (Bicubic or Nearest Neighbor) in Photoshop.

Inverse

To switch the selected and non-selected areas of an image.

Invert

To reverse an image's light and dark values and/or colors.

JPEG compression

(Joint Photographic Experts Group) A compression feature in Photoshop that is used to reduce a file's storage size. JPEG can cause some image degradation.

Kern

To adjust the horizontal spacing between a pair of characters.

Lab

A mode in which colors are related to the CIE color reference system. In Photoshop, an image in Lab Color mode is composed of three channels, one for lightness, one for green-to-red colors, and one blue-to-yellow colors.

Leading

The space between lines of type, measured from baseline to baseline. In Photoshop, leading can be measured in points or pixels.

Lightness

(Brightness) The lightness of a color independent of its hue and saturation.

LPI

(Lines Per Inch, halftone frequency, screen frequency) The unit used to measure the frequency of rows of dots on a halftone screen.

Luminosity

The distribution of an image's light and dark values.

Marquee

The moving border that defines a selection.

Mask

An "electronic" paint that protects an area of an image from modification.

Midtones

The shades in an image that are midway between the highlights and shadows.

Mode

A method for specifying how color information is to be interpreted. An image can be converted to a different image mode (RGB to Indexed Color, for example); a blending mode can be chosen for a painting or editing tool.

Moiré

An undesirable pattern that is caused by improper halftone screen angles during printing or when the pattern in an image conflicts with proper halftone patterns.

Object-oriented

(also known as vector) A software method used for describing and processing computer files. Object-oriented graphics and PostScript type are defined by mathematics and geometry. Bitmapped graphics are defined by pixels on a rectangular grid. Photoshop images are bitmapped.

Opacity

The density of a color or shade, ranging from transparent to opaque. In Photoshop, you can choose an opacity for a painting or editing tool or a layer.

Path

A shape that is comprised of straight and/or curved segments joined by anchor points.

PICT

A Macintosh file format that is used to display and save images. Save a Photoshop image as a PICT to open it in a video or animation program. The PICT format is not use for color separations.

Pixels

(Image elements) The individual dots that are used to display an image on a computer monitor.

PPI

(Pixels per inch) The unit used to measure the resolution of a scan or of a Photoshop image.

Plug-in module

Third-party software that is loaded into the Photoshop Plug-ins folder so it can be accessed from a Photoshop menu. Or, a plug-in module that comes with Photoshop that is used to facilitate Import, Export, or file format conversion operations.

Point

A unit of measure used to describe type size (measured from ascender to descender), leading (measured from baseline to baseline), and line width.

Polygon

A closed shape composed of three or more straight sides.

Posterize

Produce a special effect in an image by reducing the number of shades of gray or colors to a specified—usually low—number.

PostScript

The page description language created and licensed by Adobe Systems Incorporated that is used for displaying and printing fonts and images.

Process color

Ink that is printed from four separate plates, one each for Cyan (C), Magenta (M), Yellow (Y), and Black (K), and which in combination produce a wide range of colors.

Quick Mask

In Photoshop, a screen display mode in which a translucent colored mask covers selected or unselected areas of an image. Painting tools can be used to reshape a Quick Mask.

RAM

(Random Access Memory) The system memory of a computer that is used for running an application, processing information, and temporary storage.

Rasterize

The conversion of an object-oriented image into a bitmapped image. When an Adobe Illustrator graphic is placed into Photoshop, for example, it is rasterized. All computer files are rasterized when they're printed.

Registration marks

Crosshair marks placed around the edges of a page that are used to align printing plates.

Resample

Change an image's resolution while keeping its pixels dimensions constant.

Resolution

The fineness of detail of a digital image (measured in pixels per inch), a monitor (measured in pixels per inch—usually 72 ppi), a printer (measured in dots per inch), or a halftone screen (measured in lines per inch).

Glossary

RGB

Color used to produce transmitted light. When pure Red, Green, and Blue light (the additive primaries) are combined, as on a computer monitor, white is produced. In Photoshop, RGB Color is a three-channel image mode.

Saturation

The purity of a color. The more gray a color contains, the lower its saturation.

Scan

To digitize a slide, photograph or other artwork using a scanner and scanning software so it can be displayed, edited, and possibly output from, a computer.

Scratch disk

(also known as virtual memory) Hard drive storage space that is designated as work space for processing operations and for temporarily storing part of an image and a backup version of the image when there is insufficient RAM for those functions.

Screen angles

Angles used for positioning halftone screens when producing film to minimize undesirable dot patterns (moirés).

Screen frequency

(screen ruling) The resolution (density of dots) on a halftone screen, measured in lines per inch.

Selection

An area of an image that is isolated so it can be modified while the rest of the image is protected. A moving marquee, which denotes the boundary of a selection, can be moved independently of its contents.

Shadows

The darkest areas of an image.

Spot color

A mixed ink color used in printing. A separate plate is used to print each spot color. Pantone is a commonly used spot color matching system. (see Process color) Photoshop doesn't generate spot color plates.

Thermal wax

A color printing process in which a sequence of three to four ink sheets are used to place colored dots on special paper.

TIFF

(Tagged Image File Format) A common file format that is used for saving bitmapped images, such as scans. TIFF images can be color separated.

Tolerance

The range of pixels within which a tool operates, like the range of shades or colors the Magic Wand tool selects or the Paint Bucket tool fills.

Trap

The overlapping of adjacent colors to prevent undesirable gaps from occuring as a result of the misalignment of printing plates or paper.

24-bit monitor

A monitor with a video card in which each pixel can store up to 24 bits of information. The video card contains three color tables for displaying an RGB image, one each for Red, Green, and Blue, and each containing 256 colors. Together they can produce 16.7 million colors. On a 24-bit monitor, smooth blends can be displayed, so dithering isn't necessary.

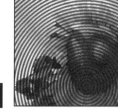

APPENDIX C: COPYRIGHT PROTECTION

Ten questions and answers about copyright

Written by Tad Crawford

Why is copyright important?

If you are a creator of images (whether Photoshop user, photographer, designer, or fine artist), copyright protects you from having your images stolen by someone else. As the copyright owner, you may either allow or prevent anyone else from making copies of your work, making derivations from your work (such as a poster made from a photograph), or displaying your work publicly. Your copyrights last for your lifetime plus another fifty years, so a successful work may benefit not only you but your heirs as well. If you are a user of images, it is important that you understand the rights and obligations connected with their use so you don't infringe on the copyright of someone else and expose yourself to legal or financial liabilities.

What is an infringement?

Infringement is unauthorized use of someone else's work. The test for infringement is whether an ordinary observer would believe one work was copied from another.

Is it an infringement if I scan an old image into Photoshop and change it?

If the image was created in the United States and is more than 75 years old, it is in the public domain and can be freely copied by you or anyone else. You will have copyright in the new elements of the image that you create.

Is it an infringement if I scan a recent photograph into Photoshop and change it?

The scanning itself is making a copy and so is an infringement. As a practical matter, however, it is unlikely you will be sued for infringement if you change the photograph to the point where an ordinary observer would no longer believe your work was copied from the original photograph.

What does "fair use" mean in terms of copyright?

A fair use is a use of someone else's work that is allowed under the copyright law. For example, newsworthy or educational uses are likely to be fair uses. The factors for whether a use is a fair use or an infringement are: (1) the purpose and character of the use, including whether or not it is for profit (2) the character of the copyrighted work (3) how much of the total work is used and (4) what effect the use will have on the market for or value of the work being copied.

Can I use a recognizable part of a photograph if the entire source photograph is not recognizable?

You would have to apply the fair use factors. Obviously, factor (3) in the previous answer relating to how much of the total work is used would be in your favor, but if the use is to make a profit and will damage the market for the source photograph it might be considered an infringement.

What are the damages for infringement?

The damages are the actual losses of the person infringed plus any profits of the infringer. In some cases (especially if the work was registered before the infringement), the court can simply award between $500 and $20,000 for each work infringed. If the infringement is willful, the court can award as much as $100,000.

Do I have to register my images to obtain my copyright?

No, you have the copyright from the moment you create a work. However, registration with the Copyright Office costs $20 and will help you in the event your work is infringed. To obtain Copyright Application Form VA (for Visual Arts), write to the Copyright Office, Library of Congress, Washington, D.C. 20559 or call (202) 707-9100. Ask for the free Copyright Information Kit for the visual arts and you will receive many helpful circulars developed by the Copyright Office.

Do I need to use copyright notice to obtain or protect my copyright?

It is always wise to place copyright notice on your work, because it is a visible symbol of your rights as copyright owner. Prior to 1989 the absence of copyright notice when the images were published or publicly distributed could, in certain circumstances, cause the loss of the copyright. Since March 1, 1989, the absence of copyright notice cannot cause the loss of the copyright but may give infringers a loophole to try and lessen their damages. Copyright notice has three elements: (1) "Copyright" or "Copr" or "©" (2) your name and (3) the year of first publication.

How do I get permission to reproduce an image?

A simple permission form will suffice. It should set forth what kind of project you are doing, what materials you want to use, what rights you need in the material, what credit line and copyright notice will be given, and what payment, if any, will be made. The person giving permission should sign the permission form. If you are using an image of a person for purposes of advertising or trade, you should have them sign a model release. If the person's image is to be altered or placed in a situation that didn't occur, you would want the release to cover this. Otherwise you may face a libel or invasion of privacy lawsuit.

Digital watermarking

The Embed Digimarc filter embeds nearly invisible copyright information and a contact address into a Photoshop image. The watermark can't easily be removed by reworking the image in Photoshop, it will be present in any copy or any printout of the image, and it will even be retained if the printed piece is redigitized by scanning, so your image will always retain its original copyright.

NOTE: To install the Detect Watermark filter, copy it from the Application CD-ROM (from the Goodies > Optional Plugins > Digimarc/Detect Watermark folder) to the Photoshop Plug-ins folder.

To create a valid copyright, you must register with and pay a fee to Digimarc Corporation. They will enter your personal information into their database and issue you a unique creator ID, so your watermark will contain your personal contact and copyright information.

To embed a watermark:

1. Open a flattened version of the image to be watermarked.

2. Choose Filter > Digimarc > Embed Watermark.

3. If you don't yet have a personal Creator ID, click Personalize **1**, then click Register to connect to the Digimarc Web site or phone Digimarc at the number listed in the dialog box.

4. Enter your Creator ID number **2**, then click OK.

5. Choose Type of Use: Restricted for limited use, or Royalty Free for unlimited use.

6. *Optional:* Check the Adult Content box (this option is not yet available).

7. Enter a Watermark Durability value, or move the slider. Enter 1 or 2 to create a nearly invisible mark that work best

(Continued on the following page)

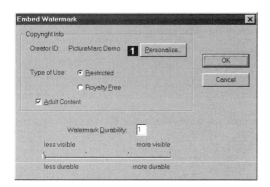

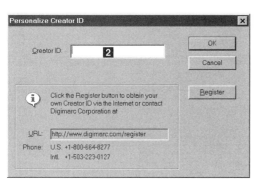

Digital Watermark

with high-end printing. Enter 3 or 4 for a more visible mark that is more suitable for multimedia or online formats, where you might need to convert the image to various bit depths. Keep in mind that a watermark with a low Durability value might be ruined by image editing.

8. Click OK.

The Digimarc filter must be available to view a watermark symbol already embedded in an image. The title bar of an image that contains a watermark will display a copyright symbol ©.

To read information about a watermark:

1. With the image containing the watermark open, choose Filter > Digimarc > Read Watermark. A dialog box displaying Creator ID and other information will open.

2. *Optional:* If you want to have information faxed back to you, dial the phone number listed in the Watermark Information dialog box.

or

If you're currently hooked up to the Web via a browser, click Web Lookup to open the browser, then navigate to the Digimarc Web site, where you'll see the creator information.

3. Click OK to close the Watermark Information dialog box.

Alicia Buelow
336 Arkansas St.
San Francisco, CA 94107
415-642-8083
e-mail: buelow@adobe.com

Jeff Brice
2416 NW 60th Street
Seattle, WA 98107
206-706-0406
e-mail: cyspy@aol.com

Diane Fenster
287 Reichling Ave.
Pacifica, CA 94044
415-355-5007
e-mail: fenster@sfsu.edu
http://www.sirius.com/~fenster

Louis Fishauf
Creative Director
Reactor Art + Design Limited
51 Camden Street
Toronto, Ontario
Canada M5V1V2
416-703-1913 x241
e-mail: fishauf@reactor.ca
http://www.magic.ca/~fishauf/
http://www.reactor.ca

Wendy Grossman
355 West 51st Street
New York, NY 10019
212-262-4497
http://www.renard
represents.com
(pages 41, 132, and color section)

John Hersey
546 Magnolia Avenue
Larkspur, CA 94939
Voice 415-927-2091
Fax 415-927-2092
http://www.hersey.com
e-mail: ultraduc@hersey.com

David Humphrey
439 Lafayette Street
New York, NY 10003
212-780-0512
e-mail: humphrey@is2.nyu.edu
(page 81)

Liana Levin
105-40 63rd Avenue
Forest Hills, NY 11375
718-459-7313
(pages 265, 266)

Min Wang
795 Coastland Drive
Palo Alto, CA 94303
Voice 415-321-4294
Fax 415-321-6246
e-mail: mwang@adobe.com

Annette Weintraub
Professor
Department of Art
City College of New York
138th St. and Convent Avenue
New York, NY 10031
Voice 212-650-7410
Fax 212-650-7438
e-mail: anwcc@cunyvm.cuny.edu
http://www.artnetweb.com/art-netweb/projects/realms/notes.html

Seasonal Specialties
Jennifer Sheeler, Creative Director
Barbara Roth, Art Director
Lisa Milan, Senior Designer (1997 catalog)
Seasonal Specialties LLC (@1996 All Rights Reserved)
11455 Valley View Road
Eden Prairie, MN 55344
Voice 612-942-6555
Fax 612-942-1801
jen.sheeler@seasonalspecialties.com
barb.roth@seasonalspecialties.com
lisa.milan@seasonalspecialties.com

Directory of Artists

Lifeline, ©1996 Annette Weintraub

Thank you

Trish Booth, Roslyn Bullas, Corbin Collins, Hannah Onstad, Mimi Heft, Nolan Hester, Keasley Jones, Cary Norsworthy, Gary Paul Prince, and the rest of the gang (hope-we-didn't-leave-anyone-out) at Peachpit Press, for always being helpful and on the ball.

Tad Crawford, attorney, author, and Allworth Press publisher, for contributing the *Ten Questions and Answers About Copyright.*

Adobe Systems, Inc. for technical support.

Gene Chin, instructor at The New School Computer Instruction Center in New York City, for producing the screen captures and revising the text for this edition.

Johanna Gillman, New York City-based artist, wonderful friend, and designer, for her layout services.

Adam Hausman, Macintosh systems specialist, for his layout services.

Darren Roberts and *David McManus,* Parsons School of Design instructors, for their comments on the Web & Multimedia chapter.

Judy Susman and *Dara Glanville* for painstakingly tending to proofreading and copy editing details.

And *Teddy* and *Christ Lourekas,* for all their love and babysitting during this busy, busy, busy year.

Photo credits

Nadine Markova (Mexico City), pages 64, 101

Paul Petroff (Great Neck, New York), pages 47, 61, 63, 80, 100, 102, 205

John Stuart (New York City), page 238

Cara Wood (New York City), page 163

All the other images originated from stock photos (PhotoDisc) or from photographs taken by or owned by the authors.

Excaved, ©1996 Annette Weintraub

Index

Index

Index

Index

Index

Psst! Want to contact the authors?

Call Peachpit Press (1-800-283-9444), and
ask them for our current e-mail address.
By the way, what do you think of this book?
And…what should we write about next?